REFLECTIONS ON LIBERTY, DEMOCRACY AND THE UNION

To Dr John Lukacs

With admiration and regard

Bob McCartney

April 2001.

REFLECTIONS ON LIBERTY, DEMOCRACY AND THE UNION

Robert McCartney

Maunsel & Company, Dublin
an imprint of Academica Press, LLC Bethesda
Bethesda Dublin Oxford

Published by Maunsel & Company
Imprint of Academica Press, Bethesda

Library of Congress Cataloging-in-Publication Data
McCartney, Robert.
    Reflections on liberty, democracy, and the union /Robert
       McCartney.
       p. cm.
    Includes bibliographical references and index.
    ISBN 1-930901-12-7
    1. Ireland—Politics and government—1949 2. Northern
    Ireland—Politics and government. 3. Unionism (Irish politics)
    I. Title.

DA963 .M35 2001
320.9415—dc21   2001018207

*For my wife, Maureen, at once my most severe critic
and my greatest support, and for the British on the
island of Ireland who believe in the cause of the Union.*

Contents

Acknowledgements

This book expresses my personal reflections on vital political principles: the value of democracy; the balance between liberty and authority; the right of the majority to rule; the subjection of such rule to the inalienable human and civil rights of minorities; and the imperative of the just enforcement of the rule of law. Yet without the counsel and criticism of others, and in the absence of informed discussion and debate, this volume might never have been written. To all of those who played a part, my gratitude.

In particular, I wish to express my sincere appreciation to Mr John O'Sullivan for his contribution of such an eloquent Foreword. To all of those within the United Kingdom Unionist Party whose encouragement and support have sustained me through dark days, my deepest thanks. I am especially indebted to Conor and Màire Cruise O'Brien for their friendship and advice and for sharing their real and enlightened love of Ireland, which remains untarnished by any narrow nationalism. For their tireless assistance in tracking down, dating and analysing my disparate writings, sincere thanks are due to my parliamentary researcher, John Cobain, with the able assistance of David Schofield and Mark Coalter. For her tireless efforts in turning my barely legible manuscript into pristine print, no praise is too great for Anne Moore, my loyal secretary for thirty years. I express great thanks to my editor, Joseph Skelly: as a friend, confidant, critic and counsellor, he not only gave this book shape and form, but lent its author hope and encouragement. I wish to acknowledge the enthusiastic support of Robert West and the entire team at Maunsel Press, including Robert Mahony and Ginger McNally. My appreciation is extended to Field Day Publications, in whose series the pamphlet *Liberty and Authority* first appeared. Finally, thanks are owed to those newspapers and magazines in which some of the material in this volume was originally published, notably the *Belfast News Letter, Belfast Telegraph, Daily Telegraph, Sunday Telegraph, Observer, Times, Spectator* and the *Irish Times.*

Abbreviations

CLMC	Combined Loyalist Military Command
DAAD	Direct Action Against Drugs
DUP	Democratic Unionist Party
INLA	Irish National Liberation Army
IRA	Irish Republican Army
MP	Member of Parliament
NIO	Northern Ireland Assembly
PUP	Progressive Unionist Party
RTE	Radio Telefis Eireann
RUC	Royal Ulster Constabulary
SDLP	Social Democratic and Labour Party
UDA	Ulster Defence Association
UDP	Ulster Democratic Party
UDR	Ulster Defence Regiment
UFF	Ulster Freedom Fighters
UUP	Ulster Unionist Party
UVF	Ulster Volunteer Force

Foreword

'The Irish complain that the English know nothing of history', said the acerbic Irish novelist, Honor Tracey, some years ago; 'that is quite true—and greatly to the advantage of the Irish'. If that is true of the history of remote events, it is even more so, alarmingly, of the history of Northern Ireland in our own time.

A dispassionate investigation of what the average well informed English reader of serious newspapers (or even of the *Guardian*) believes about Northern Ireland today would uncover a vast collage of centrist prejudices about the tribal sectarians of Ulster, coupled with self-flattering images of the fair-minded English trying vainly to reconcile them through a benevolent peace process. This reader would probably 'know' that the Unionists greatly misgoverned Ulster right up to the Belfast Agreement (in fact, the last Unionist administration at Stormont was abolished in 1972 and the first power sharing Northern Ireland executive was established in 1973 and collapsed in 1974). He would reluctantly acknowledge that the strong support given to Sinn Fein/IRA by the nationalist population made the entry of terrorists into government inevitable (in fact, Sinn Fein regularly got derisory votes in both Ulster and the Irish Republic until the London and Dublin governments gave terrorists respectability and an aura of political success by negotiating with them). He would argue that the Belfast Agreement, though it has some minor flaws, has nonetheless brought a lasting peace to Ulster (in fact, murders, beatings and forced exiles continue as the terrorists intensify their control of sectarian ghettoes; the terrorist armies steadfastly refuse to surrender their weapons; and the evidence is mounting that the 'extremists', such as the Real IRA, enjoy considerable help from the 'moderate' terrorists in preparing for a further offensive). And if corrected on all these points, he would irritably reply that when all was said and done, the problems of Ulster could nonetheless be traced to continuing Unionist intransigence in resisting measures to correct discrimination against the Catholic minority (in fact, successive British governments since 1972 have enforced strict anti-discrimination laws; the Unionists have granted not only a power sharing administration in which former terrorists serve as Ministers, but also cross-border institutions that give Dublin a role in governing Northern Ireland; and the nationalists have granted only the somewhat barbed concession that they will absorb Ulster into a united Ireland only by consent).

A well informed American reader would have a slightly different list of prejudices. While subscribing to most of those above, he would deny fair-mindedness to the English and treat Unionists and Protestants largely as the pawns of a London government in the final stages of imperial dissolution—if he recognized the existence of Ulster Protestants at all. One Irish American observer, the columnist Jimmy Breslin, managed not to include a single Protestant in his novel on the post 1968 Troubles, *World Without End, Amen*—surely a case of Hamlet without the gravedigger.

To such observers of the Ulster scene, Robert McCartney's book will come as a revelation—and a necessary curative for their illusions. Here, in the urgent practical prose of daily journalism, pamphleteering and the hustings, is the real history of Northern Ireland from 1985 to the present. Beginning with the Anglo-Irish Agreement and taking us up to the present slow-motion collapse of the Belfast Agreement, Mr McCartney shepherds us through every twist and turn of the spiraling political decline of British, Irish and, finally, American statecraft as applied to the Ulster Troubles. If his account departs drastically from the picture sketched above, it is because it shows the world turned right-side up. Whereas the conventional account depicts wise governments in Washington, London and Dublin coaxing an intransigent Unionist majority into conceding the social and national rights of an oppressed nationalist minority, Mr McCartney shows timid governments being driven by intransigent terrorists into removing the democratic rights of the law-abiding majorities in both Catholic and Protestant communities. Mr McCartney is perhaps the best lawyer in Northern Ireland—a very high tribute indeed—and he examines government documents and political speeches with a lawyer's eye for misleading concessions and dangerous codicils. As he demonstrates repeatedly in his critical examination of the speeches and documents thrown up by such events as the New Ireland Forum Report, the Hume-Adams dialogue, the Downing Street Declaration and the negotiations leading up to the Belfast Agreement, whenever the three governments have had to choose between appeasing terrorists and meeting the wishes of democratically elected politicians, they have almost invariably chosen to appease the terrorists.

That choice, repeatedly made, has in the end produced a malign and unstable paradox. Outsiders first began to take an interest in Ulster in the mid-sixties precisely because the Stormont government had gerrymandered its constituency boundaries to ensure the largest possible Unionist representation (though everyone concedes that an entirely fair system would still have delivered Unionist landslides). The Belfast Agreement gerrymanders on a far larger scale in order to ensure that even those terrorists with minimal electoral support are guaranteed a place in government. The voters are thus denied what is perhaps the primary democratic right: the ability to throw the rascals out. Judged from a democratic standpoint, then, the present situation is actually more objectionable than the status quo of 1966. With all its admitted flaws, the Stormont parliament of those times was not actually rigged to ensure that unrepentant terrorists would be Ministers of the Crown—even when almost no one voted for them. Yet that is the constitutional position in Ulster today.

What makes this outcome particularly unsettling is that Ulster has a longer and more vigorous tradition of democratic politics than almost any other part of the English-speaking world. Ulstermen supported the French Revolution (somewhat naively in my own view, but then that is also true of many of the French revolutionaries); they backed the American Revolution (more consistently with their own principles); indeed, they were leaders in the rebellion against George III and contributed mightily to the debates and struggles that created the Great Republic; and even today they are far more civic-minded than people in other parts of the United Kingdom in the age of managerial politics. They argue, debate policy and hold their leaders to account. And as Mr McCartney establishes—for this is a work of political theory as well as of recent political history—their defence of the Union is rooted in this long Anglo-American democratic tradition. It is part and parcel of a politics of civil liberty, political democracy and free vigorous debate that used to be the common property of the English-speaking world. The purely sectarian element in such politics—its hostility to 'Rome rule'—is a shrinking historical curiosity in democratic Unionism and is preserved mainly in loyalist terrorism (precisely the political forces protected by the electoral arrangements of the Belfast Agreement). Stifling democracy in Ulster for the sake of a temporary ceasefire is not only a bad bargain (since who can hold armed terrorists to democratic account?), it also suggests that a great liberal tradition in world politics has forgotten its own principles or, worse, considers them unimportant compared to the great objective of having a quiet life.

As Mr McCartney establishes on almost every page, the problem may not be that Ulster cannot be trusted with Anglo-American democracy, but that Anglo-American democracy has lost the moral self-confidence to insist that the solution to inadequate democracy is even more of the same.

John O'Sullivan
United Press International
Washington, DC·
February 2001

I

INTRODUCTION

One

Liberty, Democracy and the Union

INTRODUCTION

Reflecting upon the course of my professional and political life, it is clear that three major themes have consistently taken centre stage: liberty, democracy and the Union of Great Britain and Northern Ireland. These priorities have inspired my pursuits in the private sector and in public service, as a barrister, politician, member of the British Parliament and leader of the UK/Unionist Party. The principles of liberty, democracy and the Union have animated my defence of civil society in Ulster, my concern for the welfare of all of the citizens of Northern Ireland and my commitment to the security of the United Kingdom. They have also informed my interpretation of how relations between the United Kingdom and Ireland, and between the British and Irish people, can best be placed on a firmer footing, the kind of strong foundation that will promote real peace and lasting stability throughout the British Isles.

Liberty, democracy and the Union of Great Britain and Northern Ireland are, by their very nature, complex political concepts. They encompass sophisticated constitutional issues, nuanced political principles and subtle legal arguments. The ideas of liberty and democracy, for instance, find expression in various forms not just across the globe, but even throughout Great Britain and Ireland. Within the United Kingdom itself, the notion of the Union means different things to different people, a trend that has accelerated in the past few years as a new framework of devolution is assembled across Britain. All three themes are vulnerable to suppression by populist ideas of what amounts to social peace. Understanding them thus demands serious study, systematic inquiry and reflection upon their value. So, in addition to defending these ideals in my public life, I have attempted to analyse them over the past fifteen years in a sustained series of political writings. The pieces that I have produced have taken various prose forms. They include chapters in books, political pamphlets, an academic review of the inherent tension between liberty and state authority, major speeches, party documents, submissions to government bodies and numerous articles published in newspapers and magazines throughout the United Kingdom and Ireland, such as the *Belfast News Letter, Belfast Telegraph, Daily Telegraph, Sunday Telegraph, The Times* and the *Irish Times*.

A selection of these writings is gathered together in this volume. What unifies this representative cross-section of my work is its examination of the central place of liberty, democracy and the Union in the political life of the United Kingdom—and also in Ireland and the

United States. While exploring these wider themes, this collection addresses more specific topics as well. First and foremost, it sets out a rational and, I hope, persuasive case for Unionism. It delivers a democratic defence of the Union. It unapologetically asserts that only the maintenance of the Union can best serve the interests of democracy in Northern Ireland. Securing this aim requires Unionists to embrace a pluralist, liberal, non-sectarian Unionism. Major strides have been taken in this direction in recent years. Unionists in Ulster can thus fairly justify the significant contribution that they have made throughout the twentieth century to the growth and development of the great tradition of Anglo-American democracy.

There is still more distance to travel, however. An exploration of the nature of pluralist Unionism is thus one of the main features of this book. It is also is a central tenet of my political philosophy. This volume, consequently, clearly sets out my point of view and sketches the contours of my political thought. It establishes the imperative of liberal Unionism, while considering other issues vital to our national life, such as civil liberties, church-state relations, trade, commerce, the legal system, the European Union, the peace process in Northern Ireland, terrorism, policing and media manipulation. As a whole, the ideas, policies and precepts expressed in this collection offer a democratically principled model for ensuring the success of Unionism, and the long term survival of the Union, within the matrix of contemporary British politics, Anglo-Irish affairs and North-South relations.

I have also endeavoured to paint a fair and balanced picture of the history and politics of Northern Ireland and to offer an honest, even-handed assessment of Unionism in Northern Ireland, ignoring neither its weaknesses nor its strengths, its faults nor its achievements. Unionism is discussed not just in its Northern Irish setting, but also in its wider—and proper—British context. Such an analysis will, I trust, broaden our understanding of Unionism, deepen our appreciation of its provenance, legitimise its core constitutional principles and underscore its British character. It also reminds us that Unionism in Northern Ireland is not simply a provincial reflex, but an integral component of a larger Unionist tradition that underpins the existence of the United Kingdom itself.

*   *   *

Unionists have consistently taken pride in both their British identity and British political heritage. But these fundamental features of Unionism do not, by any means, preclude Irish nationalists from playing a full part in the affairs of Northern Ireland. In fact, it is essential that they do so. It is true that, historically, Unionism has not made this clear enough to nationalists, so its recent efforts to welcome them on an equal basis into every sphere of public life in Northern Ireland must be encouraged in the strongest possible terms. At the same time, the intrinsic Britishness of Unionism has been underestimated, overlooked and often ignored by Irish nationalists, especially in the South. This outcome is partly the result of a history and political culture that blinds many people living in the Republic of Ireland to the complexities of Unionism. True, this myopia is less severe now than in past decades, due in large part to the efforts of a small band of Southern intellectuals, scholars and journalists who have challenged the received assumptions of Irish nationalism *vis-à-vis* Unionism. Still, the political ambience that blurs the vision of many Southerners gazing northwards receives serious attention in this volume. In the process, this book explains Unionists in Northern Ireland to Irish nationalists—and vice versa. It also reveals to the latter exactly how their actions and attitudes affect the sensibilities of Northern Protestants.

One of the traits of Irish nationalism that has particularly unsettled Unionists since the partition of Ireland in 1922, and has consistently bedevilled North-South relations as a result, is the dark impulse of irredentism—in both its constitutional and violent manifestations. The interaction of these two strains of Irish *revanchism* has historically produced a combustible admixture. Sparked off by its constitutional catalyst, violent Irish irredentism inevitably assumes the shape of republican terrorism, which has been one of the primary engines of the Troubles. Republicanism, in turn, feeds off of its mirror image, Ulster loyalism, which is unquestionably inimical to the finest traditions of Unionism, democratic pluralism and civil society in Britain. The aberrant cultures of republican and loyalist paramilitarism constitute the gravest threats to democracy, liberty and the Union in Northern Ireland. A policy of appeasing terrorists for political ends, and debasing the rule of law, may simply exchange political terror for its social variant of Mafia-like criminality. These ideas are closely scrutinised in this volume, which is, *inter alia*, a robust argument against political terrorism in all of its guises as well as the paramilitary oxygen that fosters it. This book strongly upholds the rule of law, which over the past thirty years has served as a firewall against terror. Without it, liberty and democracy in Ulster will have no present foundation or hope of posterity.

Since the early 1990s the British and Irish political establishments, aided by the Clinton administration in Washington, have sought to end terrorism in Northern Ireland by engaging in a much vaunted peace process. Its thinly disguised agenda, however, is detrimental to the maintenance of the Union. Several aspects of this misguided enterprise are adverse to Unionist interests and are subjected to close examination here. These threats include the functional institutions established by the Belfast Agreement, such as the cross-border bodies overseen by the Council of Ministers. These structures were preordained in the Anglo-Irish Agreement of 1985 and are modelled on parallel structures in the European Union. They may, in fact, be used to transport Northern Ireland out of the United Kingdom and into united a Ireland. Another deleterious dimension of the peace process is its blatant appeasement of terrorism, which not only corrupts democracy, but frustrates liberty, since terror can never be placated. Equally harmful is the slick political spin that has been employed to sell the peace process to a weary public anxious for a return to some semblance of normality.

Because of the threat that it poses to the Union, the peace process illustrates the characteristic weakness and self-interest of successive British governments which, since 1921, have periodically failed to reciprocate the profound allegiance of Unionists in Northern Ireland to the Union. For this, I believe, they are justly taken to task. British officialdom has not always acted in good faith *vis-à-vis* Northern Ireland's constitutional status within the United Kingdom, and its commitment to the Union has often appeared conditional. This intermittent indifference is highlighted not as an end in itself, but as a stark reminder to the London government that the state of the Union in Ulster has immediate implications for the state of the Union overall. Loosening the bonds with Northern Ireland, especially in the context of constitutional devolution at home and closer integration in Europe, may release centrifugal forces elsewhere across the United Kingdom that will jeopardise the very existence of the Union itself. In this regard, it is well to remember that Northern Ireland lies not on the periphery of the Union, but at its very core.

REFLECTIONS ON LIBERTY, DEMOCRACY AND THE UNION

The foregoing principles and priorities are explored throughout this book. Each section focuses upon one central, or several interrelated, themes. Part II comprises *Liberty and Authority in Ireland*. This treatise, penned in 1985 when I was a member of the Ulster Unionist Party and the Northern Ireland Assembly, formed part of a series of political pamphlets published by the Field Day Company of Londonderry. It reflects on how the various political traditions in Ireland have grappled with the most serious conflicts arising in any democracy, those between majority and minority rights, church and state, a negative freedom guaranteeing civil liberties and a positive freedom ensuring self-determination. It argues that Anglo-American liberal democracy offers the most promising model for resolving these tensions in favour of individual liberty. It also maps out a vision of a modern, pluralist Unionism inspired by liberal democracy's greatest theorists, including John Locke, Edmund Burke, John Stuart Mill and Isaiah Berlin.

As a committed Unionist I am keenly alive to Irish revisionist designs on Northern Ireland. Part III, therefore, addresses the peril that Irish irredentism poses to Unionism in Northern Ireland. This phenomenon manifests itself in both straightforward and subtle ways. Several variations are addressed in 'Priests, Politicians and Pluralism', including the hidden agenda of the New Ireland Forum, the nationalist project of the early 1980s whose three final irredentist proposals provoked Margaret Thatcher's famous reply, 'Out, Out, Out!' This chapter also analyses the Roman Catholic hierarchy's submission to that Forum, especially its disturbing assertion that the 'rights of a minority are no more sacred than the rights of a majority', a statement that not only contradicts the constitutional norms of liberal democracy, but exposed the myth that the Forum could produce any blueprint for a new, pluralist Ireland. The next essay, 'Barry's John', is a review of an early political biography of John Hume. I have never been convinced that John Hume's overt political ecumenism had any real depth or that anything but the advocacy of Irish irredentism lay beneath it.

The final chapter in this section is a critique of the Anglo-Irish Agreement of 1985. Its starting point is the *revanchism* of Articles Two and Three of the Irish constitution. Declared a 'constitutional imperative' in a 1990 Irish Supreme Court case, this legal irredentism was unprecedented in a European context. It was also institutionalised in the Anglo-Irish Agreement, which did enormous harm to Unionist relations with the Republic of Ireland by establishing incipient structures with the long term capacity to transfer Ulster into a united Ireland. Now, it is true that Articles Two and Three of the Irish Constitution have recently been amended so that they express an aspiration to Irish unity. But even this revised constitutional irrendentism remains unparalleled throughout Europe; closer to home, it is anachronistic, destabilising and detrimental to developing greater rapport between Unionists and Irish nationalists.

BRITISH CITIZENSHIP AND PLURALIST UNIONISM

From 1982 to 1986 I was a member of the Ulster Unionist Party and the Northern Ireland Assembly. After the Assembly collapsed in 1986 I grew disillusioned with the UUP's drift towards the kind of devolutionist policy encapsulated in the Anglo-Irish Agreement. I, therefore, helped to launch the Campaign for Equal Citizenship—and was elected its president. This movement called on national parties in Great Britain to organise in Northern Ireland for the first time, believing that such a new political paradigm could simultaneously stabilise society and underpin the Union. This campaign is explored in Part IV. Never for a moment was it about the ascendancy of one community over the other, a fact made expressly clear in the speech 'We Have a Vision', which publicly launched the campaign. Its primary aim was to secure equality of rights between Protestant Unionists and Catholic nationalists in Northern Ireland and between the people of Northern Ireland and the rest of the United Kingdom. Written in 1986, this address still resonates today, for the concept of equal citizenship remains an imaginative framework for resolving the sectarian animosities that divide Northern Ireland.

Growing further disenchanted with the Ulster Unionist Party's failure to defend the Union, I made a speech at the party's annual conference in the autumn of the same year supporting a motion for the adoption of a clearly defined policy of political integration with the national parties of the United Kingdom. This address constitutes chapter seven, 'Equal Citizenship and Ulster Unionism'. The object of the policy I advocated would have been the strengthening of the Union at the cost of the gradual withering away of the party. Over forty percent of the delegates gave me their support, despite the opposition of all of the party's elected representatives and its executive committee. The fatal weakness of the party was exposed. The desire of many of its members for the spoils of office in a devolved administration was to provide the bait for luring them ultimately into the Belfast Agreement. The party apparatchik took their revenge by expelling me, allegedly for encouraging the electorate to support other parties.

The chapters in the next section (V) were thus written in a changed political and personal context. I ran for Parliament in the 1987 general election as a 'Real Unionist' against the sitting Independent Unionist MP for the North Down constituency, Mr James Kilfedder. While I did not win the election, the reduction of Kilfedder's vote constituted one of the biggest electoral swings in the United Kingdom. More important, my expulsion from the UUP left me free to speak my mind with untrammelled frankness. In the late 1980s and early 1990s I wrote a series of newspaper articles critical of political developments in Northern Ireland, several of which are gathered together in Part V, entitled 'The Shape of Things to Come'. The first chapter, 'Unionist Leaders will Doom the Union', challenges the UUP's growing sympathy for devolutionist proposals on the grounds that such schemes reinforced the baleful precedent set by the Anglo-Irish Agreement. The next essay, 'Hume, Adams and Clausewitz', is about the Hume-Adams dialogue of 1988. It assesses the ominous tone of this disturbing rapprochement, its implications for Unionist interests and John Hume's stealthy strategy to undermine the Union—all of which are illuminated by the nineteenth-century political masterpiece, *On War*. The chapter 'Babbling Brooke' confronts the public relations campaign launched in 1990 by Peter Brooke, then the Secretary of State for Northern Ireland, to secure the devolution objective which forms the central core of the Anglo-Irish Agreement. This policy was consistent with Mr Brooke's shocking declaration in 1990 that the British government had 'no selfish strategic or economic interest in Northern Ireland'—an extraordinary statement to make about a sovereign part of the United Kingdom. This essay and the two preceding it, like the entire previous section, assert that equal citizenship, not devolution, can provide the most satisfactory answers to many of the difficult political questions hanging over Northern Ireland today.

In retrospect, the three chapters in Part V illustrate that rational analysis can provide the basis for the discernment of future political developments. Likewise, several other selections in this volume—on the Anglo-Irish Agreement, the Hume-Adams dialogue, the peace process, consent, the Framework Documents, decommissioning, devolution—demonstrate that a serious, systematic appraisal of the available evidence often makes it possible to forecast the general course of political events in Northern Ireland. This evidence is not guarded like a state secret deep in the corridors of Whitehall, but is at hand to all citizens in a democratic society, where governments must operate in an open and accessible fashion. But making proper use of it requires discrimination and a willingness to eschew sentimental populist hopes in favour of rationality. Indeed, this faculty—logically assessing facts and conditions on the ground to ascertain the probable shape of things to come—must be utilised more frequently in order to preserve civil society in Northern Ireland.

*   *   *

In June 1995 I won a Parliamentary by-election in the North Down constituency following the death of James Kilfedder and thus took up a seat at Westminster that I have held since. In the spring of 1996 I became the leader of the newly formed UK/Unionist Party. This organisation immediately provided an institutional structure that could support the political precepts cherished by myself, my party colleagues and many of my constituents, while simultaneously conveying them to a larger audience; it also enabled us to find common cause with other likeminded Unionists.

Against this background, Part VI, 'New Unionism, Pluralist Unionism', further elucidates the priorities that inform my approach to politics, my tenure in the House of Commons and the new model of Unionism I endorse. In the first chapter of this section, written soon after my 1995 by-election victory, I assert that a Union based upon any form of sectarian ascendancy is not only undesirable, but unjust, and that a new Union must be predicated upon the principles of pluralism. These ideals recognise a wide difference of opinion on a broad range of topics and accommodate all views, save those that in their public expression are harmful to the well-being of others. This new Unionism must be inclusive rather than exclusive and dedicated to the interests of both Catholics and Protestants, nationalists and Unionists. These themes resonate in the second chapter, 'A Union with Room for All', which describes my vision of a Union that cherishes the civil and religious liberties of all the citizens of Northern Ireland—and their cultural identities as well: the rhythm of the Lambeg drum must be heard alongside the beat of the Bodhran. Next is a UK/Unionist Party election manifesto drawn up for the 1997 general election; it translates the foregoing ideas into practical politics and demonstrates how the UK/Unionist Party is true to the principles of a non-sectarian Unionism.

THE PEACE PROCESS AND THE UNION

Part VII challenges the British and Irish governments' stewardship of the peace process in Northern Ireland by highlighting its profound shortcomings: the danger it poses to the Union; its undermining of democracy; its appeasement of terrorists. The first selection, 'The Threat to the Union', evinces how the Downing Street Declaration puts it beyond debate that the British government shares with its Irish counterpart, the SDLP, the British Labour Party and Sinn Fein/IRA the view that a united Ireland is the only solution to the Northern Ireland conflict; these groups differ only on how and when it is to be achieved.

The next chapter, 'Sovereignty and Seduction', unmasks how the peace process facilitates the silent, inexorable transfer of sovereignty over Northern Ireland from the United Kingdom to Ireland.

The following essay debunks the nationalist concept of parity of esteem, which has been elevated into a sacrosanct principle during the peace process. It proposes exactly how Unionists should respond to the nationalist demand that the aspiration for a united Ireland be accorded equal legitimacy to the Unionist preference for the Union. What Unionists must do is make it clear that they will fully support total and equal rights for everyone in Northern Ireland, but they will concede nothing on the majority's democratic right to choose who will govern them. The basic principle in a democracy is that the will of the majority determines who will govern. This right of the majority, of course, is subject to the guarantee of certain fundamental liberties, such as those set out in the United States Bill of Rights. But what positively is not a civil right is the demand of a minority to choose who will govern, as opposed to how it will be governed. Accordingly, in this essay I call for an end to the pervasive Unionist guilt complex, a debilitating mode of thinking that has been exacerbated by nationalist propaganda.

While the foregoing exposition refutes untenable nationalist demands, the next chapter, 'Appeasement in our Time', draws historical parallels between the British government's policies during the 1930s and the 1990s. It was written in June 1996, soon after an IRA bomb devastated the centre of Manchester. British officialdom's initial response to this latest outrage was one of robust defiance. Still, the essay anticipates that this atrocity, and others like it, would gradually erode the British government's resolve, for its record suggested that a climb-down would inevitably take place. More specifically, it would eventually accede to Sinn Fein/IRA's political demand of entry into all-party talks without decommissioning its weapons. The chapter also asserts that Sinn Fein/IRA, having demonstrated in Manchester the efficiency of its bomb making capabilities, would nudge events in its preferred direction by declaring a ceasefire, which would provide the Irish and British governments with a pretext to welcome Sinn Fein into negotiations. The IRA's latent threat of renewed violence, meanwhile, would act as a lever to extract further concessions throughout the negotiating process.

In May 1996 the UK/Unionist Party won three seats to the Northern Ireland Forum, the vehicle for all-party talks, and I was named leader of our party's delegation. In July 1997, two months after I was reelected to Parliament, the UK/Unionist Party withdrew from the negotiations when it became clear that the British and Irish governments were going to permit the political representatives of paramilitary organisations to enter them in their substantive mode without decommissioning their weapons. The chapter 'Why the UK/Unionists are not at the Talks' explains my party's position. We exited the negotiations for two main reasons. The first is a matter of deep principle: it is wrong, absolutely and always, to negotiate with armed and unrepentant terrorists in a democracy. Northern Ireland is not South Africa, where the great majority of people did not have the right to vote. The lesson of history through the centuries is that appeasement does not work. Attempts to reward violence lead only to more violence, until the terrorists achieve their aims. It is these considerations that formed the second reason for the UK/Unionist Party's withdrawal from the talks: we refused to adopt the cynicism of other parties. Since we were convinced that the negotiations could not be successful without substantially weakening democracy and the Union in order to buy peace, we could not, in all conscience, join in. To do so would mislead our supporters and many others as to the true beliefs and intentions of our party.

All of that said, the UK/Unionist Party believes that a just resolution to the conflict in Northern Ireland is possible, so long as it adheres to two widely accepted international principles. First, existing boundaries must be respected: it is the right of majorities to determine the political and national identity of the state of which they form part. And second, the rights of minorities to full and equal respect within the law must be upheld—unequivocally and without exception.

The final chapter of this section takes up a new theme. During the spring of 1998, the Northern Ireland Chamber of Commerce invited various party leaders and public officials to discuss their views on the state of Northern Ireland's economy. In my own address I disputed the peace process-induced notion that Northern Ireland's economy can flourish in a united Ireland. I asserted, instead, that the economic future of Northern Ireland lies, as it always has, in its association with Britain as an integral part of the United Kingdom. For Northern Ireland's captains of industry to buy into the economics of Irish unity would be to risk the prosperity of one-and-a-half-million people for the financial gambles of a few. It would be to equate the possibilities of marginal gain with the probabilities of economic disaster and would, in the process, prejudice the constitutional wishes of the majority of our people.

*   *   *

Section VIII comprises two political pamphlets published in 1997: *The McCartney Report on Consent* and *The McCartney Report on the Framework Documents*. These tracts, in combination, refute the claim that the peace process can simultaneously turn aside terrorism, preserve liberty and safeguard the Union. The first report details how the vaunted principle of consent—the proposition that there will be no change in the status of Northern Ireland as part of the United Kingdom without the agreement of a majority of the people living there—has been reduced to no more than a hollow guarantee. Few Unionists are fully aware of the ongoing process for modifying and diluting this principle to the point where it will soon present no obstacle to the unification of Ireland. The British and Irish governments, assisted by the SDLP, have put in place political institutions that will gradually evolve into a factually and economically united Ireland that will render the final consent to the transfer of legal constitutional sovereignty a mere formality.

The political apparatus being constructed to nullify Unionist consent is scrutinised in *The McCartney Report on the Framework Documents*. It consists of institutions like the North-South Ministerial Council and cross-border bodies with executive powers. These structures, which are modelled on similar ones within the European Community whose real objective is a single, politically federated state of Europe, rely on the theory of functionalism. Functionalism is the centralisation of two or more independent sovereign states via an interlocking web of practical and financial institutions that results in common consultation on the harmonisation and, ultimately, executive control of the administration of the relevant states. Once effective functional and economic union has been completed, theoretical considerations of national sovereignty become irrelevant, and political union will follow inevitably of its own accord.

*   *   *

Part IX investigates one of the most glaring flaws of the entire peace process: the issue of arms decommissioning, especially the British and Irish governments' abject failure to demand that paramilitary organisations relinquish their illegally held arsenals before their political representatives were permitted to participate in all-party talks. In the chapter 'Decommissioning and Democracy', a document composed during an early phase of the Stormont negotiations (Autumn 1996) and presented to Senator George Mitchell, the chair of the talks, the UK/Unionist Party sets out its approach to decommissioning within the context of the peace process. It asserts that decommissioning, resistance to it and the failure to insist upon it cannot be considered in isolation from the political objectives of the major participants or their strategies and tactics for achieving them. For instance, regardless of the denials of the British and Irish governments that their policies are not influenced by terrorist activity, no one believes this to be true. The reality is that they simply cannot publicly admit that political violence pays.

The next selection, 'Democracy will Die without Decommissioning', cuts right to the heart of the matter: the requirement for all paramilitary groups to decommission their weapons as a prerequisite for their political wings taking part in government is not a precondition imposed by other parties, it is a fundamental demand of democracy itself. The final chapter, 'Democracy and Terror', reprints the remarks that I made while introducing a motion into the Northern Ireland Assembly calling on it to expel any political party inextricably linked with a terrorist organisation retaining arms, for such a party would be incapable of giving an absolute commitment to the democratic process. This resolution received the unanimous support of the pro-Union parties, but did not pass because John Hume's SDLP failed to give it the cross-community support it required under the Assembly's rules of procedure.

THE POST-AGREEMENT POLITICAL LANDSCAPE

The penultimate section of this book, 'Defending Democracy, Sustaining the Union', surveys the post-Belfast Agreement political landscape. The opening chapter recalls some of the setbacks visited upon the cause of the Union by the peace process. Regrettably, divisions within Unionism have contributed to the ongoing success of Irish republicanism. For their part, republican terrorists, and their loyalist counterparts, continue to tear asunder the fabric of civil society in Ulster. The second essay, 'Placating Terror Will Cost Dearly', warns that the utopian future envisioned by the most ardent advocates of the peace process is fast turning into a macabre nightmare. An increasing tide of paramilitary criminality, punishment beatings and drug culture is overwhelming the entire social sub-structure of Northern Ireland; the rule of law has simply ceased to operate in many parts of the province.

The next two chapters demonstrate that one of the most flagrant features of the peace process—the proposed wholesale reform of the Royal Ulster Constabulary—will hasten the slide into lawlessness. 'The Royal Ulster Constabulary and the Future of Democracy' constitutes the UK/Unionist Party's formal submission to the Independent Commission for Policing in Northern Ireland (the Patten Commission). It asserts that

Sinn Fein/IRA's call for 'the root and branch destruction of the RUC', and their assertion that anything less will cause the Belfast Agreement to fail, illustrate their determination to fatally demoralise the single organisation which can frustrate the triumph of terror. 'Patten's Flawed Vision' delivers a stark warning: destroy the morale of a police force and you remove its capacity to discharge its duties, both of combating crime and protecting society from political terrorism. Yes, sensible reforms of the RUC are necessary, but the present policies of the British government have done much to achieve what terrorists have failed to accomplish, namely, the destruction of the morale of a police force which has averted a descent into chaos.

The essay 'Devolution and Deception', written soon after the Northern Ireland executive collapsed in February 2000, outlines the unlikely prospects for successful self-rule in Northern Ireland. Devolution in Scotland and Wales rests upon the premise of the electorate being able to replace those in government. In Ulster, however, the system has been artificially rigged to prevent the democratic transfer of power. Any elections in Northern Ireland following a period of patently incompetent government will almost certainly result in the return of the same parties in broadly the same ratio, who will, in turn, again nominate their ministers to the largely unchanged executive. The next entry, 'Unappeasable Revolutionaries', evaluates the deal that led to the reinstatement of the Northern Ireland executive in the late Spring of 2000 and offers a realistic, hard-headed analysis of Sinn Fein/IRA's post-Agreement strategy. Several commentators have implied that the IRA's statement at this time—the full implementation of the Agreement will provide a political context in which Irish republicans and Unionists can peacefully pursue their respective political objectives as equals—is some novel concession to democracy. They are wrong. It is simply a reiteration of Sinn Fein's view of the Agreement as nothing more than a transitional phase en route to a united Ireland. In the meantime, paramilitary prisoners guilty of the most heinous crimes have been released back into society without serving their full sentences, which is the topic of the final essay, 'The Ends Never Justify the Means'. Not only is the title of this chapter correct, but rarely do dishonourable means achieve their ends. This will almost certainly prove to be the case in relation to an unjustifiable policy that sends criminals back among the people whom they terrorised in direct contravention of the rule of law.

*   *   *

The final part of this volume (XI) analyses the growth of a disturbing political phenomenon encouraged by New Labour and the government of Tony Blair: the relentless use of media manipulation and political spin. The first essay, 'Politics and Public Relations', cautions that while information control has largely been associated with totalitarian regimes of the right or the left, it would be naive to consider that governments claiming to be democratic are immune from utilising propaganda as a means of achieving policy objectives. The increasing sophistication of communications technology and the concentration of media control in a diminishing number of hands makes the potential for the distortion of public opinion a matter of crucial importance for the protection of democracy.

The next two chapters draw out this analysis further and apply it to Northern Ireland. When Tony Blair talks about New Labour, everything in it is in terms of the future. The institutions of the past—whether they be Old Labour, the House of Lords, the Constitution, the trade unions or even the Monarchy—have all become dispensable. This is also the case with the Union. Thus during the referendum on the Belfast Agreement nothing was allowed to compete with the government's message that it should pass. By early 1998 the Northern Ireland Office had its own hand-picked propaganda department dedicated to implementing its policies. Politicians who advocated a 'no' vote in the referendum were prey to the dark arts of political spin: they were tarred with epithets like 'rejectionist Unionists' and 'obstructionists', even by former terrorists accorded celebrity status by government spokesmen.

Where a state imposes such penalties, either directly or indirectly, upon those who oppose it; where a compliant media lends itself, knowingly or unwittingly, to the uncritical approval of government policy; where those in positions of influence allow themselves to be used as opponents of democratic dissent—then in such a state liberty and freedom may ultimately perish. But these principles need not be consigned to the past. The Epilogue to this volume sets out how they can not only inspire the present, but endure for future generations. Several options are discussed. Chief among them, and one of the most essential means for ensuring the survival of liberty and democracy, must be the maintenance of the Union of Great Britain and Northern Ireland.

II

LIBERTY AND AUTHORITY

Two

Liberty and Authority in Ireland[1]

INTRODUCTION

The conflict of the liberty of the individual with the authority of the majority in Northern Ireland and the Republic represents the battleground not just of people and parties, but of two ideologies about the nature of man. According to one perception, man is seen as a free spirit, naturally good, but stunted, limited and frustrated by archaic and restrictive institutions—whether of church or state—masquerading as the source and repository of sacred traditions and values. Man is seen by the other ideology as a creature of limited freedom, only partly good and whose only salvation is within the great authoritarian frameworks of states, churches or parties. It is argued that only authority gives the strength and security needed to resist the dangerous liberties touted by conscienceless individuals. Up to the early nineteenth century, supporters of both views were of the opinion that reason and discipline were the methods for both finding and applying the solution to man's problems. The abandonment of such rational methods in favour of romantic and irrational influences gave birth to the nationalism and fascism of the later nineteenth and twentieth centuries.

The growth of a nationalist movement in Ireland with an inherent anti-liberal and irrational content coincided with the emergence of an authoritarian Church as the *de facto* state religion of the overwhelming majority. The interaction of these factors produced such homogeneity of social and cultural values, and such an absence of ideological difference, as to make a form of government in the Republic based on parliamentary democracy appear to work, but only at the price of a continuing sacrifice of the individual liberties of the minority. Particularly in the Republic, the authority of the state and the Church was to overwhelm the individual. The very success of this authority was to be one of the greatest single obstructions to the nation's irredentist claim to incorporate the territory and people of Northern Ireland into a united Ireland.

THE DEMOCRATIC RULE OF THE MAJORITY VERSUS MINORITY RIGHTS

The democratic right of the majority to rule and the perception of freedom as the sum of the fundamental human rights of the individual are often the contending liberties locked in sometimes mortal conflict in

---

[1]*Liberty and Authority in Ireland* (Londonderry: Field Day Pamphlet, 1985).

Ireland. Mr Justice Robert H Jackson of the United States Supreme Court considered that the most delicate, difficult and shifting of all the balances which the Supreme Court is expected to maintain is that between liberty and authority. In case after case in which so-called civil rights are involved, the question boils down to one of the extent to which majority rule will be set aside.

There is no necessary connection between democratic rule and the liberty of the individual. The answer to the question, 'who will govern me?' is logically distinct from the question, 'how far does government interfere with me?' Freedom in the latter sense of an absence from interference and the preservation of a free area of action for the individual was thought by John Stuart Mill to be the only freedom which deserved the name, i.e., that of pursuing our own good in our own way. Liberty in this sense is the answer to the question, 'what am I free to do or be?' This, in Isaiah Berlin's terminology, is the negative, or Millsian, freedom of being free from state interference. It is the freedom which most frequently protects and guards individual and minority rights.

The function of the rule of law as the instrument of government is to regulate the conduct of individuals in relation to each other and to prevent the collision of their interests. As Mr Justice Jackson puts it:

> The legal profession in all countries know that there are only two real choices of government open to a people. It may be governed by law or it may be governed by the will of one [man] or a group of men. Law, as the expression of the ultimate will and wisdom of a people, has so far proven the safest guardian of liberty yet devised.

Well enough, one might say, but what of the laws themselves? That there must be curbs to individual freedom is self-evident. The laws affecting these curbs depend on the given society's determination of good and evil based upon its values—moral, religious, intellectual, economic, even aesthetic. To protest against laws governing censorship and personal liberty, as did WB Yeats, Sean O'Faolain and others in the Republic of Ireland, presupposes the belief that the forbidden activities are fundamental needs of men as men in a good or, indeed, any society. To defend such laws is to hold that these needs are not essential and cannot be satisfied without sacrificing other values which are regarded as more important than individual freedom—values determined by some standard that is not merely subjective, but is an objective standard for which some status, empirical or *a priori*, is claimed, be it the dogma of a Church, the authority of revealed scriptures, the cultural heritage of a nation or the ideology of a political party.

*   *   *

The right of liberty to choose to live as one desires must be weighed against the claims of many other values, of which equality, justice, security or public order are but examples. The requirement for compromise is a necessary truth. Edmund Burke thought all government, all human benefit and every human virtue was founded on compromise and barter. The determination to preserve absolute categories, or ideals, at the expense of human lives and happiness is found in equal measure not only in the political extremes of left and right, but in other less evident centres of authority in Ireland, like the churches. Sabbitarianism and laws against contraception are examples of this absolutist determination. The argument that freedom may be denied in the defence of freedom has been used in Northern Ireland, whether with political justification or not, by successive governments and with the overwhelming concurrence of the majority. Neither the dilemma nor the solution by authority is novel; nor is it limited to Northern Ireland.

It is not so easy, as some people believe, to determine what serves liberty best by restricting executive authority. The removal of Japanese immigrants, including those who were citizens of the United States, from the American West Coast in World War II was rationalised as a service to ultimate liberty. Abraham Lincoln, like Franklin Delano Roosevelt a great servant of freedom, nevertheless suspended the Writ of Habeas Corpus and resorted to wholesale arrest without warrant, detention without trial and imprisonment without judicial conviction. These policies were condemned by Chief Justice Taney. But as Justice Jackson later observed, it was difficult to be certain whether liberty would have survived if Lincoln had scrupulously observed the Chief Justice's principles and, equally so, if the Chief Justice had adopted Lincoln's philosophy as that of the law. The basis of the argument for past or present emergency legislation is that it is required by the majority to defend their freedom to determine by whom they will be governed as well as how they are to be governed. Such laws are, to a degree, a reflection of majority rule and what is conceived by that majority as the ultimate freedom.

The present laws of the Republic of Ireland owe much of their content to the nationalist and theological values of the state's founding fathers. The political necessity of creating as rapidly as possible a fully independent and sovereign state with a unique and separate national identity was only possible by obeying a political imperative hostile to pluralism. This course was facilitated by the religious homogeneity and cultural consensus of a population that was 93% Roman Catholic. Nationalism and the national religion, with it's *a priori* values on doctrine, law, education and social behaviour, were to become partners in power. The social legislation of the 1920's and 1930's, culminating in the 1937 constitution of the Republic, not only rendered the exercise of certain individual liberties unlawful, but also unconstitutional. Everything has a price, and the price of such a sovereign, national, independent state was then, and is now, partition. The 1937 constitution, described by FSL Lyons as a compendium of Catholic social teaching, did guarantee equal rights before the law, but that law was powerfully tinged by Catholic influences. Protestant parents had no rights against Catholic principles. The balance between the liberty of the individual and the authority of the majority came down crushingly in favour of authority. Some would argue that over a period of sixty years nationalism, as institutionalised in the Republic of Ireland, has proved the Unionist suspicion that Home Rule was Rome rule.

*   *   *

Freedom in the negative, or Millsian, sense of being free from interference by the state has often little to hope for from the rule of majorities. Democracy, as such, is logically uncommitted to this type of freedom and, as we have seen, it has, in certain historical circumstances, failed to protect that freedom—a failure which has, nevertheless, not entailed the rejection of democratic principles. In an age of mass media, almost any government can cause its subjects to generate any will that the government wants. To make the will of authority the will of the people is to establish the triumph of despotism by forcing the slaves to declare themselves free. If democracies can suppress negative, or personal, freedom without ceasing to be democratic, what would make a society truly free? Isaiah Berlin suggests two interrelated principles. Firstly, that no power, not even that of a majority, can be regarded as absolute; only rights are absolute. Secondly, that there are frontiers not artificially drawn within which the individual liberty of men should be inviolable. A comparison between the application of these principles in a pluralist United States and the concerted and sustained attempts to frustrate them in the theocratic ethos of the Republic of Ireland dramatically illustrates the degree to which negative freedom has been a casualty at the hands not only of irredentist nationalism, but also of a highly conservative Irish hierarchy.

NATIONALISM, THE NATION-STATE AND POSITIVE FREEDOM

If freedom in the negative, or Millsian, sense answers the question, `what am I free to do or be?' freedom in another sense answers the question, `who is to govern me?' This is the concept of positive freedom. The development of this positive freedom to be one's own master is often ultimately expressed in the collective self, or will, of a group, an interest or a nation. The individual's desire for recognition and status becomes the wish for the emancipation of his class, his community, his coreligionists or those claiming to share his national identity. It manifests itself not only in the minority of Northern Ireland, but in the Sikh and the Basque. So much is the collective status of the group interest desired that the negative freedom, or liberty, of the individual may be willingly sacrificed for it. It becomes preferable, even desirable, to be bullied, misgoverned, tyrannised by someone of the same group, interest, religion or national identity by whom the individual is recognised as a man and an equal, than to be well and tolerantly governed by someone from an allegedly higher and more remote group who does not recognise the individual for what he himself might wish to be—perhaps, in Northern Ireland terms, that chimera the 'first class citizen'. First class, in this sense, does not mean equal access to law, to rights, to opportunity. It means the triumph of the group's objective to determine by whom it shall be governed. Upon this altar the group will happily sacrifice not only individual liberty, but economic benefit. Although the individual may not obtain freedom in the negative sense at the hands of his group, they are his group, and he can identify with them. Upon such terms, in an extreme way, may a kneecapping imposed by a terrorist kangaroo court acquire a virtue among some which is denied by them to the considered judgment of a non-jury court. In this sense, Jean Jacques Rousseau could exult 'that the laws of liberty might prove to be more austere than the yoke of tyranny'.

This positive freedom means that theoretically all, and not just some, have a share in the public power which is entitled to total control over every aspect of the life of every citizen. It is absolute power exercised by the sovereignty of the people on behalf of all and over everyone. It can, and from time to time does, destroy the liberty of the individual. And why should an individual who has been robbed of his freedom make any distinction between oppression by a popular government, by a despot or even by a set of oppressive laws? Nor can it be argued that majority consent to the loss of individual liberty miraculously preserves such liberty simply because it is the majority's will. An equal right to oppress or interfere is not equivalent to liberty.

Oscar Wilde, who had much cause to know, thought that the only despot who tyrannised over body and soul alike was the people.

*   *   *

Negative freedom is, in essence, the rules for the control or curbing of power. The positive freedom of those who seek the recognition and dominance of their group is the acquisition and use of power and, if necessary (and it always seems to be necessary), the suppression in some degree of the individual's liberty. The relationship or, indeed, the conflict between these freedoms seems to highlight the fundamental political issues in Ireland. The failure to see the basic difference between them is nowhere more evident than in the confusion between the desire of Northern Ireland's minority for civil liberties and individual rights and its aspiration for Irish unity. The dilemma of liberal Unionism is its support for the former with all that it entails, in opposition to an non-Catholic ascendancy in Northern Ireland, and its rejection of Irish unity, which would entail being governed for the foreseeable future by an authoritarian and non-pluralist state.

The present situation is, of course, not a static one. The declaration of a constitutional crusade in the Republic (a crusade which is presently in abeyance), the degree of urban opposition to the abortion amendment, the virtual abandonment of a censorship which had made the South a laughing stock in the civilised world and the mounting pressure for reform in the field of family and domestic law are all indicators of a pluralist awakening. It would be premature to believe that the slow-moving tide of pluralism and liberty of conscience is either irresistible or continuous. Catholic Ireland does not exist in splendid isolation, but in the zeitgeist of contemporary world Catholicism. The forces of conservatism are far from spent. The impetus to reform initiated by Vatican II is ebbing, and John Paul II may yet emulate the reaction of Pio Nono. The future of liberty in Ireland may well be a race between a slowly developing pluralism, which will allow the Republic to grow into a modern political state, and some violent and bloody catastrophe engendered by nationalist extremists bent on the acquisition of positive freedom and the use of power it will provide—a catastrophe that may well obliterate the institutions, interests and values which a nationalist state and ultramontane political and religious conservatives seek to protect and isolate from a changing world.

The origin of much of Sinn Fein's motivation, both in method and ideology, lies in the nationalism which created and formed the ethos of the Republic. Only by an examination of this phenomenon can there be any prospect of finding a reconciling antidote.

*   *   *

According to Isaiah Berlin, the historic fusion of nationalism with the doctrine of the supremacy of the state created an idea of nationhood which possesses four major characteristics, characteristics which, on any objective view, nationalist Ireland clearly displays. Nationalism, it must be emphasised, is an ideology which is quite distinct from the concept of patriotism. It requires a conviction that men belong to a particular human group of which the individual parts are shaped in their character and can only be fully understood in the group context. This context is defined by common territory, customs, culture, laws, folk memories, language and artistic and religious expression, all of which shape not only individual human beings, but their purposes and their values. The preoccupation of Irish nationalists with the national territory, the national language, the Gaelic cultural identity and a constitution framed around a national religion is undeniable. To suggest that national boundaries have no academic currency, that Ireland historically was never a nation or that modern Gaelic culture is largely a product of a nineteenth-century romantic revival is to speak heresy.

Secondly, nationalism predicates a pattern of life in a society which depends for its values upon its own organic roots. In the case of conflict with other values—intellectual, religious, moral or personal— not springing from the same source, the supreme values of the nation must prevail. The essential human unit is not the individual, but the nation. The individual's values are not revealed to him by rational analysis, but only by an awareness of which he need not even be conscious. It is enough for him to sense the unique web of unanalysed complex relationships, which bind him to the organic whole of the nation. The exchange between the militant Irish nationalist and his Anglicised Catholic friend in Eimar O'Duffy's novel, *The Wasted Island*, published in 1919, sums it all up:

> You know little and care less for her traditions; you don't observe her customs; you don't think as she does; your heroes are not her heroes and your flag is not her flag; and instead of that patriotism which is a natural feeling innate in every normal man, you have a bastard thing you call "loyalty" . . . which is nothing more in reality than the fealty which a garrison owes to its paymasters . . . It's a question of life and death with us; a war between two civilisations, with our national language and customs, our very name and existence, at stake; and so long as the struggle goes on, nothing else in the world matters to us.

The third characteristic of nationalism is the idea that the most compelling reason for holding a belief, following a policy, fighting for a cause or attaining an objective is simply that the belief, policy, cause or objective is the nation's. They are not pursued because they lead to happiness, peace, justice of liberty or are even valid in their own right. They are pursued because they are the values of the individual's group or, for the nationalist, the nation. If they are not followed, the individual will be cut off from the particular form of social life into which he has been born. A twig, as Berlin puts it, broken off from the tree of life.

The final trait of nationalism is that in a situation where the needs of this organic state are incompatible with the goals of other groups, then the nation has no choice but to compel such groups to yield, by force if necessary. Nothing that obstructs or prevents the nation's supreme goal can be allowed to have equal value with it. There is no criterion or standard deriving its values from some external source other than those intrinsic to the nation. All values are referable only to the specific society or national organism. This loyalty to the *Volk* and its culture as the true carriers of national values and the national will is directed against the forces of disruption, forces often described in pejorative terms as 'cold' intellect, 'analytic' reason, 'alien' influences, 'rootless' cosmopolitanism, all of which ignore the differences of culture and tradition.

*　　*　　*

The rhetoric of romanticism, honed and systematised by nationalist propagandists like Mussolini and Goebbels and encapsulated in the anathemas of irrationalist and fascist writers, was all directed, as Berlin points out, at reason and the Enlightenment. The prophecy of Heine in the early nineteenth century that the romantic faith of Fichte and Schilling would one day be turned, with terrible effect, by their fanatical German followers against the liberal culture of the West was in the process of fulfilment. This battle of ideas raged in Ireland, but WB Yeats, George Bernard Shaw, George William Russell (AE) and, later, Sean O'Faolain, Frank O'Connor and others could not stem the flood of national sentiment. In 1923 Shaw could rage:

> Nationalism must now be added to the refuse pile of superstitions. We are now citizens of the world, and the man who divides the race into elect Irishmen and reprobate foreign devils (especially Englishmen) had better live on the Blaskets, where he can admire himself without much trouble . . . We must realise that national independence is now impossible.

Russell, writing in *The Irish Statesman* in January 1924 and anticipating by forty years McLuhan's aphorism that the media, and particularly television, would make the world a global village, argued passionately for the coexistence of Anglo-Irish culture with that of the Gaelic *Volk:*

> We believe we want world culture, world ideas, world science, otherwise Irish would not be a nation, but a parish. We believe ourselves that the ideal of Irish culture relying upon its own resources is impossible, but a culture more vital is possible, indeed certain, by the wedding of Gaelic culture to world culture.

In the following year, during his famous Senate speech on divorce, WB Yeats made a similar plea for an enlightened outlook when he attacked the 'exceedingly oppressive legislation' which would deprive the minority of 'rights which it has held since the seventeenth century'. All was in vain. The trait of nationalism that allows nothing to obstruct the national goal or to have equal value with it was triumphant. In the years between 1927 and 1937, when the new constitution restated the ultimate goal of a politically united Ireland and gave constitutional status to Catholic moral and social thinking, the remaining pockets of cultural resistance were mopped up. In 1929, a year after the politically disillusioned Yeats had retired from both the Senate and public life, censorship was introduced. The tyranny of the people was mounting. In 1932 de Valera came to power with a political team most of whom had been schooled at the Gaelic League. He and other former excommunicants attended with the zeal of converts to every detail of orthodox Catholic social teaching. In 1933 a tax was imposed on English newspapers. The Criminal Law Amendment Act of 1935 prohibited the sale or distribution of contraceptives, while the Public Dancehalls Act of the same year regulated these places of sin to the satisfaction of the Roman Catholic hierarchy. Ireland was to be made a land fit for saints and scholars, but only Catholic saints and Gaelic scholars. It was an Ireland that owed but little to Grattan, Flood, Emmet or Henry Joy McCracken, to say nothing of Tone or Davis. Sean O'Faolain tells of the things which he believes Wolfe Tone would not have tolerated in modern Ireland: 'The least sign of sectarianism, Puritanism, middle class vulgarity, canting pietism, narrow orthodoxy, whether of Church or state.'

Certainly, there was little sentiment in Wolfe Tone's nationalism, a view well reflected in his abrupt dismissal of the Harpers

Festival of 1792 as 'strum, strum and be hanged'. According to Tone, the enlightened men of the two great sects which divided the nation were to form the national union. These enlightened men comprised only the combined Catholic and Dissenter middle classes. The third sect, the 'Protestants', were dismissed as 'a colony of strangers' dependent on England and opposed to republican principles. Despite his much quoted commitment to substitute the common name of Irishman in place of the denominations of Protestant, Catholic and Dissenter, there is little evidence of any place being found for the Protestant. The area of future interest between Dissenter and Catholic he left undefined, but the future conflict he vaguely prophesied. The Dissenters, as genuine republicans, acted, according to Tone, upon 'reason and reflection'; Catholics, however, were 'impelled by misery and inflamed by detestation of the English name'. The reason and reflection of the same Dissenters was to find its logical expression in the founding and development of concepts upon which the pluralism of the United States was to be erected. The descendants of those who remained in Ulster were, in very different circumstances, to be the rock in the road to the national ideal of those Catholics whose nationalism was a response to England's patronising and disparaging attitude towards the traditional values of their society. The wounded pride and sense of humiliation among their most socially conscious members, coupled with the emergence of their church, literally from the hedge, would produce the anger and self-assertion that were among the necessary components of traditional nationalism.

PARTNERS IN POWER: CHURCH AND STATE IN THE REPUBLIC

Political and ideological stability is the basic requirement of the Church in order to ensure the continuum of its power. When necessary, the Church will withdraw its support for a political ideology or interest when a competing ideology or interest is clearly in the ascendant. FSL Lyons remarks on the paradox that the Irish Catholic hierarchy had been one of the main agents of Anglicisation for most of the nineteenth century. Yet once Ireland began to be regarded as a Catholic nation, the Church became a major influence in the moulding of the nation's separate identity in a form very different from the vision of a Wolfe Tone or a Thomas Davis. The attraction of the latter as the progenitors of the true strain of Irish republicanism led Dr Garrett FitzGerald to declare a constitutional crusade. However, the political reality of the power of the Church as a pillar of the nation-state led to his pledge on the abortion amendment to that constitution, and so his crusade promptly perished.

Religion is said to be the cement of social order. In 1936, 93.4% of the population of the Irish Free State was Catholic; the current figure is nearer 97%. Such a proportion of nominal Catholics is perhaps not unique, but Ireland is unusual in possessing a high percentage of committed and practising Catholics. The Church's price for providing the social solidarity and commitment to the new order in Ireland after 1922 was to be paid for by the state in the coin of a subservient Catholic orthodoxy. The priorities of individual freedoms and liberty of conscience were to be sacrificed for values which were regarded as being higher and which were determined by no subjective standard, but by the objective requirements of the Church's doctrine and dogma. Nor was it sufficient that the social values and teachings of the Church should be simply reflected in the Republic's laws; they were hallowed by their incorporation into the constitution. The 1937 constitution guaranteed those values by giving the Church such a powerful control over education and the social services that the values of one religion would be permanently cemented into the fabric of the state. Irish education became not merely denominationally controlled, it became clerically controlled. Viewed objectively, the Church is in a position of entrenched power, because of the control it exercises indirectly through the minds and attitudes of the faithful. As a result, it can virtually direct policy on matters which the Church considers essential to the maintenance of its own position and interest. Since the source of this power is the sum of the individual Catholic's commitment to the Church's teaching, education is essential for its maintenance. As JH Whyte stresses in his study *Church and State in Modern Ireland:*

> The remarkable feature of educational policy in Ireland has been the reluctance of the state to touch the entrenched position of the Church. . . not because the Church's claims have been moderate; on the contrary, it has carved out for itself a more extensive control over education in Ireland than in any other country in the world. It is because the Church has insisted on its claims with such force that the state has been extremely cautious in entering its domain.

'Give me the child and I will be accountable for how as a man or woman he or she votes on certain issues', might well be the Church's motto. It is true that the Republic is a democracy with an independent judiciary, a government answerable to a freely elected parliament and a constitution which guarantees freedom of speech and of association. But democracies, as we can see, are not logically committed to individual liberty. The triumph of religion is to educate the faithful to declare that the only freedoms of value are those within the dogma of the Church. In this sense, the Church is overwhelmingly committed to the democracy of majority rule. Despite the assertion of the hierarchy to the New Ireland Forum of its desire for a clear distinction between Church and state, and that the Constitution was for the people to decide and the laws for the legislators, such casuistry will not square with the facts. The Church is willing to sacrifice the appearance of power if it may continue to enjoy the substance, and the hierarchy did not hesitate to inform the Forum of what might result if legislation embodying subjective standards of individual liberty were to be introduced: 'We do feel bound, therefore, to alert the consciences of Catholics to the moral and social evils which, as experience elsewhere shows, follow from certain legislative enactments. We do naturally expect these to be given mature and serious consideration by Catholics'.

The hierarchy's written submission declared that in reaching conclusions about the common good, governments are required to take serious account of the views of the majority which help to constitute the 'community', or the 'common civilisation', within which pluralism is practised. Pluralism, it seems, may be tolerated where the minority is big enough to do something about it, but not, apparently, where the offence it would give to the moral principles of the majority of the citizens would be disproportionately serious. In such circumstances, the hierarchy suggested that it is not unreasonable to insist that minorities sacrifice their principles and their liberty of conscience in the interests of the common good. To support this argument, the hierarchy, perhaps subconsciously, misled in citing a judgment of a Justice of the United States Supreme Court, who in 1944 stated that a majority are not to be denied the political power to erect laws simply because such laws would offend the consciences of a minority. Significantly, the hierarchy did not point out in their written submission to the New Ireland Forum that the judgment of Mr Justice Frankfurter was repudiated by all of his fellow judges who heard the same case in the Supreme Court. Delivering the majority judgment, Mr Justice Jackson unambiguously rejected Frankfurter's view and stated:

> The very purpose of a Bill of Rights was to withdraw certain subjects from the vicissitudes of public controversy, to place them beyond the reach of majorities and officials and to establish them as legal principles to be applied by the courts. One's rights to life, liberty and property, to free speech, a free press, freedom of worship and assembly and other

fundamental rights may not be submitted to vote, they depend on the outcome of no elections.

In clear terms, the effect of the United States' Bill of Rights and, in particular, the First Amendment, was to protect the liberty of minorities and individuals from the very tyranny which the hierarchy's view would engender. In the opinion of the Supreme Court, there were areas of individual liberty which were more sacred than the rights of the majority. The very purpose of the First Amendment was to prevent what John Stuart Mill described as 'the tyranny of prevailing feeling and opinion which encroaches upon men's activities beyond the sacred frontiers of private life'.

*   *   *

The oral presentation of the hierarchy to the New Ireland Forum was designed to soften the harshness of its written submission, a submission which even dismayed nationalist politicians. However, the hierarchy's oral presentation merely emphasised the basic difficulties. Bishop Cahal Daly declared that the Catholic Church in Ireland has no power, and seeks no power, except the power of the Gospel it preaches and the consciences and convictions of those who freely accept that teaching. Pluralists have never suggested that it has any direct power, but the power it declared itself to possess and the educational infrastructure which supports its values are necessarily overwhelming in a Republic whose population is now 97% Catholic.

In an effort to placate Northern Protestants, Bishop Daly stated: 'What we do here and now declare, and declare with emphasis, is that we would raise our voices to resist any constitutional proposal which might infringe or might imperil the civil and religious rights and liberties cherished by Northern Protestants.' The implications of this declaration bear examination. It appears to imply quite positively that Northern Protestants presently have rights and liberties which are not available in the Republic to anyone, including their coreligionists. Are Northern Protestants to be allowed contraception, divorce, abortion in limited circumstances, but these rights are not to be available to Southern Protestants or Catholics living anywhere in a united Ireland? If such civil and religious rights and liberties are so cherished as to be protected, why should they not be currently available in the Republic, and who or what interest group would oppose their implementation? And if we accept that a constitution is a living and developing concept, then rights cannot be static. Are only present rights, therefore, to be protected? And by what subjective or objective moral standards are new rights to be admitted? It seems probable that it was precisely their fear of the right of privacy becoming an admitted right which prompted the forces of Catholic reaction to launch the campaign that led to the abortion amendment. And this reactionary fear could only be quelled by putting the issue beyond the possible power of an independent judiciary.

*   *   *

This issue is a fundamental reflection on the nature and purpose of the state and those who form it, because it clearly shows that those exercising power in the Republic have subconsciously taken upon themselves the responsibility of ensuring that the Irish people remain not only Christian, but Roman Catholic. The state is not only not neutral as between religion and irreligion, it is not even neutral as between one religion and another. There is no halfway house. And until it is recognised that the function of the state is simply to regulate the lives of its citizens so as to control by compromise and agreement conduct infringing the rights of others, there will remain the battle between liberty and authority. It needs to be clearly recognised that the achievement of objectives said to be moral is a matter for churches, philosophers and the consciences of individual citizens. It is emphatically not the business of the state.

Catholic theologians in different countries, and particularly in the United States, have argued forcefully for the pluralist viewpoint. The arguments advanced by a Jesuit professor of theology, John Courtney Murray, are particularly cogent. Writing on the First Amendment as an article of peace, Murray crystallises the issue:

> Religion itself, and not least the Catholic Church, has benefited by our free institutions, by the maintenance, even in exaggerated form, of the distinction between church and state. Within the same span of history the experience of the Church elsewhere, particularly in the Latin lands, has been alternately an experience of privilege or persecution. The reason lay in a particular concept of government. It was alternatively the determination of government to ally itself either with the purposes of the Church or with the purposes of some sect or other (sectarian liberalism, for instance) which made a similar, however erroneous, claim to the full and final truth. The dominant conviction, whose origins are really in pagan antiquity, was that government should represent transcendent truth and by its legal power make this truth prevail. However, in the absence of social agreement as to what truth really was, the result was to involve the Catholic truth in the vicissitudes of power. It would be difficult to say which experience, privilege or persecution, proved in the end to be more damaging or gainful to the Church.

The governments of the Republic since 1922, unlike some of their American counterparts, have undertaken to represent the Catholic version of transcendental truth, hence the Church's patent involvement with the aims of Irish constitutional nationalism, its bitter opposition to Sinn Fein and its investment of the aspiration for Irish unity with a moral value which it denies to the maintenance of the Union. The Church is not neutral as between unity and union. It is difficult to see how the Church could be neutral in its historic context as a vital component in the emergence of the Republic of Ireland as a nation-state.

RIVALS FOR POWER: CONSTITUTIONAL NATIONALISM AND SINN FEIN

Sinn Fein and its terrorist wing, the IRA, represent positive freedom to be one's own master in its most distorted and theoretical form. A relatively small group in terms of electoral support, they nevertheless claim to represent the real self of the people and the pure spirit of Irish nationalism. Like Robespierre and Saint Just, they express the philosophy that, in the cause of the Irish millennium, all means are justified for those who personify the struggle. By labelling those who oppose them 'enemies of the people' or 'legitimate targets', they place such opponents beyond the pale of humanity or justice. The same genuine idealism and quasi-religious revolutionary fervour which lent respectability to the exponents of terror in the France of 1792 is now used by Sinn Fein to give its leaders a sense of total superiority over their victims and to transmit a feeling of righteous virtue to justify their excesses. This assumption—that they alone know what the people really want—enables them to justify murder, oppression, torture and extortion in the name of, and on behalf of, the real self, the spirit of the Irish people. The murder and mutilation of members of the minority community in Northern Ireland by the IRA is reminiscent of Bukharin's Bolshevik argument that 'proletarian coercion in all its forms, from executions to forced labour, is, paradoxical as it may sound, the method of moulding communist humanity out of the human material of the capitalist period'. Is the future humanity of Sinn Fein's united Ireland to be moulded out of the human material of the Catholic ghettos by similar methods?

There is scarcely any area of individual liberty or negative freedom upon which Sinn Fein and its military wing are not prepared to trample in their ruthless pursuit of positive freedom and the absolute power it will provide. The threat to personal freedom posed by Sinn Fein has been accentuated by their decision to utilise not only terror, but the democratic process of the ballot box as part of the revolutionary process. Like Engels, they believe that the parties of order will perish under the legal conditions which they themselves have created. In its declared objective of taking power in Ireland, Sinn Fein will use irredentist Irish nationalism, with all its romantic, emotional and irrational associations, as an instrument for establishing a totalitarian authority. Irish nationalism is their badge of justification, the hallmark of their legitimacy and the Trojan Horse that will enable them to destroy liberal democracy, imperfect though that democracy may be, in the Republic of Ireland. Nor will the Church be spared the vicissitudes of involvement with power, a possibility of which the hierarchy is by no means unaware.

*   *   *

Although the objective of Sinn Fein is to take power in Ireland, its field of operations in Northern Ireland is ultimately circumscribed by the Unionist population. Yet it is only in Northern Ireland that the realisation of the myth can actually be attempted, and so the constitutional nationalist parties are forced to compete in an irredentist contest they cannot hope to win. As long as Sinn Fein and constitutional nationalism share an objective which is sanctioned by the constitution of the Irish Republic, the political legitimacy of Sinn Fein is irrefutable. Sinn Fein's contempt for successive governments of the Republic and for the Church, with whom it must compete for authority and legitimacy, is scarcely veiled by the necessity for some temporary accommodation with their shared nationalist objective. Continuing instability in Northern Ireland is the key to destabilising the Republic, whose commitment to nationalism is, paradoxically, its Achilles heel.

It is arguable that the very insistence of nationalism on a unanimity of outlook, reflecting only the Catholic view of transcendent truth and an almost universally shared myth of geographical unity, has caused the stagnation of the conflict of genuine ideas and values, a conflict which provides a true democracy with its political dynamic. Two ultra-conservative and, essentially, identical parties have offered the people of the Republic no real choice about either ideology or policy. Partnership with the Church excluded all but a neutered from of socialism. Elections became simply a competition to decide who would share the spoils of office for a time, and the missing political dynamic was replaced by the pursuit of the national aspiration, or myth, of unity as a substitute. Nationalism could not be allowed to die, for there was nothing else. The actual pursuit of Irish unity was modified into the political fiction of verbal republicanism, and the balance between that fiction and the philosophy of armed struggle has always been sensitive.

Liberty in contemporary Ireland is now in grave danger. Grave because the fabric of the Republic, its society and its democratic institutions are presently so fragile that the parties of so-called constitutional nationalism must move closer to the Sinn Fein line of a relatively immediate unitary state. But they refuse to recognise the problems they face. Pluralism is a necessary pre-condition to unity, yet neither the Church nor the vast majority of the people it influences will allow that price to be paid by the state. Since Unionist consent is said to be necessary, Unionists are assured that once such consent is given, a pluralist constitution will then be available. The New Ireland Forum not only did not apply its intellectual resources to an analysis of the nationalist ideology underlying its position, but it also avoided completely the issue of church and state relations which might have sundered a nation already teetering on the brink of instability.

The economic, social and political problems of the Republic provide the material which an unchecked Sinn Fein may yet detonate. This is because Sinn Fein feeds off shared nationalist myths and, simultaneously, offers a programme of social reform which would fill the void let in the Republic by the absent political dynamic. Nor does it hesitate to oppose the Church and support divorce and contraception. Alert to the urban weakness of its opponent and confident that devotion to the nation will pardon almost any sin, Sinn Fein is not in partnership with the Church for the support of the faithful—it is in competition for their minds. The time of Sinn Fein could not be more opportune, and the fate of individual liberty and democracy never more in doubt. If these are to be preserved to any degree, the Republic must begin to replace the myth of unity with the politics of social and economic justice for all classes. It must commence the creation of a pluralist and open society in which the Church, while rightly guarding its won flock and maintaining its own moral control, cannot involve the secular arm of the state to either remove temptation or supplement internal discipline. Education and social welfare must become the prerogative of the state.

NORTHERN IRELAND: THE UNENDING SIEGE

James I of England thought that the plantation of Ulster would win the rude and barbarous natives from their depraved manner of life to English 'civility' and establish 'the true religion of Christ among men . . . almost lost in superstition'. The native Irish 'stood upon their keeping' to plunder the planters at every opportunity and were, in turn, viewed as human wolves to be tracked to their lairs and slain. Because they were men 'well settled in their religion', the planters' God was an austere and unrelenting

Protestant whose transcendent truths were revealed not in dogma, but in scripture. Fundamentals of fear, suspicion and triumphalism still inform irrational Unionism to the present day. These irrational Unionists see no essential virtue in the Union if it does not guarantee a non-Catholic ascendancy. But there was a tradition of a different kind of union which manifested itself in the Enlightenment of the eighteenth century, though many Enlightenment ideas can themselves be traced to the Protestant English nationalism which developed during the Puritan revolution of the seventeenth century. This English nationalism had closer religious associations than the later nationalisms of a more secular age and placed more emphasis upon individual rights and the common nature of humanity than upon national identities and cultural divisions. It is, perhaps, most clearly expressed in the political philosophy of John Locke, a philosophy stated in three essential principles. First, no man has such complete wisdom and knowledge that he can dictate the form of another man's religion. Secondly, each individual is a moral being responsible before God—and this presupposes freedom. Thirdly, no compulsion that is contrary to the will of the individual can secure more than an outward conformity. This was the basis upon which the liberty of English nationalism was to influence American and French nationalism in the eighteenth century. American pluralism was to grow from the triple seed of the Puritan revolution, Locke's political ideas and the rational analysis of English liberty by contemporary French philosophers such as Montesquieu, Thomas Jefferson and Tom Paine were to underwrite this liberal and humanitarian nationalism, which was a product of reason and the Enlightenment and not of romance and cultural identity. It was on this view of liberty that Wolfe Tone's Dissenters reasoned and reflected as genuine republicans.

The constitutional comparison of Ireland's situation with that of Britain's American colonies did not go unnoticed in Ireland, and nowhere more so than in Ulster, which, during the preceding fifty years, had provided the overwhelming bulk of Irish immigrants to America. There was no support in Ireland for the British cause in the American colonies, except, perhaps, among the Catholic middle class, with their innate suspicion of the colonists' republican principles. In 1798, the Year of Liberty, the revolutionary republican theme of civil and religious liberty for all found its only clear expression in the Protestant Ulster of the Northeast. The rebellion in Wexford of those Catholics impelled by misery and detestation of the English was to become a piked crusade against Protestants. It has become popular to view the '98 Rebellion as some golden age, when there was an enduring comity of interest between

Dissenter and Catholic, but that is not so. The Act of Union, described by Cornwallis as a union with a party and not with a people, delay in Catholic emancipation caused by Irishmen rather than by the English, the advent of Daniel O'Connell and the growth of romantic, cultural nationalism in the nineteenth century were to carry Catholic Ireland almost as far away from the Dissenters of 1798 as the native Irish had always been from the austere and awful Protestantism of Mountjoy and Cromwell.

*   *   *

The nineteenth-century clash of liberalism and nationalism found its expression also in the minutiae of Ulster's Protestant theology. Henry Cooke, the Protestant demagogue of his day, enshrined his version of the planter Presbyterian myth when he addressed the General Assembly of the Church of Scotland in May 1836. Cooke declared that:

> Our Scottish forefathers were planted in the wildest and most barren portions of our lands . . . the most rude and lawless of the provinces. Scottish industry has drained its bogs and cultivated its barren wastes, has filled its ports with shipping, substituted towns and cities for its hovels and clachans and given peace and good order to a land of confusion and blood.

It was the theology of the children of Ham; a frontier Christianity of 'praise the Lord and pass the ammunition' that was to find expression also in the laagers of Blood River and help to lay the foundations of modern apartheid in South Africa. It was also a theology of division—of race, culture, values and identity—which denied the universality of man's nature and his individual worth. The *Northern Whig* rejoined that Cooke's activities were 'a regularly concocted Tory scheme . . . to attack Popery as a means of opposing justice in Ireland'. The *Londonderry Journal*, in a comment reminiscent of contemporary attitudes which resemble Cooke's, stated that he 'and his adherents have acquired a hold of the minds of the worst educated and most unreasoning of the Presbyterian laity'.

The Protestant sectarianism of Cooke's following, and the siege mentality it engendered, were simply nationalism writ small. Its modern supporters have not been unfairly described as Protestant Sinn Fein. Cooke, the Presbyterian Pope, offered as his variant of transcendent truth which should inform the minds of the legislators not the dogma of the Church, but the authority of revealed scriptures. Opposing disestablishment of the Church of Ireland, he argued that voluntaryism would forbid the state from legislating upon such subjects as marriage and the use of the Lord's Day. Is it surprising that the same attitudes supported by the same philosophy should plague Ireland to the present day? Or that there should be such unanimity between conservative Protestant and Catholic theology as to the role of the state as the moral guardian of the people?

Contrary to popular and unfounded belief, it was not Cooke who changed the political direction of Ulster Presbyterians from the liberalism of 1798 to its subsequent conservatism. That change was directly attributable to Gladstone's conversion to Home Rule in 1886, a conversion which virtually destroyed political liberalism among Ulster Presbyterians. With few exceptions, Protestants saw Home Rule as Rome Rule. The subsequent history of Ulster and, ultimately, Northern Ireland was essentially that of a people under ideological siege from an emerging Ireland flushed with nationalist enthusiasm and fuelled by a cultural identity, a political outlook and an authoritative theology which they could not share.

In these circumstances, Ulster Protestants did what besieged people always do. They settled, *pro tem,* their internal quarrels, as had Anglicans and Dissenters in Londonderry two centuries before, and imposed the rule that those who are not for us are against us. In defence of what they perceived to be their ultimate liberty, they circumscribed the individual liberty of others within the metaphorical city. There are those who believe that liberty might equally have been preserved by granting it, and whatever arguments may be advanced in defence of an attitude perhaps justifiable in 1926, they could not avail in 1966, when the besiegers had at least temporarily quit the walls. This defensive attitude can, however, now be argued as justifiable once again. The Northern Ireland Unionist is threatened from within by the activities and violence of republican terrorists. Externally, he is threatened by what he sees as a sectarian Republic, which, in its claim to his territory, legitimises the internal violence and to which the minority look for support. This continuous external pressure polarises the communities and makes rational discussion or concession virtually impossible. The solution is not to be found in superficial political formulae. Upon John Locke's second principle it may be said that no compulsion that is contrary to the will of the Unionist people can secure more than an outward conformity. John C Calhoun observed that the American constitution 'is superior to the wisdom of any or all of the men by whose agency it was made. The force of circumstances, and not foresight or wisdom, induced them to adopt many of its wisest provisions'. The circumstances of a tragic contemporary Ireland impose the necessity for creating a social environment protected by law in which people of differing religious faiths and of conflicting moral values may live together in peace. The establishment of mutual values and pluralist societies, both in Northern Ireland and the Republic, is a necessary precondition to peace, let alone unity.

THE UNION AND LIBERTY

The United Kingdom of Great Britain and Northern Ireland is, with all its faults, a pluralist state. Its Catholic millions and their Irish coreligionists who have chosen to live there find no oppression, nor in real terms do they suffer any social or political disadvantage. It is also true that the state fails to provide in its laws a source of external discipline for the maintenance of morals as approved of by churches. The same may be said of the United States of America. But those British laws ensured within Northern Ireland a significant measure of freedom, which a devolved legislature motivated by its own version of transcendent truth frequently failed to provide within the limits of its delegated powers. Indeed, it is the present determination of the government of the United Kingdom to ensure the fundamental rights of the minority which creates the political tension between that government and the forces of an irrational and sectarian Unionism which sees the Union merely as a convenient constitutional device for maintaining a non-Catholic ascendancy. The true and essential Union is not an exclusive union of loyalists or Protestants, but a union between peoples who believe in liberal democracy and civil and religious liberty for all in the fullest sense of a pluralist society.

Current support for the Union, and current opposition to unity, can only be postulated in terms of liberty, upon the loss of individual freedom from state interference. The defence of human rights is properly one of the great topics of our times, and the churches share this enthusiasm. Human rights provide the content of much of the politicisation of Christianity; but the practice of adding religious authority to political campaigns for human rights has been described as both divisive and partial. In reality, human rights issues become the means by which Christians express their endorsement of the political values of their own society. Nowhere has this attitude been more evident than in the Irish hierarchy's investment of the political aspiration for a united Ireland with the qualities of a human right and its failure to accord a similar value to the maintenance of the Union. In the words of a Jesuit theologian, the Reverend J Kerkhofs, 'while the Church in recent times has increasingly been a defender of human rights in society, she remains very reluctant to grant these rights to actual members of the Church . . . the right to be pluralist and different is a basic human right rooted in the Gospel message'.

*   *   *

Individual freedom and the circumstances which best sustain it are not static. If the present union now offers the people of Northern Ireland a greater measure of personal liberty than is to be found elsewhere in Ireland, it may not always be so. It is not impossible for some militant tendency of the left or some equally anti-libertarian party of the right to subvert Britain's liberal parliamentary and pluralist tradition. It is equally possible that the Republic of Ireland may, under the influence of what is best in Anglo-American ideas, become increasingly pluralist, and that theocratic influences may diminish. Those who believe in liberty will always have to seek union with those who share that belief. As Isaiah Berlin states:

> Principles are not less sacred because their duration cannot be guaranteed. Indeed, the very desire for guarantees that our values are eternal and secure in some objective Heaven is perhaps only a craving for the certainties of childhood or the absolute values of our primitive past. To realise the relative validity of one's convictions and yet stand for them unflinchingly is what distinguishes a civilised man from a barbarian. To demand more than this is perhaps a deep and incurable metaphysical need; but to allow it to determine one's practice is a symptom of an equally deep and more dangerous moral and political immaturity.

Ireland, in its search for the positive freedom of an independent sovereign state governed by 'its own', has had to pay the price for that positive freedom not only in terms of the circumscribing of individual freedoms, but in the exclusion of those who valued their personal liberties and who were not prepared to sacrifice them as the price of belonging to a nation they did not see as theirs. The price of reconciliation, let alone unity, is the establishment of pluralist states, in both North and South.

If Parnell's statement that 'no man has a right to fix the boundary of the march of a nation' is the summation of Irish nationalism, then the answer of a dissenting Unionism must be that no nation has the right to set limits upon the development of the individual liberty and unique nature of a man.

III

ULSTER UNIONISM
AND IRISH IRREDENTISM

Three

Priests, Politicians and Pluralism[1]

INTRODUCTION

In 1983 the four main Irish nationalist parties—Fianna Fail, Fine Gael, Labour and the SDLP—formed the New Ireland Forum, which has been assigned the task of developing an agreed approach to a Northern Ireland settlement. The submission of the Roman Catholic hierarchy to the Forum, however, has brutally exposed the myth that it can produce any blueprint for a new Ireland. In clear and unequivocal terms, the hierarchy has spelled out its message that a New Ireland based upon pluralism has no place in its future scheme of things. 'The rights of a minority', according to the hierarchy, 'are no more sacred than the rights of a majority'. Implicit in this statement is the principle that in any new, or united, Ireland the majority will be a Roman Catholic majority.

A forty-year-old judgement by one of the most ultra-conservative of United States Supreme Court judges, Felix Frankfurter, is used by the hierarchy to ram home the point that such a majority are not to be denied the political power to erect laws simply because such laws offend the consciences of a minority. What the hierarchy do not tell us is that the opinion of Mr Frankfurter was repudiated by the majority of his fellow Supreme Court judges in the very same case. Indeed, this overriding judgement destroys the very argument on which the hierarchy's case is based. The hierarchy was, nevertheless, in the terms of its submission, telling the politicians of the Forum in no uncertain terms that it was not prepared to underwrite any offer that would obstruct or prevent a Catholic majority from imposing the dictates of its conscience or theology upon a Unionist minority.

THEOCRACY AND PLURALISM

Despite the assertion of the hierarchy that it considers it inappropriate that it should make any recommendations regarding possible political structures or arrangements, it does not hesitate to indicate clearly what the Forum may not do. Only the gullible and the naive would deny the enormous political influence of the hierarchy upon the laws and constitution of the Republic. Successive governments of the Republic have acknowledged, by their actions, that to confront the Church is to court political extinction. The recent referendum on abortion proves the

---

[1]Written in 1984, this essay was reprinted in John Wilson Foster (ed.), *The Idea of the Union: Statements and Critiques in Support of the Union of Great Britain and Northern Ireland* (Vancouver: Belcouver Press, 1995).

point. It was not sufficient to make abortion unconstitutional. Abortion had to be made unconstitutional upon terms that precisely reflected Roman Catholic theology. The amendment of the constitution was secured by ignoring the reasonably expressed, but differing, views of respected leaders of other churches. Such leaders can hardly be dismissed as representatives of 'fraternities of friendly rapists or bigamists'; but dismissed, nevertheless, they were.

Even a cursory analysis of the hierarchy's paper on pluralism reveals at once its intolerant and authoritarian attitude. Before deciding whether any group has a right to be heard as an expression of pluralist opinion, it seemingly has to undergo a number of subjective tests. The group will not qualify as a religion unless it is adjudged to be so by someone who has some idea of what a religion is, according to other criteria of a more ultimate, but unspecified, kind. Similarly, a group is not Christian unless it complies with some nebulous grouping of Christian churches who, doubtless themselves in turn, have to be ultimately vetted by the one true Church. Even if the tests of religion and Christianity are surmounted, there is the further requirement of being theologically sound. Moon worshipers would, of course, fail on all three grounds, though probably Presbyterians, members of the Church of Ireland and Methodists could only be toppled on the third.

At each point the subjective values and conscience of the individual are subservient to the objective dictates of authority. This writer offers no prizes for recognising the identity of the ultimate authority on these matters. The limitations imposed on religious pluralism are, apparently, those of the 'moral law', 'the common good of all' and 'the objective moral order'. These limitations are recognised by the Second Vatican Council, and in Ireland, curiously enough, are identified with the teachings of the Roman Catholic Church. These limitations are not, however, derived from the Roman Catholic Church, but are a distillation of right reason, a process available to all, but whose conclusions happily coincide with those of the Roman Catholic Church. On this basis, the Protestant population of the Republic were subjected to censorship, bans on contraception and divorce and a constitutional amendment on abortion, which right reason neatly fitted into the exact pattern of Roman Catholic theology.

CATHOLIC MORALITY AND INDIVIDUAL LIBERTY
The question may be asked why this right reason does not lead Protestant theologians and clergy invariably to the same conclusions as the hierarchy? The answer is that upon those issues where the Protestant

churches agree with the hierarchy, their views are expressions of acceptable religious pluralism. In those cases where they do not have the concurrence of the hierarchy, the latter are forced to impose the limitations of 'the moral law', 'the common good of all' and 'the objective moral order', in which right reason and Roman Catholic theology fortuitously coincide.

It is, indeed, astonishing as to how the faithful in the United Kingdom, the United States of America, France, Germany, Holland, Spain and Italy manage to survive without the assistance of the Irish hierarchy's interpretation of these limitations on religious pluralism. The Roman Catholic Church adopts exactly the same erroneous principle as Mr Justice Frankfurter before the Supreme Court put him right. Freedom in religion is not an absolute right of the individual where, in the Church's opinion, it is subject to the abridgement of the process of the law passed by elected representatives. If those so elected subscribe to the Roman Catholic faith, then the law will reflect that. Sir Isaiah Berlin has stated that it does not matter who removes your liberty, whether a popular democracy or a tyrant, but the hierarchy obviously thinks it is quite in order to diminish your liberty provided it is done by an elected majority reflecting Catholic theology.

Unionists hold the view that the Roman Catholic Church is in such a position of entrenched power, because of the control it exercises indirectly through the minds and attitudes of the faithful, as to be able to dictate policy to the state on matters which the Church considers essential to the maintenance of its position. Such is the extent of this power that conflict between state and Church in the Republic rarely arises. Since the source of this power is the sum of the individual Catholic's commitment to Church teaching, education is essential for its maintenance. The influence of the Roman Catholic Church on the modern Irish state is not merely the powerful influence of the hierarchy operating as a major interest group in society, it is an all-embracing value system, a comprehensive body of ethical, moral and social thinking.

These values are *supra* party politics. There is no abiding theological difference between Fianna Fail and Fine Gael; they are both ultra-conservative Catholic parties. In April 1951, after the resignation of Noel Browne on the issue of the 'Mother and Child Scheme', one government minister stated in the Dail debate, 'There will be no flouting of the authority of the bishops in the matter of Catholic social or Catholic moral teaching', while that well known advocate of minority rights and pluralism, Sean MacBride, as quoted as saying, 'those of us in this House who are Catholics, and all of is in the government who are Catholics, are, as such, of course, bound to give obedience to the rulings of our Church and of our hierarchy'. The Fine Gael Minister for Finance, Mr McGilligan, and General MacEoin, the Minister for Justice, were equally shrill in proclaiming their total subservience to the dictates of the hierarchy. The Church today no longer assumes quite so high a profile, but, as Dr Garret FitzGerald well appreciates, confrontation with the Church is politically not a paying proposition.

Is it any wonder, in these circumstances, that the hierarchy are sensitive to any move that might weaken clerical control of education? The submission makes the positive claim that the values which are the inspiration of the Catholic school system are incompatible with violence, hatred or intolerance. These central Christian values include the sacredness of human life, love of all people irrespective of religious, political or other differences, reverence for truth and justice. The political reality of the education issue is the Roman Catholic Church's determination to maintain the circle that ensures political power. Education helps to guarantee the continuance of the all-embracing value system, the body of ethical, moral and social teaching that will, in its turn, make sure either through referendum or election, that the ongoing status quo is maintained.

THE IRISH HIERARCHY AND POLITICAL AUTHORITY

If the function of the New Ireland Forum is to find out what the people really want, then the hierarchy, representing some 97% of the Republic's population, has told it so in unequivocal terms. The old Ireland of twenty-six counties must stay as it is. The hierarchy will not object to the addition of another six counties upon similar terms. Everyone in the Forum wanted the Unionists to come to Dublin and name their bottom line. While there was no prospect of such a journey ever being made, it is equally clear from the submission that it would have been an absolute waste of time in any event. It rather does appear as if the priests and politicians have failed to put their act together. Charles Haughey, the Irish Taoiseach, promised us that if we consented to a united Ireland everything would be on the table, but harmonisation of laws, administrative practices and social structures might only be possible over a gradual and, perhaps, extended period. Somehow, he managed to make it all sound like a raffle being run by a fairground gypsy. Like the boa constrictor, the Republic would immediately swallow the North in a united Ireland, even though it might take twenty years to complete the digestive process.

The hierarchy's submission is totally at odds with Dick Spring's opening statement that 'notions of Church control or Church vetoes, real or imagined, should be removed in any overall vision of a united Ireland', while Dr Garrett FitzGerald must be left to reflect that the example to the world of the courage, the generosity, the imagination and intellectual honesty and sound good sense of the Irish people, which he mentioned in his opening address, is hardly demonstrated in the submission of the Republic's most powerful interest group. Dr FitzGerald had stated that the Forum might succeed, with God's help, but, if that is so, God must be operating through a very different agency than the Roman Catholic hierarchy.

The unpalatable truth is that even if Unionists had been prepared to name a pluralist price for their consent, neither the majority or the people of the Republic nor the Roman Catholic Church would have permitted her politicians to pay the price in the coin of reformed institutions. The Forum is now presented with the alternative of trying to obtain constitutional unity in the short term by means of external and other pressure, while continuing to mouth ecumenical platitudes about long term institutional reform.

CONCLUSION

Three options will probably be presented by the Forum. First, the unitary state, which is totally unobtainable and is merely listed to pad out the selection and make Unionists look churlish for not finding something to suit in such a wide range of choices.

Secondly, 'dual sovereignty', which is both logically and, in practical terms, an utter nonsense. Sovereignty is exercised over territory only to the degree that power is available to enforce its exercise. What, therefore, happens when, in the exercise of joint sovereignty, the sovereign powers disagree? In the end the question is: who will be master? In what form will this dual sovereignty be exercised? Will the Tricolour fly side-by-side with the Union Jack? In what manner will the civil and military power be constituted and to whom will it be responsible? Will there be representatives of each sovereign power in the cabinets of the other? It is impossible to believe that such a nebulous and bizarre solution has been seriously considered. It would, however, avoid any nasty business, like reforming church-state relations in the Republic.

Last but not least, the Unionists will be offered a federal solution. This choice does not even have the advantage of being novel. It is old, tired and disinterested. Terence Brown, in his book *Ireland: A*

Social and Cultural History, 1922-79, states 'that if current population trends continue, the Protestant population may disappear in the Republic at the beginning of the next century'. If there should ever be a united Ireland reflecting the views of the hierarchy's submission, then some later social commentator might be making a similar comment by the end of the twenty-first century with reference to the Protestant population in the whole of Ireland. There is, however, this to be said in fairness to the hierarchy's submission: when the last resident Prod is taking his final breath before joining the dodo bird and the passenger pigeon, he will be unable to blame the bishops, for they told him so way back in 1984.

Four

Barry's John[1]

INTRODUCTION

'Fools admire, but men of sense approve.' So wrote Alexander Pope in his *Essay on Criticism*. Barry White's admiration for John Hume, punctuated with approval, leaps almost embarrassingly from every page of his recent biography *John Hume: Statesman of the Troubles*. After reading the first two chapters, the reviewer is left to ponder if there can be any possible denouement short of canonisation. Educational and social obstacles rivalling those of Tom Brown and Oliver Twist are compounded by an army of Unionist Flashmans. True Grit plus Tom Ó Faich in the role of Dr Arnold combine to create 'SuperHume', an amalgam of George Washington, Mazzini and Martin Luther King.

This biography is clearly directed to a popular audience of existing worshippers. Written in the 'Insight' style, the modern marketing test of credibility appears to have been substituted for the rather older test of objective truth. What is disappointing in this book is the absence of any sustained intellectual analysis or evaluation of those ideas, social or political, attributed to John Hume and alleged to be novel. The assertion of an unidentified Irish delegate at a British-Irish Conference in Oxford in 1983 that every new idea about Ireland has come out of Hume's head is hardly intellectually convincing, whatever reflection it may be upon the political contents of other Irish heads.

There is no doubt that John Hume represented something of a phenomenon when he first entered nationalist politics in Northern Ireland, but then so did the one-eyed man when he entered the Kingdom of the Blind. Hume's evident intelligence, education and burning personal ambition admirably equipped him to be the political spokesman for a new generation of the Northern Ireland minority. Like the reviewer, they had benefited from the Education Act (Northern Ireland) of 1947 and were, rightly, seeking their place in the sun. Barry White's reference to the Stormont government introducing this legislation because it had no choice illustrates a less than objective attitude which, unfortunately, permeates the entire book and, ultimately, detracts from its potential value to the serious reader.

TECHNICAL DEFECTS

The technique of structuring a biography around a series of factual situations detailed by the fly on the wall method and in which the subject

---

[1] *Fortnight*, 25 January 1985.

is given an heroic part as the originator of all ideas, the draftsman of all major documents and the taker of all crunch decisions has serious defects. In many cases, the reader must simply take the writer's word for what he reads. For this reason, the contemporaneous statements of John Hume are much more valuable than the rather adulatory commentary. From these utterances, a picture of Hume's political objectives and methods emerges almost accidentally. An RTE broadcast of April 1972 reveals that Hume saw Irish unity as the only viable option and the objective for which the SDLP should then be negotiating. Even Barry White is forced to comment that this statement was a contradiction of Hume's earlier emphasis on Unionist consent before unity. All this in 1972, two years before Sunningdale and twelve years before the New Ireland Forum Report. In subsequently awarding Hume the powers of the clairvoyant or visionary, White misses the more evident point.

What the biographer fails to perceive is that John Hume was neither creating nor selling new ideas, but simply providing an infinitely better sales and market technique for the old ones. The picture that slowly surfaces, almost in spite of the author, is of a man in no way out of sympathy with any of the traditional thinking or objectives of nationalism, but vastly irritated with the persistent use of obsolete and archaic means to attain its objectives. The task of getting the nationalist boat back home was one for a political Ulysses. Few of the problems which Hume was to face with other nationalists were never about principles. Any differences with Seamus Mallon, Paddy Duffy or Charles Haughey were clearly to be about means, and any current sympathy with Dr FitzGerald is on a similar basis. Where there was an issue of principle, as with Gerry Fitt and Paddy Devlin, there was an inevitable parting of the ways.

Perhaps because Hume thinks like a Catholic-Nationalist from an area where they are in a majority, he often appears to lack the gut political perception and reality of Fitt and Devlin. His negotiating stance at Sunningdale revealed this two-dimensional attitude in ignoring the fact, despite warning, that the real guarantors of any settlement were the one million Unionists back home in Northern Ireland. It is in this area that Hume's nationalist-myth philosophy could have been profitably explored. While Hume shows his dedication to two of the traditional nationalist myths in particular, his biographer seems to miss their significance. The first is that if Britain broke the link with Northern Ireland the Unionists would accept an accommodation with the Republic. The second is that Britain has the necessary resources—

military, economic and political—to coerce the Unionists into a united Ireland or a blueprint for one.

A cynical observer might even say that the only difference between John Hume and Sinn Fein is that the latter are prepared to coerce the Unionists on their own account, while Hume, as a constitutional nationalist, would prefer the British Army to do it for him. After the Ulster Workers' Council strike of 1974, Hume the historian concluded that the British Army had once more avoided confrontation, just as they had in the Curragh incident of 1914. This was a theme to which he returned after the Anglo-Irish Summit of November 1984. The connection between this theme and the New Ireland Forum Report's fudging of the consent issue is, unfortunately, never fully developed by Barry White, even though it is allegedly central to John Hume's political philosophy. Consent for John Hume has never meant the right of the majority to refuse to give it. One wonders if the whole issue of consent was the same sort of device as Hugh Logue saw in the 1974 Council of Ireland, that is, a mere vehicle for trundling the North into unity. But then Hugh Logue, like Seamus Mallon, lacks the necessary political guile to ever get any boat back to Ithaca.

THE FATHER OF THE MAN

The child is said to be father of the man, and John Hume's education and upbringing never prepared him for anything beyond a sophisticated multi-level dissemination of traditional Catholic and nationalist values. He never bridged the ten-year gap between himself and the more secular anti-Unionists such as Michael Farrell, Eamonn McCann or even Bernadette Devlin. He has never been a political composer, but rather a political virtuoso with improvising gifts. The failure of the New Ireland Forum to meet the issue of church-state relations in the Republic mirrors faithfully his own reluctance to face up to the sort of Ireland he really wants as opposed to the sort of Ireland which he permits fellow travellers to think he wants. The John Hume of 1964, who saw in the name Londonderry a summation of the two great traditions of the city, is never compared with the Hume who sat silent while one tradition triumphed over the other in 1983 when 'London' was removed from the name of the city. While such a silence, and his party's failure to contest the 1981 Fermanagh-South Tyrone by-election (which enabled Bobby Sands, a republican terrorist on hunger-strike, to be elected to Parliament), may be justified on the basis of political pragmatism, they owe little to statesmanship or democratic principles.

The timing of this biography was perhaps a little unfortunate. The SDLP are at the nadir of their political fortunes. The achievement of many, if not all, of the civil rights objectives virtually left Irish unity as the only thing in the party's cupboard. An inability to cope with the more immediate policies of Sinn Fein for the achievement of unity left John Hume and his party to rely even more on the nationalist myth of an external solution. Such reliance has caused a disastrous rundown in the party's infrastructure, and the Republican areas of Belfast have been well nigh abandoned to Sinn Fein. The social realism of Fitt and Devlin might have saved these areas for the party, but they were sacrificed at an earlier date to the rural nationalists who, like Hume, thought like republicans in a majority situation.

John Hume may have performed the role of Moses by leading the nationalists of Northern Ireland out of their political Egypt, but at the present day he seems to have them firmly established in a political wilderness. Sinn Fein have set up a golden calf, and even his faithful Boswell, Barry White, cannot see the Promised Land. Perhaps it will take another forty years before the Republic undergoes the necessary transformation, during which time John Hume will have to play a more radical and less conservative part if he is to fulfil the role that his biographer has already chosen for him. It will be for future biographers to determine whether he has accepted the challenge.

Five

A Tale of Two Governments:
A Critique of the Anglo-Irish Agreement[1]

INTRODUCTION

In early 1990 the Irish Supreme Court handed down a landmark decision in the McGimpsey case. It decided that Article Two of the Irish constitution consists of a declaration of the extent of the national territory as a claim of legal right and that the reintegration, or unification, of the national territory is a constitutional imperative. The national territory is defined in Article Two as 'the whole island of Ireland, its islands and the territorial seas'. In simple terms, the Republic of Ireland, by its constitution, makes a legal claim to the territory of Northern Ireland and, by implication, governments of the Republic must seek to achieve that objective by their political efforts. In his written judgement Chief Justice Finlay makes it clear that in his view the government of the Republic, by signing the Anglo-Irish Agreement in 1985, was not in any way derogating from the legal claim in Article Two of the constitution, but was, in effect, attempting to resolve it by means of the machinery and consultative processes made available to it by the terms of the Agreement itself.

The Supreme Court is to be congratulated for its clear and unambiguous exposition of an issue which British and Irish politicians have attempted to hide for many years. Indeed, the suppression of what the Supreme Court has now declared to be true has been a cornerstone of every so-called initiative in Northern Ireland up to and including the signing of the Anglo-Irish Agreement in 1985.

NATIONAL FRONTIERS AND MINORITY RIGHTS

One of the root causes of World War II was the assertion by extreme nationalist leaders such as Hitler and Mussolini of the principle of national frontiers and the right of their countries to include within their national territory such parts of other states as were occupied by German and Italian nationals. Upon this basis, Hitler claimed the territory of Czechoslovakia that was occupied by Sudenten Germans. It was in the ambience of such nationalist claims that the Irish constitution was drafted in 1937. The invalidity and fallacies of such theories are now

---

[1]*Belfast News Letter*, 22 March 1990; and John Wilson Foster (ed.), *The Idea of the Union: Statements and Critiques in Support of the Union of Great Britain and Northern Ireland* (Vancouver: Belcouver Press, 1995).

universally acknowledged by every political scientist of international repute.

Although both Britain and Ireland are active participants in the United Nations, both of them, but particularly Britain, have chosen to ignore entirely the recommendations of the United Nations in drawing up the terms of the Anglo-Irish Agreement. In the Capotorti Report, prepared for the United Nations and published in 1979, the desirability of bilateral treaties between states for the protection of minorities was emphasised, but such treaties or agreements were to be subject to two important principles, both of which the terms of the Anglo-Irish Agreement violate. As the Capotorti Report states: 'the special rapporteur strongly believes that bilateral agreements dealing with minority rights concluded between states where minorities live and states from which such minorities originate (especially between neighbouring countries) would be extremely useful. It must be stressed, however, that cooperation with regard to the rights of minority groups shall be based on mutual respect for the principles of sovereignty and territorial integrity of the states concerned and non-interference in their internal affairs'.

In addition to the terms for such bilateral treaties recommended in the above report to the United Nations, it should also be noted that within the compass of the European Community, of which both Britain and Ireland are members, largely similar obligations are imposed on member states. Such states within the Community are committed to the recognition of each other's existing boundaries.

IRISH CONSTITUTIONAL IRREDENTISM

There can be little doubt that at the time the Anglo-Irish Agreement was signed, the British government was aware that the Irish government could not, by reason of Article Two of its constitution, accept the territorial integrity of the United Kingdom of Great Britain and Northern Ireland, and that the terms of the Agreement would afford to the Irish government widespread powers to interfere in the most fundamental way with the internal affairs of a part of the United Kingdom. Despite this knowledge, not only did the British government sign the Agreement, but it engaged in a massive propaganda campaign exercise to persuade the British public that it had obtained, for the first time, a new and fundamental recognition of the status of Northern Ireland by the Irish government.

In tandem with the British efforts at deception, the Irish government and, in particular Dr Garrett FitzGerald, were peddling the patently erroneous line that Article Two was purely declaratory of the Irish political aspiration for unity and was not a legal claim, in a true sense, to the territory of Northern Ireland. Both governments were very well aware that what they were stating was false or, at best, a very economical use of the truth. In the Sunningdale Communiqué of December 1973, the British government declared that 'the present status of Northern Ireland is that it is part of the United Kingdom. If in the future the majority of the people of Northern Ireland should indicate a wish to become part of a united Ireland, the British government would support that wish'.

The Irish government, for its part, merely accepted and declared that there could be no change in the status of Northern Ireland until a majority of the people of Northern Ireland desired a change in that status. It was obvious that the Irish government was unwilling to recognise the legal status of Northern Ireland as a part of the United Kingdom. When the meaning of the Irish declaration at Sunningdale was subsequently challenged in the Irish courts by Kevin Boland, the Irish Attorney General declared that 'any person living in this island and knowing our history could not possibly construe the declaration as meaning we did not lay claim over the six counties'. As one political scientist has asked about Liam Cosgrave, the Irish Prime Minister at the time of Sunningdale, was he 'merely recognising a fact he could not alter and representing this as a concession?'

In essence, the Irish declaration was little different than Articles Two and Three of the constitution, which claimed the whole island as the national territory as a legal right, but recognised the factual situation by stating that, without prejudice in the meantime, the Irish government would only legislate for the twenty-six counties over which it exercised not only legal, but factual, sovereignty.

THE ANGLO-IRISH AGREEMENT
Article One of the Anglo-Irish Agreement, signed by the British and Irish governments in November 1985, states:

> The two governments:
>
> (a) affirm that any change in the status of Northern Ireland would only come about with the consent of the majority of the people of Northern Ireland;

(b) recognise that the present wish of the majority of the people of Northern Ireland is for no change in the status of Northern Ireland;
(c) declare that if in the future a majority of the people of Northern Ireland clearly wish for and formally consent to the establishment of a united Ireland, they will introduce and support in the respective Parliaments legislation to give effect to that wish.

What was immediately clear was that while the Agreement spoke of no change in the status of Northern Ireland, it neither determined nor declared what that status was. Far from being a measure that, as Tom King, the Secretary of State for Northern Ireland, asserted in Parliament strengthened the Union, it in fact even weakened the Sunningdale position, where the British government was at least willing to declare openly its definition of Northern Ireland's status as being part of the United Kingdom.

The political dishonesty of the whole business was plain from the very start in that the title of the Agreement was different in the Irish and British versions. The Irish copy declared that the Agreement was made with the Government of the United Kingdom, while the British version declared the Agreement to be made between the Government of the Republic of Ireland and the Government of Great Britain and Northern Ireland. When Mr Charles Haughey, then in opposition, questioned the Agreement in the Dail as being tantamount to an abandonment of the national claim to Irish unity and the recognition of British sovereignty over Northern Ireland, the then Minister for Foreign Affairs, Mr Peter Barry, assured him that the Agreement is 'as it must be, of course, totally consistent with the constitution and, therefore, with Article Two'. It was thus evident, almost from Day One, that the Irish government was fully determined to maintain the legal claim to the territory of a neighbouring state and fellow member of the European Community.

A CONSTITUTIONAL IMPERATIVE

What the Supreme Court's decision has now made clear beyond argument is that Article Two of the Irish constitution assigned to the Irish government a constitutional imperative to work towards the making good, in fact as well as in law, of the Republic's claim to the territory of Northern Ireland. Against this background, who can really deny that whatever theoretical distinctions may be made as to how this legal claim is to be translated into fact, the IRA derived constitutional legitimacy in its attempts to achieve by terror what the constitution of the Republic declared to be its legal entitlement. The object of the Republic's constitution is a united Ireland; the object of the Provisional IRA is a united Ireland; and the declared policy of the SDLP, led by John Hume, is a united Ireland. All efforts to achieve an internal solution of Northern Ireland's problems within the United Kingdom are doomed to failure, because of the opposition of these three groupings. None of them can permit a solution to the problems of Northern Ireland other than by way of Irish unity. Their combined opposition has forced weak and vacillating British governments to enter into agreements which no other European state would have tolerated.

Despite the obvious use of which the British government might have made of the recommendations of the United Nations and the terms of membership in the European Community, it has declined to do so. Much is made by the Republic of the fact that the Anglo-Irish Agreement is an international treaty registered with the United Nations, but the British government has failed to take any steps, either at the United Nations or at Strasbourg, relevant to the abject failure of the Republic to honour the Agreement's terms. The truth is that following the recent extradition debacle, the Irish government must now feel assured that there is no breach or insult, be it ever so gross, that will persuade the British government to react positively.

The reason for this weakness on the part of the British government is not difficult to define: the British government has long since ceased to regard Northern Ireland as properly within the territory of the United Kingdom or its citizens as real British citizens. Any government only defends the territory over which it seeks to maintain its sovereign jurisdiction, and sovereign states only reject claims to such of its territory as it truly sees as its 'own'. The uncertainties and doublespeak of the Agreement's terms presented no real difficulty for the British and Irish governments, or even the SDLP, since all of them were privy to the 'realities' and hidden agendas concealed behind the public facade.

CONCLUSION

The ambiguities were a necessary cosmetic veneer in an effort to persuade not only the Unionists, but large sections of British public opinion and the media, that what had been done had a measure of principled political decency which, in truth, it wholly lacked. Over the last several years this veneer has cracked and peeled and revealed the reality of the Agreement's terms for the unpleasant and shabby things they are. One can only hope, even at this late stage, that the truth, as partially demonstrated by the Irish Supreme Court's decision, is capable of awakening some vestige of political morality in the corridors of British power, and that those who support the Union, both in Northern Ireland and Great Britain, will endeavour to ensure that justice is done to the British citizens of Northern Ireland.

IV

EQUAL BRITISH CITIZENSHIP

Six

We Have a Vision:
The Case for Equal Citizenship[1]

INTRODUCTION

The Campaign For Equal Citizenship is not about the triumph or the ascendancy of one community over another. It is not about the Unionist determination to maintain the Union or the nationalist aspiration to obtain unity. It is a campaign for obtaining equality of rights as between the two communities in Northern Ireland and for obtaining equality of rights as between all of the people of Northern Ireland and their fellow citizens in the rest of the United Kingdom of Great Britain and Northern Ireland.

It is my belief that since the creation of the state of Northern Ireland in 1921 the denial of such equality of citizenship to the entire people of Northern Ireland has been the fundamental cause of the division, the confrontation and the sectarian violence which has disfigured almost every aspect of life in this province. This denial of equal citizenship has had very different effects upon the two communities, but its combined effect has been to institutionalise and entrench the differences between them. Its effect has been to ensure, through an inherently unstable party political structure, that the very best that can be hoped for is a precarious coexistence within an acceptable level of violence. It has created a situation where only the positive dominance of an insecure majority could give to the state a semblance of stability. When such dominance was broken by its creator—the British government—the essential fraud and infeasibility of devolved government was totally revealed.

Before the objects of this Campaign for Equal Citizenship can be fully appreciated, it is necessary for us to understand the answers to a number of basic questions. In what manner is the value of our British citizenship different from the rest of the British people? How did such difference in the value of our citizenship come about? What have been the effects upon both communities of these differences? Why is the only hope for ultimate peace dependent upon the elimination of these differences and the granting of full equality of citizenship to all the people of Northern Ireland?

---

[1]This chapter is based on a speech delivered to a meeting of the Campaign for Equal Citizenship at the Ulster Hall in Belfast on 3 July 1986.

WHAT IS THE VALUE OF OUR PRESENT CITIZENSHIP?

Our British citizenship is devalued to the status of total sham because we cannot vote to elect our own government since the parties that could form governments—the Conservative Party, the British Labour Party and, latterly, the SDP—refuse to contest elections here or even to allow British citizens living in Northern Ireland to join them. British governments cannot deprive us of our right to vote, but, by excluding us from parties, they can effectively render such votes valueless. Governments are formed from parties who have to account to the electorate for their policies. But since neither Conservative nor Labour governments are accountable to the electors of Northern Ireland, they can treat our votes with contempt—as they have done in the case of the Anglo-Irish Agreement. Since we are excluded from parties, we are excluded both from the use of power and even the influencing of power. Since none of the British parties compete for our votes, they can agree to ignore our wishes. A Welshman, a Scot or an Englishman can aspire to the highest political offices of the state, but an Ulsterman can only do so if, like Mr Brian Mawhinney, he leaves Northern Ireland, lives in England, joins a major party and is elected by English electors. He then, by some magical process, becomes fit to be a junior minister in the Northern Ireland Office.

Our Parliament does not discuss our affairs. Legislation for Northern Ireland is not passed in the same manner as laws intended for the rest of the United Kingdom. For Northern Ireland, ministers simply place Orders in Council before Parliament for acceptance or rejection. Such orders cannot be amended. These Orders are neither debated nor passed like Acts of Parliament applying to the rest of the United Kingdom. They are simply endorsed, usually in the early hours of the morning, by an unaccountable government majority. It is the total negation of parliamentary democracy.

There is in Northern Ireland no local government democracy. All the most important local government functions—education, housing, health and social services—are in the hands of the Area Boards and the Housing Executive, the majority of whose members are non-elected appointees of the Northern Ireland Office. These appointees, worthy though they may be in some cases, are not elected by the people and are not responsible to the people. Only the most trivial local government functions remain the responsibility of our elected representatives. We are allowed to be responsible for the clearing of our refuse and the burial of our dead. Democracy in Northern Ireland is a fraud and a sham, but what is most frightening is that the vast majority of people are not even aware of it. The ultimate triumph of the despot is to persuade the slaves not only to believe that they are free, but to actually declare that they are free. The vast majority of our people are unaware of the degree to which they have been disenfranchised.

HOW HAVE WE LOST OUR RIGHTS?

If you are now convinced that as a British citizen living in Northern Ireland you have no effective political rights, you are entitled to ask how did this come about? In 1921 Ireland was divided, not upon the basis of some sectarian head count, as some would have us believe, but upon the basis that there were two separate peoples: those who saw themselves as British and those who saw themselves as Irish. Their values, their allegiances, their cultures and, often, their religions were quite separate and distinct. Edward Carson endeavoured to persuade the British government that they should recognise this principle and grant full equality of citizenship to all the people of what was to become Northern Ireland. In May 1920, in the House of Commons, he had this to say:

> It has been said over and over again, "you want to oppress the Catholic minority; you want a Protestant ascendancy over there". We have never asked to govern any Catholic. We are perfectly satisfied that all of them, Protestant and Catholic, should be governed from this Parliament and we have always said it was the fact that this Parliament was aloof entirely from these racial distinctions and religious distinctions which was the strongest foundation for the government of Ulster.

The initial policy of the British government was to get rid of the whole of Ireland and, if they could not do it in one piece, then they were quite prepared to wait in order to finally dispose of the rest of the business. In the meantime, the new state of Northern Ireland would be maintained in an artificial limbo under a devolved government. The citizens of Northern Ireland had to be given the right to vote in Westminster elections, but, by excluding them from the main party system, such a right could be effectively nullified. The new state could only be stabilised by permitting the majority to rule, and, so long as they effectively maintained an acceptable level of public order, the British government was prepared to ignore any excesses. The entire political community had been deprived of their real political rights, but the Unionist community enjoyed the position of 'trustees' in what was to become a political prison.

*   *   *

In 1921 the British government's solution for the Irish Question was Home Rule. The activity of Ulster Unionists partially frustrated the proposed scheme, and the 1921 settlement was one which put Northern Ireland into the category of 'unfinished business'. Northern Ireland was to be kept artificially separate and undisturbed until British interests or policy required a reappraisal. Lloyd George had been confident that the business would finish itself within five years and said as much to Michael Collins. Winston Churchill was prepared to finish it in 1940 in exchange for the Irish Free State's abandonment of its neutrality in favour of the Allies. Currently, British policy, and that of the United States, would best be served by a stable united Ireland within the fold of NATO. This view is not necessarily shared by the British people, but it is favoured by some politicians, by large sections of the media, by many civil servants and is the declared objective of some of the major British parties. It is a policy which can only succeed by prostituting political principle to political expediency and policy.

Since it cannot be done in one move without provoking civil war and destabilising the whole of Ireland, the policy moves upon three principles. Firstly, the people of Northern Ireland, but particularly the Unionists, must be portrayed through the media as unreasonable, difficult and different. Their behaviour can be categorised as 'rebellious' and worthy of harsh treatment. The object is to persuade the British electorate that the Unionist people, though technically British citizens, do not really conform to standards that require them to be treated as such. To this process, the conduct of some of our political dinosaurs make a large contribution. Secondly, by excluding Northern Ireland MPs from participation in government through the major parties like everyone else, the political establishment has neutralised their influence. No longer, like Carson, could an Ulster MP become a cabinet minister. Except on the rare occasion of a hung parliament, the influence of our MPs became totally marginal. The Conservative Party, cynical as always, bought the loyalty of Unionist MPs by allegedly supporting the Union, but carefully prevented Unionists from being able to do that job themselves from inside the Conservative Party. Thirdly, devolved government was the strategy which, for fifty years, prevented Northern Ireland from becoming as much a part of the United Kingdom as Scotland or Wales. It kept us artificially separate and distinct and, since 1972, has allowed successive British governments to subject the Unionist population to unremitting political, economic, media, cultural and even legal pressure to assume an Irish dimension or identity in place of a British one, which is being systematically dismantled.

In 1921 the British government imposed a devolved government upon Northern Ireland simply because it suited the then current British policy. Its effects were to be disastrous for both Northern Ireland communities.

WHAT WERE THE EFFECTS OF DEVOLVED GOVERNMENT UPON BOTH COMMUNITIES?

From the Unionist viewpoint, the fact that Northern Ireland was to be governed differently from the rest of the United Kingdom was an immediate qualification of the status of British citizens in Northern Ireland. Such distinction was, and remains, the badge of difference. The realisation by Unionists that their presence within the United Kingdom was, to some degree, conditional, created within them an anxiety about their constitutional future that, in many cases, amounted to paranoia. Anxiety, fear and lack of confidence ensured that generosity was minimal towards a minority who felt bitter at their exclusion from an Irish state. This political anxiety among Unionists about the future of the Union so dominated all other political issues that normal functional politics were dwarfed into insignificance. The creation of a Catholic state for a Catholic people in the rest of Ireland guaranteed the equal and opposite theme for Northern Ireland. The basis for sectarian confrontation was rapidly laid down and just as rapidly built upon. From the nationalists' viewpoint, their disappointment at exclusion from the Irish Free State and the British belief that Northern Ireland would not survive encouraged them in an abstentionist policy in almost every aspect of the Northern Ireland administration. The powers given to the Unionist majority, particularly in the field of internal security, and the Northern Ireland government's need to establish stability reinforced the polarisation of the two communities and, inevitably, led to the allegations of oppression and discrimination about which Carson had warned.

While all of this was going on, what was the British government doing? Having created a situation that could only work if the majority were in a dominant role, it promptly passed a ruling that matters properly within the competence of the Northern Ireland government were not open for debate in the House of Commons. It thus totally distanced the Westminster government from the affairs of Northern Ireland and about those affairs it wished to know as little as possible. There can be few better examples of total political cynicism than this creation of Lloyd George, but it was a prostitution of political principle to political policy that every subsequent British government, including the present one, has acquiesced in. British government policy excluding Northern Ireland from its proper place in the United Kingdom is the biggest and most important factor in the current problems of Northern Ireland.

THE DEVOLUTION REMEDY

Since 1921 devolution has enshrined the government policy for Northern Ireland of 'equal but separate', which has effectively deprived us of our civil rights. Devolution still remains the central core of that policy, as illustrated by the Anglo-Irish Agreement. Unionists were deluded into believing that a devolved government was the best guarantee that their wish to remain within the United Kingdom would be respected. Fortunately, after Sunningdale and Hillsborough a decreasing number of political dinosaurs cling to that illusion, which the British government still encourages. However, even if the Anglo-Irish Agreement was annulled tomorrow, the search for peace and stability would have to go on. Unionists' anxiety about their constitutional future, and the minority's desire for their proper place in the affairs of the state, would have to be met. The answer to that search would not be, even in those circumstances, devolution of a legislative and executive kind. Devolution has foundered on the rock of the division of the community, which devolution itself created.

To return to a local parliament, either with or without power sharing, would be a return to the same conditions that have caused the murder and misery of the last seventeen years. There would be a renewal of block sectarian voting, Unionist against nationalist, Catholic against Protestant. The perpetual struggle for ascendancy of the two identities, the two cultures, the two aspirations, would inevitably continue.

All the citizens of Northern Ireland would be condemned to another prison sentence of second class political status, unable to play any effective part in the normal political debates which focus the interest and attention of our fellow citizens in Great Britain. The social, industrial, economic and environmental issues of our lives would continue to be subordinated to the constitutional issues of union and unity, and Westminster policies and decisions in these vital matters would be applied to Northern Ireland without discussion or debate. While pygmy politicians in Northern Ireland debated parochial and parish pump issues, the entire community, in real terms, would be governed from Westminster like a half-alien dependency.

*   *   *

In a devolution situation, Northern Irish political parties must attempt the impossible. They must each contain within their own membership the whole range of political opinion, from extreme right to extreme left. They must, at the same time, be essentially either Catholic or Protestant. It is a political contortion achievable only by the sacrifice of involvement in the real issues of politics and by the wholly unjustified assumption of correspondence between political opinion and religious belief. It has been rightly said that this closed system of constitutional parties imposes restrictions on people which amount to an attack on their liberty. The people of Northern Ireland are the victims of a 'Catch 22' situation. First, they are denied the right to vote for a national party that may form a government; second, they are condemned to vote for a local party upon the single issue of union or unity.

Why, for example, can one not be openly Catholic and Unionist or Protestant and nationalist? How does a strongly conservative Catholic industrialist, sympathetic to the present government's economic policies, find satisfaction in voting for the SDLP? How can a Unionist socialist register his convictions about the structures of education or the privatisation of industry by voting for a conservative party. The scandal of the situation is revealed when one considers that a Unionist population that has shared the worst unemployment record in the United Kingdom has consistently, throughout the fifty years of Stormont, voted for a party which supported various Conservative governments that were, in many instances, responsible for that situation, when, rationally, they should have been voting Labour with their Catholic, working class neighbours.

Does the SDLP support the British Labour Party because of the latter's socialist ideology, or are the Unionists voting broadly Conservative because of Tory policy? The answer in both cases is no, they are not. Their connections are based upon the real, or imagined, support of those British parties for the maintenance of the Union or support for Irish unity.

None of the various attempts to solve the problem of government in Northern Ireland has ever faced up to the difficulties inherent in the province's political party system. Such attempts have all been concerned to secure coexistence with the minimum of friction. The Anglo-Irish Agreement is the latest of these Heath-Robinson structures based on the absurd notion that reconciliation, peace and stability can be obtained by confirming and strengthening the claims and the aspirations of rival cultures and traditions. This scheme breaks none of the old moulds or offers any fresh initiatives. It is simply the latest ploy for keeping Northern Ireland as an artificially separate part of the United

Kingdom, a region outside the whole mainstream of politics and forever asserting its loyalty to comfort its insecurity.

One of the most compelling sources upon which I have drawn heavily—Edgar Haslett, a non-party Unionist committed to equal British citizenship for people living in Northern Ireland—puts it like this: 'It has been said that if power sharing would work there would be no need for it. The same is true for all other recommendations aimed at uniting Unionists and nationalists.'

THE UNITED-IRELAND REMEDY

If devolved government, whether of the power sharing or majority rule variety, is not the answer, what about a united-Ireland solution? It might be argued that in a united Ireland the constitutional issue would disappear and the Protestants could join the liberal crusaders of Dublin in search of a pluralist state. It is an option which I honestly believe is not only unattractive to the vast majority of Protestants, but to a very significant number of the minority. The Ulster political parties, limited though they may be, at least have the excuse of a terrorist campaign and a foreign territorial claim. The parties of the Republic do not even have that excuse for their stunted sectarian parochialism. There is no incentive for the citizens of a pluralist state such as the United Kingdom to become citizens of a state dominated by a constitution which the late Professor FSL Lyons described as a compendium of Catholic social teaching, a state held in the grasp of an authoritarian church. I have written repeatedly on this issue over the last five years and I quote from an article written in February 1984:

> The unpalatable truth is that even if the Unionists had been prepared to name a pluralist price for their consent [to a united Ireland], neither the majority of the people of the Republic nor the Roman Catholic Church would have permitted her politicians to pay the price in the coin of reformed institutions.

In both the abortion referendum of September 1983 and the divorce referendum of May 1986, the people of the Republic, with the encouragement and support of the Roman Catholic Church, overwhelmingly rejected pluralism as the price for a united Ireland, despite, in the latter referendum, the persuasive efforts of both Garrett FitzGerald and John Hume that a 'yes' vote would assist the Anglo-Irish process. The rejection was decisive by a vote of almost 2 to 1. In September 1983 an *Irish Times* editorial declared after the result of the abortion referendum that the Border, after 60 years, had finally been confirmed by the votes of the Irish people. If that was so, then the effect of the divorce referendum is to engrave such confirmation upon tablets of stone.

Not only is there no social incentive to embrace the united-Ireland solution, there is absolutely no financial or economic one. The financial problems of the Republic are enormous: a rising and uncontrollable unemployment rate, a mountainous burden of foreign debt, the heaviest taxation in Europe and an escalating drug and crime problem. Not only is there no attraction for the Unionist population, but there is certainly none for the North's nationalists. In a united Ireland, the Protestants might just be substantial enough in numbers to secure their interests, but the group which would be nobody's darling would be the Northern minority.

THE EQUAL CITIZENSHIP SOLUTION

The only option which has a sound logical, moral and political basis is one which would provide for equal citizenship within the United Kingdom. Some people refer to this option as integration, although I believe that this term can be used emotively in a way which prevents both communities from fully appreciating the concept.

Northern Ireland already forms part of a modern, pluralist, democratic state, and yet its citizens are prevented from playing a proper part in the life of that state. Nowhere is the determination to keep Northern Ireland artificially separate so clearly shown as in the failure of the British parties to organise here or to accept Northern Irish people as party members. We pay exactly the same taxes, we are, in general terms, subject to the same laws. We are affected by the same decisions on a number of issues, from defence to nuclear power. But we are excluded from voting for a party which may form the government and which takes decisions on these matters. Instead, we are offered local parties which are quite incapable of reflecting our opinions on any of these issues. Any form of devolved government would again commit us to this political prison. Is it any wonder our politicians become so intellectually and politically shrunken when they are confined within such narrow cells.

Imagine, therefore, the scope and the excitement that might be offered if the British parties were to organise here. The political life of the province could be transformed. Imagine the opportunity for Catholics and Protestants to share in a political ideology, whether of the left, the right or the centre. Imagine the true integration of a community on the common ground of making Northern Ireland a better place in accordance with political, rather than sectarian, principles. It would offer some real prospect of achieving peace, stability and reconciliation. It is a vision which would force all the parties to our problems to declare themselves.

The SDLP would have to declare whether their prime objective was equality of opportunity, equality of justice, equality of civil rights for the minority community or, on the contrary, to state that these matters were really secondary to the nationalist aspiration for a united Ireland.

Unionists would have to decide whether they were really in support of the Union, because it maintained a link with a secular, pluralist and democratic state, or whether their true objective was a non-Catholic ascendancy, and, if the Union did not provide that, they might have to go it alone. The choice for me of a Roman Catholic theocracy or a fundamentalist Protestant statelet is equally unacceptable.

The government of the Republic would have to declare that while the United Kingdom was capable of governing one million Southern Irish Catholics now living in freedom and prosperity in Great Britain, it was incapable of governing fairly and justly the Catholic minority in Northern Ireland in similar fashion. The Republic's declared concern for the continuing nightmare of the North's minority could then be judged as either genuine or merely as a vehicle for an irredentist foreign policy.

Finally, the British government would have to declare itself. It could no longer play the role of 'honest broker' or of 'Pontius Pilate'. It could no longer maintain the fraudulent pretence that the people of Northern Ireland are as British as Margaret Thatcher's Finchley electors, while, at the same time, excluding them from full equality of citizenship. Northern Ireland could no longer be kept as an artificial satellite outside the rest of the United Kingdom. The British government could no longer prostitute the principle of equal rights for British citizens to an outdated, outworn and a failed political policy for Northern Ireland.

The adoption of a policy of equal citizenship would herald the dawn not only a new era of political hope, it would herald a new age of political honesty.

WHO WOULD OPPOSE EQUAL CITIZENSHIP AND WHY?

The challenge to the solution of integration, or equal citizenship, as I prefer to call it, would come from a number of predictable sources. The identity of such groupings is as readily ascertainable as their arguments, but both identity and the arguments bear examination.

There would be opposition from the government of the Republic and from the SDLP, but, as I have already illustrated, the very nature of their objections would force them to declare the nature of what really, what truly, motivates their political agitation. Are they sincerely in search of peace, reconciliation and stability or are they simply engaged in a disguised operation to manipulate a fraudulent consent for a united Ireland that is in nobody's interest. If they are sincere on the issue of a united Ireland only by consent, if they are sincere about their search for peace and stability, how can they object to the wish of the present majority to remain within the United Kingdom as citizens with full and equal rights, while all await majority consent for an All-Ireland solution? Equality of citizenship would be on the basis that it would remove nationalist fears and complaints about discrimination and Protestant/Unionist domination. Even political nationalism would not be lost to them should they wish to ignore membership of the major parties and go it alone like the Scottish and Welsh nationalists at Westminster. The choice would be theirs, but the people would have that choice.

There is equally no doubt that opposition would emerge from the Unionist community. One of the by-products of the Anglo-Irish Agreement has been the emergence of a form of Ulster nationalism that was always latent in Unionism. For many Protestant extremists, their view of the Union was simple. The Union was a convenient constitutional device for maintaining a Protestant ascendancy over the Catholic minority. If the Union didn't serve that purpose, then for such so-called Unionists its value was questionable. The psychological damage which the Anglo-Irish Agreement caused to all Unionists had a particularly virulent effect on this group. They talk the language of devolution, but the spirit is that of a Unilateral Declaration of Independence. Ian Paisley has made political use of this emotion, but has been politically astute enough to shrink from its consequences. Others may not be so squeamish.

Opposition would also emerge from a variety of groups dedicated to the idea of consensual, or even socialist, politics of a non-sectarian nature. These groups believe that integration into the major British parties would mark the end of their local power. The Alliance Party offers only limited scope for non-sectarian politics and, indeed, its only reason for being is that Northern Ireland's citizens are treated less equally than those in Great Britain. The Alliance Party may accommodate Catholic and Protestant, but it cannot accommodate Catholic conservative and Protestant socialist and it can never aspire to form a government of the state of which its electors form part. The

Workers Party, with whose socialist policies many Protestants as well as Catholics would have sympathy, has also chosen to bind its base by binding itself to a constitutional commitment.

*   *   *

All of these groups would have different reasons for supporting a devolved government, but the very variety of reasons and their objects in using it would ensure it took on the character of a Tower of Babel. The SDLP would wish to use a power sharing assembly as a Trojan Horse for Irish unity. The DUP would wish to use a majority-rule assembly with security powers to reinstate Protestant supremacy. The Alliance Party would wish to use their votes to control the balance of power and obtain for themselves an importance that their popular support would never justify. Each and every one of these objectives were demonstrated to the full in the attitudes of these parties in the Northern Ireland Assembly. All of this opposition places far too high a value on a local assembly, in which, as one shrewd commentator puts it, 'too many politicians have to chase too few political ideas in an assembly which is as expensive as it is unnecessary and which has within it the seeds of its own decay'.

The Provisional IRA and the INLA would, undoubtedly, be opposed to equal citizenship. They exist upon, and feed off of, both the real and imagined grievances of the minority community, and if none existed they would be forced to invent them. A policy of full equality of citizenship would, nevertheless, be a serious blow to their morale, though initially they might well escalate both their violence and their propaganda.

*   *   *

The biggest opposition to this campaign, however, will come from the entire population which has the most to gain. It is not the active opposition of those with a personal or political axe to grind. It is the passive opposition from an apathetic mass of politically indifferent, largely middle class people. Their response is simple. Integration, or equal citizenship, is the best solution, the fairest solution, the logically and politically unanswerable solution, but the British government will never give it to you, for Margaret Thatcher and even Tom King have spoken. These are the very people who bitterly complain about lack of leadership and lack of policy. These are the very people who smugly and complacently eschew any part in the nasty business of politics. These are the very people who have the education and intelligence to make money and be successful, but who lack the spirit and the will to claim, nay, to demand their constitutional rights. Do they wish to be slaves? Do they desire to be serfs? Is it their will to remain disenfranchised? Or is it simply that, because of their wealth and their position, they have no hunger to be equal?

I believe that such is the justice, the logic, the morality, the political sense of the case for equal citizenship that it must succeed. If we find men and women who can measure up to the quality of the cause, then success will assuredly be ours.

This campaign cannot offer to nationalists the promise of fulfilment for their unity aspiration. This campaign cannot offer to Unionists an eternal guarantee for the maintenance of the Union. This campaign can offer to both nationalists and Unionists the equality of citizenship that can enable them both to realise their full political potential without sacrificing their principles.

We in this campaign offer a vision of what is possible. We are not so naïve as to believe that it is a magical formula that can achieve instant success in a seemingly intractable situation. We appreciate that it will require resolution and determination. We know that there will be doubts and disappointments. We believe that it is a vision of hope that, with faith and charity, can be made to work—for clearly nothing else can.

WE HAVE VISION

The constitution of the United States declared that all men were born equal, but for nearly sixty years afterwards some men were treated as equal but separate. The constitution of the United Kingdom gives all its citizens the same right to vote for members of Parliament, but for sixty-six years the people of Northern Ireland have been treated separately and the effectiveness of their vote nullified. Both the majority and the minority in Northern Ireland have suffered economic and social deprivation in an area with the highest unemployment in the United Kingdom. Both communities have been denied their civil and constitutional right to vote for a party that conceivably might form a government. They have been condemned to vote for Lilliputian parties devoted almost entirely to their own sectional interests, unrelated to any ideology or policy beyond union and unity. The majority have been persuaded by limited power and marginal economic advantages that they are, in some way, ascendant over the minority. In confronting each other, they have ignored their common loss of rights. Let no Unionist believe that the British establishment thinks much better of him than his nationalist neighbour. In sum:

We in this campaign have, like Martin Luther King, a dream.

We, like Martin Luther King, have a vision.

It is a vision in which the entire community in Northern Ireland have an equal place.

It is a vision for equality of citizenship not only between Protestant/Unionist and Catholic/nationalist, but between both of them and the rest of their fellow citizens in the state of which they now form a part.

It is a vision in which we can all have hope for a better future, because it is based on equality and fairness.

It is a vision not about union or unity, but about equal rights and in which Protestant, Catholic and Dissenter can place their faith, without concession.

It is a vision which, with tolerance and charity, can be made to work.

Go out and tell your families, your friends, your workmates, your professional and business associates.

Go out and share your vision and impart your dream.

Go out prepared to work to make this dream come true.

Seven

Equal Citizenship and Ulster Unionism[1]

INTRODUCTION

Fellow Unionists, today you are participants in what may prove to be an historic occasion for the future of Unionism. What you resolve today may have a crucial influence on the future of your children and even upon your children's children. The decision which you take ought to be above petty politics or personalities, for it is a decision about the future of your state. In a land without a vision, the people perish. In a party without a policy, the people despair. This party presently has neither vision nor policy. If there are those among you who know what the policy of this party is supposed to be then I should wish to hear it, for I know not what it is. Many believe that this party is suffering from political paralysis. Some say that the only discernible policy is that of Micawber: an endless waiting in the hopeless expectation that something will turn up. Almost literally anything will do, such as a Haughey government in Dublin, a defeat of the Conservative Party, a hung parliament in Westminster, perhaps even the hope that God may be a Unionist who will divinely intervene. Anything, in fact, will suffice that will absolve this party from adopting a resolute policy of its own.

Yet throughout all these years the historic policy of Unionism, the political strategy fashioned by Edward Carson for the Ulster people, has atrophied for want of men with courage great enough to use it. This specifically is the policy of equal rights and equal citizenship for the people of Northern Ireland within the United Kingdom. It is a policy which rejects the petty political huckstering of a sectarian provincial devolved government. On 23 September 1912 Edward Carson offered your forebears a policy and a vision. He stated it in clear and direct terms:

> Our demand is a very simple one. We ask for no privileges, but we are determined that no one shall have privileges over us. We ask for no special rights, but we claim the same rights from the same government as every other part of the United Kingdom. We ask for nothing more, we will take nothing less.

Five days later, on Ulster Day, 28 September 1912, in the greatest political demonstration ever held in the United Kingdom, 471,414 people pledged to stand by one another in defending for themselves and

---

[1] Address to the Ulster Unionist Party Conference, 8 November 1986.

their children their cherished position of equal citizenship within the United Kingdom.

Against this historical background, I hereby propose a motion calling on the Ulster Unionist Party to embrace the clearly defined objective of political integration with the national parties of the United Kingdom. In this resolution I am asking you to endorse no new policy. I am not even presenting an old policy in different words. I am asking you to raise again the standard of your forefathers. I am asking you to restore their policy of equal rights and equal citizenship as the declared, the defined and the united policy of this party. This party came into existence for the sole purpose of maintaining the Union, but there are those who would sacrifice the Union as the price for its purposeless existence. The policy of equal rights for British citizens is not only simple, it is right. It is a policy that can succeed, because it is both honourable and unanswerable. Those without courage or resolution say, 'you will never get it'. But what alternative do they offer? Their only alternative is second-class citizenship in a devolved sectarian prison, while awaiting ultimate political extinction in a united Ireland.

THE LIMITS OF DEVOLUTION

Devolution, however, is dead, because the terms upon which it is attainable are unacceptable to the Unionists of Northern Ireland and any terms upon which some would accept it are totally unobtainable. But even the best terms are those of second class citizenship and division. There is no resolution on devolution before this party conference because its terms are incapable of formulation.

Devolution is not Union, it is difference. It was thrust upon Carson and Ulster against their wishes. Its aim in 1921 and its aim today is to separate us from the politics, parties and institutions of our fellow British citizens in the rest of the United Kingdom. The Anglo-Irish Agreement is the fruit of that separation, and the central core of that Agreement is again the bribe of devolution in a weakened power-sharing arrangement that amounts to the formal institutionalising of sectarian differences. The Anglo-Irish Agreement, hateful though it is and destroyed though it must be, is merely a symptom and not a cause. Even now there are those so blind that they fail to see this distinction. Yes, we must destroy the Agreement, but that must not prevent us from formulating a policy to eliminate the thing which created it. If we fail to destroy the disease, its symptoms will merely break out afresh in some other and more virulent form. Devolution is no bulwark for the Union if it is vulnerable to something no more lethal than a Prime Minister's pen.

There are those in this party who, incapable of formulating a policy of their own, will shelter behind the smokescreen of alleged party unity and say, 'first let us deal with the Agreement, then we will form a policy'. By the time that happens, it will be too late, and they will be busy shamelessly selling us into second class citizenship in some debased form of devolved arrangement.

The choice is stark. Either we decide upon a policy of full and equal union, and seek it not from British politicians but from the British people, or else we follow the emotional, violent madness of Ulster nationalism through the blood of a civil war into a re-partitioned and independent state—but a state minus the border areas of South Armagh, Fermanagh and Londonderry, West of the Foyle. We must instead place our trust and our faith in a resolved and determined policy of our own to persuade the British people that British citizenship means equal citizenship for all the people of Northern Ireland within the United Kingdom. The time has come for us to tell the British people what exactly we will say 'yes' to. I believe that such a policy can gain us votes from every section of the Northern Ireland people as they realise the awfulness of the alternatives.

VISION, HOPE, RATIONALITY
We must give our people a vision. We must substitute hope for despair. We must offer a rational policy, instead of blind intransigence. We must offer a policy of full integration into the political institutions of the United Kingdom as the only policy for this party. If, despite our utmost efforts—for the task will be formidable—the British people reject our honourable demand for equal citizenship, then we shall have established the moral platform upon which we may determine the destiny and constitutional future of our people.

I ask this conference to give our people both a policy and a vision. I ask this conference to endorse a policy that will give us full and equal citizenship that will bind us to the people, parties and institutions of the United Kingdom. Let us embrace this vision now.

V

THE SHAPE OF THINGS TO COME

Eight

Unionist Leaders' Strategy will Doom the Union[1]

INTRODUCTION

In 1984 I wrote a passage in the Ulster Unionist Party's policy document, *The Way Forward*, about the strategic objectives of Irish nationalism. One of these objectives was to pressurise Unionism into consent to a united Ireland by producing within Unionist ranks a feeling of rejection and isolation, coupled with anti-British sentiment, in the hope that these feelings would weaken the Union. Once, of course, the Union is broken or even seriously threatened, the process of wearing down Unionist resistance to Irish unity would be accelerated.

The second major objective of nationalism, and a consistent part of John Hume's grand strategy, has been to use the Protestantism of the majority as the weapon to destroy their Unionism. In 1982 Mr Hume gave an address to a mixed audience in St Anne's Cathedral directed to those in the Protestant community whom he considered to have a wider vision. He appealed to such people to step forward and present nationalists with proposals for a New Ireland that were acceptable to Protestantism, as opposed to Unionism. This statement, made two years prior to the report of the Irish Forum, reveals John Hume's strategy. A united Ireland with suitable constitutional adjustments, which even Charles Haughey has offered to make, could accommodate Protestants, but it could never accommodate a single Unionist. This simple fact, which seems to have escaped the minds of the current Unionist leadership, was pointed out by the *Guardian* soon after the New Ireland Forum Report was published. Paragraph 5.4 of the Forum Report stated: 'a united Ireland would necessarily accommodate all the fundamental elements in both (the nationalist and Unionist) traditions'. But the *Guardian* illustrated the basic absurdity of this claim by pointing out that the most fundamental element in the Unionist tradition was the Union of Northern Ireland with Great Britain, an element which could not possibly be accommodated in a united Ireland.

REDEFINING UNIONISM

Peter Smith, recognised as the party intellectual at Glengall Street, saw this issue quite clearly in November 1984 and echoed the *Guardian's* point in his excellent review of the Forum Report. The bitter irony is that he appears to have now forgotten it completely, for the Ulster Unionist Party, by redefining the objects of Unionism, is currently presenting

---

[1]*Belfast News Letter*, 14 April 1987.

Irish nationalism with its greatest opportunity. The maintenance of the Union is, apparently, no longer the primary object of the Ulster Unionist Party, whose main purpose now is 'the protection of the interests of the Protestant community in Northern Ireland' (Peter Smith, *Belfast Telegraph*, 10 April 1987). If the protection of Protestant interests accurately represents the present strategy of Glengall Street, then one can have little hesitation in saying the Union is doomed. Northern Ireland is no longer, to use Peter Robinson's phrase, teetering on the window ledge of the Union, for Glengall Street is preparing a parachute to catapult it out onto the street.

The Anglo-Irish Agreement has produced the required degree of dejection in Unionist minds to persuade them to psychologically abandon the Union—something which Irish nationalism could never accommodate—and to now embrace the protection of Protestant interests, which a united Ireland could at least appear to include. There are certain political principles which, once conceded, can never be retrieved. To concede the Union as the main object of Unionism is one of them. Paradoxically, the cause of this latent rejection of the Union is the unwillingness of some Protestants to put their trust in a Union which requires a broad tolerance of the views of others in a pluralist state, a state operated by a Parliament which, as Edward Carson said in May 1920, knew none of the racial or religious distinctions or interests which the 'new Unionism' would seek to defend.

In truth, whatever the Ulster Unionist Party may become, whether it be the Ulster Protestant Party or the Protestant Interest Party, it will not, essentially, be a Unionist party. Frank Millar, the chief executive of the Ulster Unionist Party, speaking at Enniskillen on 30 March, heralded the 'new wave' of thinking by attacking those who allegedly sought refuge in old values and standards. This cursory rejection of the men of 1912 who swore to maintain their cherished position of equal citizenship within the United Kingdom, and of Edward Carson himself, could only come from one like Frank Millar, who declared himself to be in the business of political leadership. The question many Unionists are asking Frank Millar is: where are you leading us?

If the business of the Ulster Unionist Party is no longer the maintenance of the Union, but the protection of Protestant interests, how is this 'new thinking' likely to be reflected in the deliberations of the Unionist Task Force? Despite leaks of its proceedings, the nature of its report can only be guessed at, because one of its three members, Peter Robinson, has wisely kept his own counsel. Frank Millar has declared himself already to be 'a confirmed devolutionist', while Harold McCusker, who has announced that the simple destruction of the Anglo-Irish Agreement is no longer achievable, is openly enamoured with the devolved power sharing proposals of the Ulster Defence Association. It is almost certain that at least the majority of the Task Force will opt for some form of power sharing devolution along the lines of the UDA document and that they will recommend negotiations with some cosmetic arrangement to disguise the fact that the Anglo-Irish Agreement is still in force. This essentially seems to be the message given by Harold McCusker's 'destruction unachievable' signal.

*   *   *

Many people are also interpreting the phrase 'Unionist realism' as an acknowledgement that power-sharing in some form is on the cards. Ultimately, three factors may prevent Unionists from once again shooting themselves in the foot. They are Peter Robinson's political judgement, the SDLP's determination to safeguard their gains under the Anglo-Irish Agreement and the IRA's escalation of terror. Many Unionists are distressed that at a time when an increasing number of people from all creeds and classes are backing the equal citizenship option, which the Secretary of State is now willing to consider, and at a time when an increasing number of the nationalist community are terrified by the economic consequences of Irish unity, the Unionist leadership should be so reluctant to adopt the one policy that their opponents would find unanswerable, namely, equal British citizenship for all residents of Northern Ireland.

Nine

Hume, Adams and Clausewitz[1]

INTRODUCTION

Carl von Clausewitz, in his treatise *On War*, defined that activity as a continuation of politics by other means. He considered war to be an act of violence intended to compel the opponent to fulfill the aggressor's will. War was simply a real political instrument to continue political commerce by other means. The securing of the policy objective was always to be the determining factor in its use. When Clausewitz wrote in 1832, the situation was different from any of the terrorist wars of the twentieth century, for in his day those who desired the policy objective also controlled the apparatus of war by which it might be achieved. It is this difference which lies at the root of John Hume's alliance with Gerry Adams since the beginning of this year. So much of their dialogue—passages of which have been reported in the media—confirms what most people already know: that both of them share the same policy goal of a united Ireland in circumstances where the formal British political and military presence will be removed so as to permit the will of nationalist Ireland to be imposed upon the pro-Union majority in Northern Ireland.

POLITICS AND TERRORISM

The struggle to obtain this policy goal is being waged at two levels. At the largely political level, the forces of constitutional nationalism are spearheaded by John Hume and the SDLP and backed by the Irish government and fellow-travellers in the major parties of the United Kingdom. At the level of terrorist war, the armed struggle of the Provisional IRA is continuing this political commerce under the auspices of Sinn Fein. What, therefore, is lacking in this arrangement is a unity of political control over terrorist means. Hume clearly believed that a point had been reached where the failure to subordinate the war machine to the policy objective was becoming counter-productive. 'The armed struggle was inflicting the greatest damage on unifying all the people of Ireland and had to end so that political progress could be made.' He then confirmed what the political progress was to be: 'The SDLP's basic view was that the Irish people as a whole had a right to national self-determination. This [outlook] was shared by Sinn Fein and a majority of people on the island.'

Few people would deny that Hume and the SDLP have been the principal beneficiaries of IRA terror. Each outrage executed at the risk of

[1]*Belfast News Letter*, 9 September 1988.

death or imprisonment by the IRA's volunteers has brought further political concessions to Hume's law-abiding constitutional nationalists. It must have galled Adams as Hume and Company joined in the pious platitudes after each fresh horror and then quietly slipped off to bank the political proceeds. Hume's decision to enter dialogue with Adams was dictated by the strategic conclusion that, for the present, terrorist war had served its purpose by placing him in a position to capitalise on the political gains it had brought. Unfortunately, Hume did not control the buttons that operated the terrorist campaign. Tactically, a deal with Sinn Fein to form a pan-nationalist front and suspend the terror would have produced tremendous political dividends for Hume and the SDLP. His hope was surely that the British government, aided by the exhortations of the great and the good, would exert such pressure on the poor, leaderless and policyless Unionists that they would accept almost any political humiliation and dishonour as the price for the suspension of murder and mutilation. Hume and Adams found agreement on a number of things, principally upon the policy objective, or real question, as to how they might end the British presence in Ireland in a manner which left it stable and peaceful, i.e., with the pro-Union community doped and disarmed. Surely the position of the SDLP is now clear. Only, perhaps, the Alliance Party remains so politically virginal as to believe that John Hume's political process to obtain a peaceful and just settlement in Ireland means anything less that Irish unity after the pro-Union British have been processed into cowed docility. Hume and his party have about as much interest as the man on the moon in power sharing devolution as a means of bringing stability and peace to Northern Ireland.

The Sinn Fein assertion that the object of the Hume-Adams talks was to develop 'an overall political strategy to establish justice and peace in Ireland' is almost certainly true. In form, it is almost classical 'Humespeak' and, unlike the more direct language of Sinn Fein, contains a well recognised SDLP code for Irish unity. The talks represented an audacious political gamble by Hume, which, had it succeeded, would have concentrated in a pan-nationalist front both the united Ireland policy objective and a measure of control over the political instrument of terrorist war by which the latter might, in certain circumstances, be achieved. Hume would have become the political puppet master controlling the strings at all levels. In one stroke he would have strengthened the political arm of the SDLP and guaranteed its future electoral base. The political effect of Sinn Fein would have been neutralised while, psychologically, a resumption of hostilities by the IRA would have been enormously difficult. Hume could have exercised some control over them on the basis that their renewed violence would be rejected by a war-weary Catholic community whose prospect of political success such violence could be seen as threatening. On the other hand, the very suggestion of the resumed activity could be used to pressurise political concessions out of both the British government and the pro-Union majority in Northern Ireland. On top of all this, the risk of a split between the IRA's political and military wings would create division and weakness within that organisation.

MACHIAVELLI IN NORTHERN IRELAND
There are fundamental lessons to be learned from this Machiavellian exercise—that is, if the British government, the Northern Ireland Office and the Unionist parties have not entirely foresaken the learning process. The failure of the British government to solve the Northern Ireland problem arises almost solely form the fact that since 1921 their policy objective has been similar to that of Sinn Fein and the SDLP: they see the resolution of the Northern Ireland problem essentially in terms of Irish unity. Since the security forces are the military means of effecting policy, the British government has been in the ludicrous situation of attempting to obtain a policy result which is at odds with the use of the security forces. What the British government must now do is to adopt a political policy of treating Northern Ireland on an equal basis in every sense with the rest of the United Kingdom and fully utilising all means at its disposal to achieve that end. It can do this by making it clear not only to Sinn Fein, but also the SDLP, that their objective of a united Ireland by force or fraud has no prospect of succeeding in the foreseeable future.

There is only one way in which any real peace, stability or reconciliation can be achieved in Northern Ireland, and that is by affording all the citizens of this part of the United Kingdom exactly the same rights, including that of political party participation, that are afforded to British citizens in the rest of the United Kingdom. Until that objective is achieved, Northern Ireland will remain prey to instability, murder and terror.

Ten

Babbling Brooke[1]

INTRODUCTION

In recent weeks the British Government, through the medium of its current colonial governor, Peter Brooke, has launched a political offensive to secure the devolution objective which forms the central core of the Anglo-Irish Agreement. In this attack, unlike the Somme, where lions were said to be led by donkeys, some political jackasses are simply attempting to induce other political fools to follow them. The assault was carefully orchestrated and was preceded by the obligatory artillery barrage from the assembled press corps. It can scarcely be an accident that a particularly dull speech by the Secretary of State, containing absolutely nothing new and made to a group of anonymous businessmen in North Down, should hit the front page of not only the *Times*, but the *Daily Telegraph*. It was rather more predictable that the salvos of these heavy press batteries should be echoed by the pop gun of the *Belfast Telegraph*. All the worn out clichés were then marched forward into the attack, with windows of opportunity being thrown open by the hundred and log jams becoming unstuck by the dozen. Inevitably, one or two local politicians suffered shell shock in the noise and excitement of the bombardment. This resulted in a failure of brain-to-mouth coordination and produced statements ambiguous enough to be seized upon by the Republic's press, which then induced Charlie Haughey to say that which he almost immediately retracted. Now, all of this would be highly amusing as the plot for a Whitehall farce featuring Peter Brooke as Captain Blackadder, but as a response to a month of murder, mayhem and destruction it is a very sick joke. Worse than that, it is a cynical piece of political manipulation designed to take advantage of the natural hopes of decent people that a new year in a new decade might bring peace.

FOLKLORE AND FAIRYTALES

The real truth only becomes apparent when the artificial and manufactured myths are blown away. It is total folklore that a devolved government provides any form of bulwark for Unionists against the threat of a united Ireland. What Westminster gives it can take away, as demonstrated by both Stormont and the Northern Ireland Assembly. Neither of those institutions had any real political power. At most, they were part of the administrative apparatus for executing the policy

---

[1]*Belfast News Letter*, 31 January 1990.

decisions taken by the British government of the day. Whether that government was a Labour or a Conservative one did not matter. The devolved assembly implemented its decisions, which were made without any reference to the electors of Northern Ireland.

An equally pernicious fairytale is the one that suggests that a devolved government will, in some way, improve the present deplorable security failures. The false impression given is that if the SDLP and the Unionists get around a table, never mind into an assembly, this will, in some magical and wholly unexplained way, isolate the men of violence. There is not a shred of evidence to support this fable. Indeed, the reverse is almost certainly the case. The devolution experiment in Northern Ireland in all its forms since 1921 has never done anything but institutionalise communal and sectarian differences, differences which, under any new devolved arrangement, local politicians will continue to emphasise in order to maximise their sectarian-based support. The true, but terrible, paradox is that the sectarian bitterness engendered by devolution, and which made horrors like Darkley, La Mon and Enniskillen possible in the first place, might now be given a new lease on life because of those very horrors. The propaganda line put out by the Northern Ireland Office is that most Ulster Unionists are endlessly forgiving ecumenists who only wish to live in apolitical peace with their Catholic neighbours and whose Christian aspirations are being frustrated by both IRA terrorists and intransigent Unionist leaders. Like all effective propaganda, the skill lies in prostituting part of the truth to political policy. There is absolutely no basis for equating religious ecumenism with a power sharing policy for devolution; nor is there any foundation for the belief that a devolved government of that kind will have any effect whatsoever in reducing terrorist activity. If there is any such evidence, then the Northern Ireland Office should state clearly and openly just what that evidence is.

POLITICAL PROPAGANDA

The essence of effective propaganda is to persuade those sought to be influenced that the proposed policy is something which no decent, right-thinking person could reject. The technique employed is simple. First, the policy is declared to have as its purpose some lofty and noble object. If, for example, one is opposed to the Anglo-Irish Agreement, one may be categorised as an opponent of peace, stability and reconciliation. Similarly, 'power sharing', whatever that phrase may mean in a Northern Ireland political context, has emotional overtones of fairness and reasonableness. A Unionist who is opposed to the concept, whatever the validity of his reasons for such opposition, may be written off as a Protestant bigot unwilling to share political power with his Catholic neighbour. When one puts all the pieces of the propaganda together, the massive confidence trick reads as follows: 'All decent people want an end to terrorist violence. All decent people should be willing to share political power. If political power is shared in Northern Ireland, the men of violence will be isolated. When the men of violence are isolated, terrorism will end.'

This illogical gobbledygook is highly successful in convincing a large number of totally unthinking people. Since they do not think, but prefer to have a comfortable self-image as decent people willing to share, they do not begin to consider just what is proposed to be shared and how the sharing will be done. Nor do they contemplate what the effect of such sharing may be upon their potential future and identity and that of their children. Now, most people wish to be thought of as fair and decent, but one or two Unionist politicians have turned the cultivation of this image into an art form. A politician with a cultivated, self-conscious political decency, coupled with a desire for public recognition, is meat and drink for his political opponents and is usually a complete sucker for the propaganda message outlined above. The Republic's press and television media have become past masters in the art of massaging the ego of the decent and reasonable Unionist, so long as he is moving in what they consider to be 'the right direction'. Endorsement by the *Belfast Telegraph* and the *Irish Times* is now tantamount to official approval by the British and Irish governments. The present 'initiative' is directed towards achieving, first, negotiations and, second, consideration of a devolved administration for Northern Ireland. Unionists said to be reasonable are to be used to provide the key to open the gates or the window of opportunity, depending on how one views the prospect.

BASIC PRINCIPLES

Against this background, certain basic principles must be understood. The suspension or even abolition of the Anglo-Irish Agreement is much less important than the terms of any proposed devolved government. John Hume and the SDLP are only interested in devolution upon their terms plus the direct involvement of the Irish government in Northern Ireland's internal affairs. It was because the Northern Ireland Assembly did not provide for both that the SDLP refused to participate. Hume, Mallon and others, including the leading SDLP devolutionist, Austin Currie, have made it clear beyond argument that any form of devolved government is not an end in itself, but is only part of a process to achieve a final and lasting solution in Ireland. Translated freely from 'Humespeak', the last phrase means a united Ireland. In his dialogue with Gerry Adams, Hume stated his position in unequivocal terms: 'The SDLP's basic view was that the Irish people as a whole had a right to national self-determination. This was shared by Sinn Fein and a majority of the people on the island.'

The SDLP leader has made no secret of his willingness to abandon the Anglo-Irish Agreement if he can obtain in return an even better arrangement for furthering not only the SDLP's, but Sinn Fein's, aspiration for a united Ireland. Unionists would be making a catastrophic mistake if they accepted suspension or even abolition of one horror which is to be replaced by an even greater one. The very heart of the Anglo-Irish Agreement is a devolved government. Such an arrangement would confirm the separateness of Northern Ireland from the rest of the United Kingdom and will not dampen the terrorist campaign, but will, undoubtedly, fuel it. The greatest threat to the Union lies not within the SDLP, but with those Unionist politicians who are either so misguided or so cynically self-interested as to throw away their only card by agreeing to any form of legislative devolution. Mrs Thatcher, Lord Mackay, the Lord Chancellor, and Malcolm Rifkind, Secretary of State for Scotland, have all openly rejected devolution for Scotland on the basis that it would weaken the Union and marginalise Scottish input to national affairs. In such circumstances, who but a political amateur could believe that devolution for Northern Ireland could strengthen the Union or improve our position as part of the United Kingdom. Devolution for Northern Ireland is designed for an altogether different purpose: as a transit camp on the road to a united Ireland. The permanent institutions of the Anglo-Irish Agreement have already provided a railroad track to unity, but agreement by the Unionists to a devolved assembly would simply be providing the rolling stock to carry the people of Northern Ireland out of the Union and into a united Ireland.

THE LIMITS OF POWER SHARING

Any review of the concept of power sharing on a proportional basis immediately reveals the totally undemocratic nature of the whole idea. Free and democratic elections involve the basic principle of the capacity to change governments. The only exception to that principle is that of a national, or coalition, government for a limited period of a national emergency. In Northern Ireland no such change of government would ever be possible. Whichever way the electorate voted, there would always be the same power sharing body on exactly the same terms of reference with the same proportional distribution of jobs for the same group of boys. Each election would simply confirm the separateness and rigidity of the two communities. Moreover, what would these representatives legislate about? It certainly would not be about the economy, the Health Service, education, unemployment or the fundamental issues of the environment, but, most definitely, it would not include any legislation about security arrangements. The prospect of the SDLP and the Unionists agreeing to the deployment of the RUC, the UDR and the British Army presents a spectacle too ludicrous to contemplate. All of these important matters would continue to be dealt with by the real government formed by real political parties accountable to real electors who have the power to choose a new government if they do not like the policies of the existing one.

At a time when the whole of Eastern Europe has risen to reject the idea that the state can designate to them an unchanging party political identity and government, the people of Northern Ireland are being issued with permanent political identity cards in accordance with their baptismal certificates. The government has decreed that there shall be in Northern Ireland two communities who shall be constantly reminded of their differences. They will be identified by their places of worship and their places of education, and upon such a basis they will be ascribed politics, aspirations, allotted jobs and offered government preferment. They will be constantly reminded of their distinctive separateness by the laws and institutions which reinforce them and they will be deprived of all rights to change even the limited and stunted form of government they are permitted to vote for. Nor will they ever, in a real sense, be permitted to participate in the real parties, policies or affairs of the state of which they are said to be full and equal citizens. The presence of a Conservative Party in Northern Ireland without the presence of the British Labour Party is presently ineffective to bring real politics to Northern Ireland. Only when a government is faced at the polls by an opponent who has a real prospect of forming a government will the democratic principle of real electoral choice be seen in action.

THE IMPERATIVE OF EQUAL CITIZENSHIP
Peter Brooke may babble in New York about what the Agreement has achieved. In similar circumstances, Winston Churchill might have said of the Agreement 'that nowhere in the field of human endeavour have so many lives been sacrificed for the achievement of so little'. All the so-called achievements were accurately described in an editorial in this newspaper as a load of codswallop. When will the British government

realise that while the issues of civil rights, alleged and real discrimination, job opportunity, justice and peace are important, the British government will never achieve their solution, for their continued existence is a necessary requirement to maintain the nationalist belief that such problems cannot be solved within the United Kingdom, but only within the context of a united Ireland. The keeping open of old wounds by assiduous licking is an ancient and well-practised art in Ireland.

The people of Northern Ireland of all persuasions must, like the people of Eastern Europe, refuse to accept the predestined role cast for them by both the British and Irish governments and acquiesced in by many of their own elected representatives. They must assert their right to participate in the politics and decisionmaking process upon all the issues that will govern not only their lives, but the lives of their children. They must utterly refuse to be herded like mindless cattle into their respective ghettos, which unaccountable British and Irish politicians have prepared for them. The people of Northern Ireland must assert their rights as individuals to choose, as free and equal citizens of the United Kingdom, who will govern them. Present government policy does not provide for the growth of the people of Northern Ireland into one community. Rather, it predetermines and encourages the continued existence of two communities. Only, however, when religion is no longer the means of identifying a man's politics, and when employers are no longer given lists of schools enabling them to do so, will there be peace in Northern Ireland. The sooner the whole process of mixing Protestants and Catholics in the anonymity of socialism and conservatism begins, the sooner will there be both peace and power sharing in Northern Ireland.

VI

NEW UNIONISM, PLURALIST UNIONISM

Eleven

New Unionism, Pluralist Unionism[1]

INTRODUCTION
In the recent North Down by-election, both the Ulster Unionists and Alliance Parties played the 'Orange Card' by distorting my record. Neither party hesitated to deliberately deceive the less politically aware sections of the electorate. In outlining my political hopes for the future of Northern Ireland, the reasons for the behaviour of those parties may become clear. Over the past ten years it has become evident to many that a Union based on any form of sectarian ascendancy is not only undesirable, but unjust. Not only does it exclude those Catholics who are pro-Union but anti-Unionist, it is also a complete turn-off for all of those who consider that the communal politics engendered by such attitudes are the source of Northern Ireland's political and social instability. It has, therefore, become a political imperative that if the benefits of the Union are to be preserved, the present political landscape of Northern Ireland must be changed.

ULSTER UNIONIST RESISTANCE
It is resistance to such necessary change that feeds much of the Ulster Unionist Party's bitterness. Since 1921 that party has relied on two factors: the in-built Unionist majority; and the manipulation of pro-Union paranoia about Northern Ireland's place within the United Kingdom. This constitutional anxiety was compensated for by an extreme sectarian loyalism which became a barometer of constitutional fear. These two features were sufficient to ensure a vote without the necessity of evolving policies. The Anglo-Irish Agreement and subsequent government initiatives represent strategies designed to circumvent what they see as naked majoritarian control.

The response of the Ulster Unionist Party to these threats to the Union has been inadequate and politically incompetent. It is caught in a time warp of traditional ideas that bear little relevance to present needs and is acting like a political undertaker presiding over the funeral of the Union. In my view, the old Protestant ascendancy view of the Union ought to be buried along with much of its outdated associations. Just as the present Labour leaders have refashioned and reequipped the Labour Party's ideas, so must pro-Union leaders remodel the case for the Union so it can meet the demands of the twenty-first century.

---

[1]*Belfast Telegraph*, 19 June 1995.

PRINCIPLES OF PLURALISM

Politics are as much about perceptions as realities, and the relationship between political parties and organisations perceived—rightly or wrongly—as sectarian serve the interests of neither. The new Union must be based on the principles of pluralism, which recognise the wide difference of opinion on a broad range of topics and accommodate all save such as those that are harmful to the well-being of others in their public expression. This new Unionism must, therefore, be inclusive rather than exclusive and founded on what is best for the interests of the entire community. It must afford to all sections of the community full and equal recognition of their right to express their particular cultural and ethnic heritage. That said, this is very different from granting politically institutionalised rights to a separate state enabling that state to share in the administration of what is part of the United Kingdom.

I have no doubt that there is an expanding and increasing majority in the centre of both the Protestant and Catholic communities in Northern Ireland which is capable of political coalescence into a pro-Union pluralist majority. There is an increasing tide of public feeling that rejects the extension of accelerated Irish unity canvassed by Sinn Fein and also the extreme sectarianism of ultra-loyalism. During the recent election campaign, for example, these abstract concepts were turned into reality. In Bangor market I was taken aside by a serious-faced middle-aged man who announced that he was a Catholic, did not see Irish unity around the corner, but wanted his people treated justly and equally. He declared that he intended to break the habit of a lifetime by voting for me. 'It's down to you, Robert', was his parting shot. In the loyalist Ballybeen estate I was stopped by a man in his thirties who declared that he had always voted DUP, but would give me his vote, because 'things had to change'.

On the principle that all shades of opinion must be listened to within Unionism, I have spoken to both Ulster Unionist and Democratic Unionist Party meetings since February 1995. I have been astonished at the degree of both acceptance and enthusiasm for the need to change not only style of presentation of the case for the Union, but the case itself. Regrettably, the possibility of someone other than the Alliance Party being the agency for political progress towards reconciliation and consensus seems to fill that party with a bile reserved for no one else. It appears that the Alliance Party would rather burn the garb of reason than tolerate it being worn by another. Sir Oliver Napier, when faced by Vincent Hanna on Radio Five, tacitly admitted that special election leaflets distributed by the Alliance Party alleging that I was in favour of

Irish unity were untrue. To play the Orange Card is one thing, but to produce it from up one's sleeve is quite another.

NATIONALIST REACTIONS

It is not only the Alliance Party and the Ulster Unionists who oppose fresh and radical thinking, it is also the extremes of nationalism. The accusation is that whatever the nature of the Union, whether inclusive or exclusive, it can neither accommodate nor provide for the aspirations of nationalists, as opposed to Catholics. This suggestion is false. There is absolutely no obstacle to nationalist parties continuing to propound and canvass their political objectives by peaceful and democratic means, as similar parties do in Scotland and Wales. But the proposition that the nationalist minority in Northern Ireland requires institutional political links with the Republic to protect their rights and their identity is not one that is recognised in any other Western European democracy.

Everyone must have the same rights and the same opportunities to choose their political future, but a predetermined agenda for a single constitutional outcome is not one attractive to a free people. At a personal level, I have never received anything but generosity, fairness and kindness from the Catholic community and I am determined to do unto them as they have done unto me.

Twelve

A Union with Room for All[1]

INTRODUCTION

It is written in the Book of Proverbs that in a land where there is no vision the people perish. It is regrettable that for too long the people of Northern Ireland have been denied a vision. History will record how the good, the kind, the civil people of Ulster became the tormented children of division. Successive British governments, by their policy of political apartheid since 1921, have separated our people from their fellow British citizens in the rest of the United Kingdom and rendered them a disenfranchised minority in a country which they believe to be their own. The Irish government, which developed an exclusionary ethos validated by a partitionist constitution, likewise set the people of Northern Ireland permanently apart from the rest of the island. The inhabitants of Northern Ireland became the children which neither Britain nor Ireland chose to cherish equally. Turned away by others, they turned in upon themselves, focusing upon the things which separated them from each other and ignoring too often that which they shared in common.

A NEW VISION

For some years now, I have sought to remedy this blindness. And eyes may now be opening, for the people themselves are beginning to discern the way ahead. Like my fellow citizens of Northern Ireland, I, too, have a vision. It is one of a Union which includes all and excludes none. It is one which cherishes civil and religious liberties, not just for some, but for everyone. It is a Union founded upon the principles of pluralism, which is a philosophy that recognises the right to be different and, by acknowledging diversity, avoids division. I offer a vision of the Union which requires no one to be anti-Irish or anti-Catholic in order to participate.

I have a vision where elements of the past must be addressed if they obstruct or threaten our present welfare or our future happiness. History is of value as a source of reference for the prevention of recurring error. I advance the cause of a Union purged of the past excesses perpetrated wrongly in its name. But when history becomes a catechism of past grievances it becomes a corrosive curse, which, in Ireland, has been refined into an art form. Still, the Union must not merely be for the sanitised and antiseptic classes which have denied

---

[1]*Belfast News Letter*, 29 June 1995.

leadership to those in the ghettoes who suffer at the sharp end of violent terrorism. There must be room for all and the cultural rights of all must be respected. The rhythm of the Lambeg drum must be heard along with that of the Bodhran.

IDEAS INTO REALITY

But where do we begin the task of turning ideas into reality? What is to be the means of communicating the thoughts and concepts of pro-Union thinkers and experts to the people at large? How are ordinary people to participate in a revolution of pro-Union thinking? Some months ago, I proposed in the columns of the *Belfast News Letter* the formation of a pro-Union League. Such an organisation would enable all people who support the Union, regardless of their race, religion or sex, to come together without the impediment or baggage of any political association. The objects of the League would be to further the cause of a New Union for a New Age. A Union defined in terms of the principles already stated, which while recognising the British political identity of Northern Ireland, nevertheless, by its very nature, guaranteed the cultural and ethnic heritage and values of everyone and afforded them equal respect.

The League would be a forum for the spread and dissemination of literature and ideas. It would create an entirely new level of political and cultural debate that would transform the world-wide image of Unionism as a cult for political dinosaurs into what it should be: an honourable political cause whose pedigree lies in the age of reason and in a class far above the questionable and suspect genealogy of nationalism. The possibilities for the creation of a new wave of pro-Union confidence, enthusiasm, hope and generosity are endless.

History is not the record of some tide of inevitable certainty, but rather the swing of the pendulum, and there is much presently to suggest the swing in favour of the Irish nationalism may well be on the turn. It is my belief and conviction that, given the proper vision for the Union, circumstances may be created for ensuring that the swing of history's pendulum is now in favour of the Union.

Thirteen

The UK/Unionist Party: Pro-Union and Pluralist[1]

INTRODUCTION

The UK/Unionist Party is, as its name suggests, unequivocally a pro-Union party. It believes that a substantial majority of the people living in Northern Ireland wish to remain within the United Kingdom. The reasons for such a desire are various. They include the belief that the economic and social welfare of all the people is best served by that connection and that it is in accordance with the basic principle of any democracy that the majority of the people have the right to determine the nature and political identity of the country in which they live. This is not to suggest, though, that the majority have the right to either ignore or diminish the basic human and civil rights of others. This fundamental democratic principle has been recognised by political parties on all sides of the political spectrum, with the notable exception of Sinn Fein. Stated simply, it means that Northern Ireland will remain an integral part of the United Kingdom until a majority of the people determine otherwise. The consent to any change in that position must, nonetheless, be a real consent and not one achieved by violent coercion, economic pressure or political deception.

One of the sad features of political life in Northern Ireland is the confusion, which in many cases is deliberate, between those who support an accepted political viewpoint and those who advocate religious and sectarian division. In many quarters it has become almost impossible to be recognised as a person pledged to the maintenance of the Union without being branded a sectarian bigot. As a private citizen, a professional barrister and a public representative I have never written or uttered a sectarian sentiment, though I have been a dedicated advocate of the cause of the Union in the sphere of politics.

Neither my party nor myself as its leader have any quarrel with Roman Catholicism in any theological sense. A person's religious beliefs are entirely matters between that person and their God or their spiritual advisers. That said, it needs to be recognised that while the achievement of objectives said to be moral is a matter for churches, philosophers and the consciences of individuals, it is emphatically not the business of the state. Indeed, one of the basic objections of the pro-Union people to Irish unity is the degree to which successive governments of the Republic have enacted laws reflecting the moral and social values of one denomination.

---

[1]UK/Unionist Party Election Manifesto, Spring, 1997.

THE PEACE PROCESS

As leader of the UK/Unionist Party, my views on the Downing Street Declaration and the Framework Proposals were made a matter of public record in a series of newspaper articles long before I was elected to Parliament (several of which are reprinted in the following section). Such views, together with my lifelong opposition to sectarianism, have remained unchanged. While I welcome the support of those who share my expressed opinions on constitutional issues, such support neither commits me, or them, to any shared opinions on any other issue, whether political, social or theological. Despite my public record of opposition to sectarian politics, it has served the interest of political opponents on both sides of the divide to suggest otherwise. None of them, however, have produced one iota of evidence to support their contention.

My party's opposition to the so-called 'peace process' is based on several clear principles, none of which has any relationship whatsoever to sectarian politics. They are reviewed in great detail throughout the rest of this volume, but it is helpful to note them here. First is the conclusion that the enterprise is not, and never was, a peace process, but rather an agenda for achieving a political settlement acceptable to Sinn Fein/IRA. Can anyone doubt that unless Sinn Fein/IRA had been guaranteed Irish unity as the eventual outcome of the process, it would not have remotely considered participation in any form? Second, the Downing Street Declaration declared the United Kingdom's willingness to facilitate Irish unity and stated that Britain had no economic, strategic or selfish interest in remaining here. These words were not original, but repeated almost verbatim the statements made by Mr John Hume in the *Irish Times* in September 1988 immediately after the first of his meetings with Mr Adams. Third, the Framework Documents provided the agreed and detailed administrative machinery and institutions for effectively circumventing the principle of majority consent by means of a factual and economic unification of Ireland. Finally, the insistence of both governments, along with the representatives of pan-nationalism, that the Framework Proposals should be central to any settlement that might emerge from the Stormont talks demonstrated the determination of these parties to meet what they believed was the minimum Sinn Fein/IRA demand, namely, Irish unity by instalments.

THE UK/UNIONIST PARTY, EQUALITY AND DEMOCRACY

The UK/Unionist Party has absolutely no desire for a return to any form of majoritarian devolved government. It is committed to equality of education and opportunity and equal access to employment. It believes in the recognition and equal place of the cultural diversity existing in Northern Ireland. Still, it does not accept that the pro-Union people are some form of aberrant Irishmen who, if divorced from their own British cultural heritage, would suddenly rediscover an Irish-Gaelic identity. We are not two traditions of one people living on the one island: we are two very different and distinct peoples with different cultures and traditions, but who have many shared experiences and outlooks. What we have in common is the human experience which is shared the world over. Everyone wants the best education for their children, the best health and social care for their sick and elderly, the best employment opportunities for their young people and the long term unemployed. The real issue for the foreseeable future should be not which country we should serve, but which country can best serve the interests of our people. The UK/Unionist Party believes that those interests are presently best served within the Union with the rest of the United Kingdom. This view is shared by the majority of our citizens. It may not always be so, but for the present, our economic and material welfare corresponds with the democratic wishes of the people.

My party remains anxious and willing to have positive negotiations with those from any community who oppose political violence. But such talks and negotiations must be upon a new and realistic basis. They must be directed at institutions of government designed to serve the best interests of all the people of Northern Ireland, not merely to comply with the political needs of either the government of the United Kingdom or that of the Republic of Ireland or to fulfil the aspirations of any one party. If all parties look primarily at what best serves our people and no one else, a real and lasting settlement is possible.

VII

THE PEACE PROCESS:
THE THREAT TO THE UNION

Fourteen

The Threat to the Union[1]

INTRODUCTION

The Downing Street Declaration puts it beyond debate that the Conservative government now openly shares the view, with the Irish government, the SDLP, the British Labour Party, Sinn Fein and the Provisional IRA, that a united Ireland is the only solution to the Northern Ireland situation.[2] These groups only differ on how and when it is to be achieved. The murderous terrorism of the IRA has been rewarded with the maximum concession which a British government can make short of such as will provoke a civil war. John Major has said that the Unionists will be permitted to live in their homes so long as a majority wish to do so. The second class British citizens of Northern Ireland will be tolerated as lodgers, because they cannot be forcibly evicted, but never as family where rights require no guarantee.

UNDEMOCRATIC PRECEDENT

The British declaration that its government has no selfish strategic or economic interest in Northern Ireland is now stated policy. Such a declaration that a state has no interest in preserving the integrity of its lawful territory in accordance with the wishes of the majority of it citizens living in that part of the state is without precedent in a modern democracy. What is even more disquieting is that only one final solution is contemplated. There is no suggestion that the process is geared to any other conceivable outcome. There is no alternative, because any other outcome would be unacceptable both to Sinn Fein and the IRA, whom, John Major told viewers in his national broadcast, were the only people who can decide when the violence will end. The logic of that statement is that one either appeases them or eradicates them, and John Major has chosen to appease them. Appeasement will simply whet their appetite, and when they decide the time is right they will tighten the screw again. Nowhere is the intention to abandon the British citizens of Northern Ireland more evident than in the language of the Downing Street Declaration.

In paragraph one the people of Northern Ireland are included as the people of Ireland, North and South, while in paragraph two they are disposed of as a tradition in Ireland. Nowhere are they granted their identity as British citizens living in Northern Ireland. This denigration of

---

[1] *Belfast Telegraph*, 16 December 1993.
[2] See Appendix.

their political identity and status is relevant to another semantic fraud, namely, the constant assurance that the status of Northern Ireland within the United Kingdom will not be changed without the consent of the majority, while, at the same time, vigorously facilitating the diminution of the status of the individual British citizen within Northern Ireland.

Unionist failure to appreciate how damaging this declaration is to the future of the Union may well be fatal. The British government has pledged itself to the role of facilitator for agreed structures for the island as a whole, including a united Ireland. Paragraph four contains the most dangerous threat in that Britain has agreed to the principle that it is for the people of the island of Ireland alone, by agreement between the two parts respectively, to exercise their right of self-determination on the basis of consent freely and concurrently given. If anything smacks of the Hume-Adams partnership, this does: in one move it takes Britain off the board. The Unionists in this political chess game have lost their Queen.

THE FUTURE OF THE UNION

If the Unionists acquiesce in this policy they will be subjected to every covert pressure short of naked force to convert that acquiescence into consent. Britain, having agreed not merely to stand aside as a neutral party without selfish or other interests, but to act as facilitator, will be free to play the role of Pontius Pilate. The leadership of the Unionist Party should take care that they are not placed in the role of Brian Faulkner after Sunningdale and are seen by their constituency as dupes who have sold their birthrights as British citizens for a mess of parliamentary pottage in the shape of a select committee. As for the Alliance Party's hopes of a devolved institution, paragraph nine makes it clear that this is but a transitory stage en route to an agreed and peaceful future, which is 'Humespeak' for a united Ireland. Nor can pluralists be happy with the Taoiseach's assurances that he will examine those aspects of the Republic's laws that are inconsistent with a modern democratic and pluralist society, when such an examination will be qualified by the desire of the majority to preserve their inherited values. No prizes are offered for guessing what those might be.

The preservation of the Union lies not with politicians, but with the people. No power on earth can direct a million people, resolute in their cause and settled in their national and political identity, to go where they do not choose to go. But the people must have courageous, intelligent and articulate leadership that will restore their confidence and their self belief. One can only pray that they get it.

Fifteen

Sovereignty and Seduction[1]

INTRODUCTION

Sovereignty of a state has been defined as that area of conduct in which a state is autonomous and not subject to legal control by other states. If a government, therefore, surrenders to any other state or foreign agency effective control over any of the essential functions of government, its sovereignty is thereby diluted, for the legal control is diminished by the placing of factual power in the hands of that other state. It is by the application of these principles and their definition that the pro-Union majority in Northern Ireland is placed in its greatest constitutional danger.

The government of the United Kingdom, through its implementation of the Anglo-Irish Agreement, has already severely prejudiced its claim to be the sole sovereign power in Northern Ireland. The value of the principle of majority consent as a constitutional guarantee of British sovereignty in Northern Ireland is, by definition, limited.

JOINT SOVEREIGNTY AND CONSENT IN NORTHERN IRELAND

While a majority in a referendum may supposedly prevent sovereignty over Northern Ireland passing from Britain to the Irish Republic, the administrative structures created by the Anglo-Irish Agreement already permit both governments to create institutions that allow, without majority consent, a foreign government to exercise effective power over economic, social and cultural issues. Such structures or institutions do not require the consent of the majority and represent a transmission of sovereign power to the Irish Republic. In terms of fact, therefore, whatever the legal theory, this represents a degree of joint sovereignty, or authority, over Northern Ireland.

In a speech to the Irish Association at Dublin Castle on 10 January 1994, Mr Albert Reynolds, the Prime Minister of Ireland, made it perfectly clear that majority consent, as defined in the Downing Street Declaration, referred only to the constitutional (or soveriegnty) issue and was not required for joint institutions agreed by the governments. These joint institutions would exercise *de facto* control over the administration of certain portions of government in Northern Ireland.

---

[1]*Belfast Telegraph*, 22 September 1994; and John Wilson Foster (ed.), *The Idea of the Union: Statements and Critiques in Support of the Union of Great Britain and Northern Ireland* (Vancouver: Belcouver Press, 1995).

This view of the consent principle was repeated and endorsed by Mr Seamus Mallon in a television interview on 8 September 1994. In plain language, a process has now commenced whereby real and effective power over increasing areas of government may gradually be transferred to the Irish republic without the consent of the majority. As Mr Mallon put it: 'it would be for the two governments alone to decide how Northern Ireland would be administered and what institutions or structures they wished to create for that purpose'. Ultimately, whether the majority give their consent to the transfer of formal legal sovereignty will be of no account, for the factual transfer of sovereign power will have already been accomplished.

There is little doubt that on the present view of the situation, Mr Reynolds and Mr. Mallon have got the blueprint for the future absolutely right. Article 10 (b) of the Anglo-Irish Agreement provides that if it proves impossible to achieve and sustain devolution on a basis which secures widespread acceptance in Northern Ireland, the Inter-Governmental Conference will be a framework for the promotion of cooperation between the two parts of Ireland concerning cross-border aspects of economic, social and cultural matters in relation to which the Secretary of State for Northern Ireland continues to exercise authority.

The SDLP have clearly no intention of agreeing to any kind of devolved government which, in a real sense, is a democratic expression of the majority wishes. Without their participation, Northern Ireland will continue to be governed in secret via the Inter-Governmental Conference, by two governments neither of which have any electoral mandate from the people of Northern Ireland. The truly despotic nature of such government is demonstrated by the fact that one government pursues a constitutional imperative to absorb Northern Ireland into its state, while the other has ceded to the Irish Republic powers over part of its sovereign territory that only stop short of being 'executive' because of the theoretical sovereignty issue. (This was stated to be the case by Garrett FitzGerald, the then Taoiseach, in the Dail in November 1985.) Furthermore, the Downing Street Declaration of December 1993 pledges the British government to assist in facilitating a united Ireland. Indeed, in a speech at Dublin Castle, Mr Reynolds was of the opinion that both governments have agreed to be persuaders of Irish unity.

THE IRISH REPUBLIC IN NORTHERN IRELAND

Few people in Northern Ireland are fully aware that the Irish government presently plays a major part in almost every essential area of government and administration in Northern Ireland These dealings and activities, however, have to be kept secret from the majority of Northern Ireland's citizens, because if they were fully aware of the extent of the Irish Republic's involvement, there would almost certainly be open and, very probably, violent mass dissent. The entire process is a total violation of the most basic principles of democratic government, which could only be practised upon a community that has been effectively disenfranchised by its exclusion from the British electoral system. All three of the major nationalist parties are equally guilty in this gross breach of fundamental democratic rights.

The powers of the Inter-Governmental Conference cover a wide range of functions, including political matters, security affairs, legal issues, including the administration of justice, and the promotion of cross-border cooperation. The chief architects of the Anglo-Irish Agreement, Douglas Hurd and Sir Robert Armstrong, were determined from the outset to put in place administrative machinery for governing Northern Ireland which was of a permanent nature, such that would survive government changes and be available for use more extensively when it was politically convenient to do so. The plan was undoubtedly one of a long term strategic nature designed to service a policy of British disengagement from Northern Ireland.

The significance of the Downing Street Declaration as a complementary feature to the Anglo-Irish Agreement was that it afforded political approval to the more extensive and over-use of the 1985 Agreement's administrative structures. The peace process, the Hume-Adams dialogue, the Downing Street Declaration and subsequent diplomatic manoeuvrings of London, Dublin and Washington must all be seen as operations broadly in accordance with this policy blueprint.

The pro-Union majority are, in effect, being both sedated and hoodwinked by the assurances of London that in terms of formal sovereignty Northern Ireland remains within the United Kingdom until they consent otherwise. The real issue, however, for a free and democratic people is not the identity of the state which claims nominal sovereignty over them, but the state which effectively governs them in terms of the making or influencing of the decisions which affect every aspect of their lives. Such decisions range over a wide span of issues, from the identity of the judges who administer the law, the control of the police who enforce that law, to the curriculum which provides the nature of their children's education and the feelings of cultural and national identity which it is intended to imbue. On these matters alone, which are but examples, the fundamentals of British citizenship are being eroded.

*   *   *

As recently as 15 September 1994 Mr Reynolds returned, in an article in the *Irish Times*, to his theme of January 1994. In a reference to the building of present institutions, he was both bolder and more specific. His suggestion was that 'we [presumably the whole of the people of Ireland] would prosper better by treating Ireland within the European Union as an island economy of five million people. A high degree of North-South economic integration can be achieved under appropriate consensual institutions without any prejudice to continuing differences over sovereignty'. This comment alone emphasises Mr Reynolds' clear grasp of the reality of factual economic unity and power as against the empty shell of nominal theoretical sovereignty.

What, therefore, is the value of the so-called guarantee to retain the constitutional link with Britain when Northern Ireland would, in fact, form part of the national economy of the Irish republic? What is the value of control over such a link when it is an empty husk divested of any real substance in maintaining Northern Ireland as part of the United Kingdom? The present peace process, of which the Downing Street Declaration and articles such as that by Mr Reynolds form such a part, is not, in fact, a peace process at all. It is merely an organised and well planned progression along a pan-nationalist agenda for a united Ireland. If that is what the pro-Union people of Northern Ireland wish, then the democratic decision to follow that course should prevail. But let no one be guilty of self-deception or delusion in believing that the consent principle on the sovereignty issue is anything but an illusion designed to deceive.

SAFEGUARDING BRITISH SOVEREIGNTY

Unless the pro-Union parties in Northern Ireland obtain by careful negotiation a number of safeguards, going far beyond mere consent to the issue of formal legal sovereignty, they will have failed to protect the true essence of the Union and to ensure that the people of Northern Ireland remain full British citizens with the same rights and privileges as are enjoyed by their fellow citizens in all other parts of the United Kingdom of Great Britain and Northern Ireland.

John Major, in his recent visit to Northern Ireland, made a statement that his approach was scrupulously fair to both sides and that he seeks to recognise their legitimate aspirations. This is simply not correct. Any objective analysis of the Downing Street Declaration demonstrates that Irish unity is the only solution contemplated. What is more, in an interview in the *Daily Telegraph* on 2 September Mr Hanley, the Conservative Party chairman and former Northern Ireland minister, warned pro-Union Conservative backbenchers not to support the integration of Northern Ireland into the United Kingdom, for that would upset the balance of the peace by depriving republicans of their aspiration.

*   *   *

A scrupulously fair approach to both sides would have placed no such limitations upon the Unionist aspiration and, certainly, none is set upon the nationalist goal of unity by Dublin or Washington. But then these governments are positive in their support for Irish unity, while Britain is declared neutral on the Union. Equal rights for the British citizens of Northern Ireland were originally diminished in 1920 by the Government of Ireland Act, which set them apart from their fellow citizens on the mainland. These rights were further diluted in 1974 by Edward Heath, in 1985 by Margaret Thatcher and, most recently in December 1993 by John Major. All of these Conservative Prime Ministers are leaders of a party which a succession of Unionist Party MPs faithfully followed through the lobbies of the House of Commons.

It may be that Mr Molyneaux, the current leader of the Ulster Unionist Party, and his colleagues are privy to information lacking to the general public, and this explains their trust and support for Mr Major, without which his present policy could not succeed. In their simple faith they would do well to remember Carson's speech in the House of Lords on 14 December 1921—'What a fool I was! I was only a puppet, and so was Ulster, and so was Ireland, in the political game that was to get the Conservative Party into power'—and the prophetic words of Sir William Harcourt—'the Conservative Party has never taken up any cause that it did not betray in the end'.

Sixteen

The Pretence of Parity of Esteem[1]

INTRODUCTION

The fundamental conflict between the pro-Union British majority and the pro-unity Irish minority in Northern Ireland is about who will govern this part of the United Kingdom. This issue is purely a political one. It has, however, been deliberately confused in some quarters with the related, but different, issue of civil rights, especially the right of all citizens to be fairly governed, regardless of the identity of the governing power. The dilemma of fair-minded, pro-Union people is that while they are anxious to support fair government and equal opportunity for everyone, they are equally opposed to the political claim for Irish unity, which they believe would result in government by an authoritarian, theocratic state that is alien to both their identity and culture. This opposition is strengthened by the fear that their British identity and way of life will be subsumed in nationalist triumphalism. They are also anxious that their economic welfare will be fatally prejudiced in a united Ireland. Whether such fears and beliefs are justified may be debated, but the reality of these perceptions is undeniable.

Exacerbating these perceptions is the shared goal of the Irish government, the SDLP, Sinn Fein, the IRA and even the Irish hierarchy, namely, a united Ireland. They all desire to be governed by the Republic of Ireland rather than the United Kingdom. They also, in broad terms, act jointly in the field of civil rights insofar as these are said to affect the nationalist community. In this area, the advocacy of civil rights is often only a cover for the advancement of purely political goals. The language used to convey political claims is often that of civil rights. A settlement based on justice and peace in Ireland is 'Humespeak' for a united Ireland. As one political scientist put it: 'in reality, civil rights issues become the means by which Christians express the political values of their own society'.

RIGHTS AND REALITIES

While republican propagandists can induce the sympathy of the politically ignorant with unreal comparisons between the nationalist minority and the black populations of Alabama and South Africa, there has been no mass exodus to the Republic from Northern Ireland. In contrast, nearly one million Irish citizens, born in the Republic, are currently living happily on the United Kingdom mainland, whose

[1]*Belfast Telegraph*, 19 January 1995.

government has been solely responsible for the administration of Northern Ireland since 1972. If the issue in Northern Ireland was one of civil rights only, then this paradox seems to have escaped everyone. The Republic of Ireland seeks to be granted executive powers to protect the civil rights of Irish nationalists in one part of the United Kingdom, but requires no similar powers to protect even greater numbers in another part of the same kingdom. Why not? The answer is simple. The claim in Northern Ireland has got little to do with civil rights or civil liberties. It is an irredentist political claim to the territory of Northern Ireland, a claim disguised by the Republic's politicians as an aspiration only, until declared by the Republic's Supreme Court to be a constitutional imperative.

At long last, and in increasing numbers, pro-Union people at all levels of society and of liberal views are realising that the constant pressure for so-called civil rights, and the latest concept of parity of esteem, have got little to do with civil rights as such, but a lot to do with the political advancement of Irish unity. The issue has shifted from the purely civil rights one of fair and equal government to the purely political one of who is to govern. Successive British governments and pro-Union liberals have in the past failed to grasp that no institution of government in Northern Ireland that fails to provide immediate machinery for a Dublin executive input and for mid-to-long term institutions for Irish unity will ever meet with the approval of the Irish government, the SDLP, Sinn Fein or the IRA. The SDLP have repeatedly declared that no internal settlement is possible. In short, no concession to alleged or real breaches of civil rights are now capable of settling the Northern Ireland crisis.

This realisation is no justification for failing to ensure that every citizen is guaranteed equality in every sphere. But the pro-Union people should no longer foolishly believe that any form of positive discrimination against Unionists, or policies of affirmative action, are going to lesson nationalist demands. Meanwhile, reactions to such policies in the United States have led to their reassessment, not only of their value, but their fairness. But in Northern Ireland claims of injustice provide the dynamic for Irish unity: they will never be settled while the Union remains.

REASSESSING GUILT AND RESPONSIBILITY

Against this background, the majority in Northern Ireland, particularly the middle classes, must review their thinking, thinking that has been warped for too long by a guilt complex, induced and exacerbated by nationalist propaganda. Burdened in many cases by a falsely assumed sense of responsibility for real and imagined nationalist grievances, middle class Unionists have hidden in their closets. While privately resentful as they see their British identity slip away and the Union weaken, in public they are apologetic, thinking that they can redeem the position with kind words, ecumenical utterances and the belief that total equality of rights and opportunities will redeem their imagined guilt and satisfy the republican appetite for a united Ireland.

What Unionists should be doing is making it plain as day that they will give full and complete support for total and equal rights for everyone, but they will concede nothing on the majority's democratic right to choose who will govern them. The basic principle in a democracy is that the will of the majority determines who will govern. This right of the majority is subject to the guarantee of certain fundamental rights, such as are set out in the United States Bill of Rights. What is positively not a human or civil right is the demand of a minority to choose who will govern, as opposed to how it will be governed. If it were otherwise, then every Marxist, fascist and anarchist who had a political aspiration to be governed in accordance with his wishes could legitimise violence or withdraw his consent to be governed.

THE PRETENCE OF PARITY OF ESTEEM

The most recent piece of 'Humespeak' is the phrase 'parity of esteem', a condition to which nationalists claim entitlement. Is this a civil right, a political claim or sheer nonsense? Parity is equality, while esteem is said to mean 'to have high regard or great respect for'. It must, in this context, mean that some third party, such as the British government, will offer this parity of esteem in a comparative sense, such as 'we, the British government, have equally great respect for the nationalist objective of Irish unity as we have for the Unionist desire for union'. Now, the British government, while declaring itself neutral on Union or unity—which is surprising enough—has declared that there will be no change in the status of Northern Ireland within the United Kingdom without the consent of the majority, which is hardly an unreasonable stance if any weight is to be given to fundamental democratic principles. Both the SDLP and Sinn Fein, however, refer to this principle pejoratively as the 'Unionist veto' and are now making a linguistic flanking attack. They now require parity of esteem, or equal regard, to hold for Union and unity. And, if this is so, they argue, can there be any reason why the Republic and the United Kingdom should not jointly govern Northern Ireland? The fact that current proposals would provide for the United

Kingdom to foot ninety-five percent of the running costs would, of course, be no basis for any disparity. The real trick is to conceal the purely political motive in the language of civil rights. However, it is not people who are going to be afforded parity of esteem. This esteem is sought for a political aspiration which is contrary to the will of the democratic majority in Northern Ireland.

This technique of obtaining political advantage under the guise of respecting everyone's civil rights sensitivities was demonstrated during the Queen's University national anthem debate. Northern Ireland is part of the United Kingdom, which is a constitutional monarchy with the Queen as its Head of State. Comparisons with practices at other British universities are unhelpful. None of these institutions is sited in an area where the sovereignty and the nature of the state is under attack. All of them enjoy such complete security of constitutional future and national identity as to make an symbolic representation about that fact superfluous. In the present circumstances, to change an established practice at the instigation of those dedicated to ending the rule of that monarch in Northern Ireland was not to grant any civil right to that minority, but to surrender to that minority's political claims. The real objective was a denigration of the existing political status of Northern Ireland—and this constituted an offence to the majority of its citizens. In similar vein were the remarks of Mrs Brid Rogers of the SDLP in a recent television broadcast of the programme Question Time. When asked about the future of the Royal Family, Mrs Rogers indicated that the Royal Family did not concern her, as 'our president, Mary Robinson, is elected'.

*   *   *

The fact that certain groups and certain people do not recognise the validity of the state, its institutions or its Head is a matter of opinion which such people are entitled to hold. What it does not mean, however, is that the validity of such views should be formally acknowledged by the state whose very right to govern such views deny. Yet this is exactly what the decision of the Queen's University Senate not to play the anthem amounts to. In essence, since the national anthem offends those who do not acknowledge the right of the United Kingdom to govern, they are entitled to its removal. The Senate's decision was not a concession to neutral opinion, it was a surrender to nationalist influences within the university, which the Senate is no longer able to control.

This public confirmation of a private state of affairs has led increasing numbers of students from pro-Union families to eschew the university of their parents. The atmosphere at Queen's University, and the Students' Union in particular, is no longer neutral. It is overwhelmingly nationalist. Nevertheless, the decision of the Senate has been of service in that it has done more than anything else to bring a true appreciation of their position to the minds of the pro-Union middle and professional classes in Northern Ireland.

Seventeen

Appeasement in Our Time[1]

INTRODUCTION

The bomb recently detonated in the centre of Manchester by the IRA is an outrage that will have shocked, though surely not have surprised, the public in both Britain and Northern Ireland. Will it achieve Sinn Fein/IRA's aim of entry into the all-party talks without any commitment to decommission its weapons? The sad answer, almost certainly, is 'yes'. For although the British government's initial response will be one of robust defiance, its record indicates that, ultimately, the inevitable climb-down will take place. Here in Northern Ireland, there is a strong feeling within the pro-Union community that Sinn Fein/IRA, having exploited the media over its exclusion from the talks, and demonstrated in Manchester the efficiency of its bomb squads, will shortly declare a ceasefire, the next likely step of what is usually called the 'peace process'. The Mitchell Report's requirement for parallel decommissioning as the political talks progress is already poised for a fudged burial in a subcommittee, where Senator Mitchell's embalming skills will be utilised to give the appearance of life to that which is already effectively dead.

AN APPEASEMENT PROCESS

What is this process? There are a few moments in history when a human drama catches the spirit of the times—and explains what is really happening. Neville Chamberlain brandishing his piece of paper on returning from Munich provided one of the most famous examples. The opening day of the talks on the future of Northern Ireland provided another. The Irish Prime Minister, John Bruton, was sharing with the delegates his awareness of the grief of the bereaved, coming as he did from the funeral of an Irish policeman whose murder the IRA has belatedly acknowledged. He thought it appropriate to recall the list of elected representatives murdered by terrorists. When he came to the name of the Irish senator Paddy Wilson, silence filled the room, for there, opposite Mr Bruton and sitting as a delegate for a fringe loyalist party, sat Paddy Wilson's murderer, now on parole.

Why, one might ask, has the government set up an electoral system designed to guarantee negotiating places for such men who have scarcely any mandate other than the silence of their guns? And why has the Irish government attempted to dissociate a culpable terrorist

---

[1]*Daily Telegraph*, 17 June 1996.

organisation from the slaying of one of its own policeman? The answer is that in this 'peace process' the terrorists—through the medium of their political alter egos—are the only people whose presence is deemed absolutely essential. Representatives of democratic parties, regardless of their electoral strength, are merely the furnishings required to dress the stage upon which a deal will be struck between the plenipotentiaries of terrorism. The purpose of the talks is for Sinn Fein/IRA to legitimise its political blackmail.

While a ceasefire is in operation, the lever for concessions is the threat of renewed violence. In the absence of a ceasefire, the promise of its restoration provides the inducement to satisfy the terrorists' demands. The technique is a modern version of 'Morton's Fork'. Since Sinn Fein/IRA is democratically unable to obtain its political goals without the means to carry out their threats, there will be no decommissioning until those goals are achieved.

Prime Minister Major, in a broadcast after the Joint Declaration between the British and Irish governments was announced in December 1993, stated that only the men of violence could offer peace. This was, in effect an acknowledgement that a sovereign government was unable to enforce the rule of law and offer protection to its citizens. It is an accepted principle of democratic government that political objectives may not be obtained by the use or threat of violence. The pro-Union community, therefore, rejected negotiations with Sinn Fein/IRA while it retained its weapons. John Hume, the leader of the SDLP, initially agreed that negotiations could not proceed with weapons on or under the table. This was a sentiment which the Irish government also shared. In the face of a total refusal by Sinn Fein/IRA to countenance decommissioning, the sacrifice of democracy to violence began.

THE POLITICS OF EXPEDIENCY
The politics of expediency were about to subsume the principles of democracy. First, the Irish government and the SDLP jumped ship. The British government, for a time, clung weakly to the plank of the vital 'Washington Three' principles, which required some token decommissioning prior to Sinn Fein's inclusion. However, the insistence of Dublin and Washington was sufficient to break such token resolve. An international committee, chaired by Senator George Mitchell, President Clinton's special envoy, was summoned into being to remove the impasse.

Unsurprisingly, this body concluded that there was a 'clear commitment on the part of those in possession of such arms to work constructively to achieve a verifiable decommissioning as part of the process of all-party negotiations, but that commitment does not include decommissioning prior to other negotiations'. This conclusion was patently an error of judgement. At the moment in November 1995 when Senator Mitchell was concluding their good faith, IRA activists were planning the bomb that was to blast London's Docklands in February 1996. That bomb marked the end of the ceasefire, but not the end of the 'peace process'. For the effect of the atrocity was devastating. British morale collapsed alarmingly, and the Sinn Fein/IRA demand for a fixed date for the talks was met with disquieting haste.

The plan of the two governments for the talks was simple. First, Senator Mitchell would be chairman. The clout he could command as Mr Clinton's special envoy would ensure that all 'relevant' parties were included. Second, he was to be provided with overriding powers that would enable him to determine whether good faith beat in the breasts of those retaining weapons of destruction. What was made clear last week to the pro-Union parties, in a demonstration of naked political power, was that Senator Mitchell is going to be chairman come what may. It was a demonstration sufficient to break the will of David Trimble, the Ulster Unionist Party leader, and it is one that will almost certainly be repeated this week when Senator Mitchell's powers are conferred.

The declaration of a ceasefire will be seized upon gratefully by both governments to allow Sinn Fein entry into the talks, where it will be permitted to procrastinate over decommissioning while it assesses the benefits of participation. A negative assessment will precipitate withdrawal amid a welter of accusations and bad faith. Coincidentally, pro-Union concessions to constitutional nationalism in the interests of peace will never be recoverable.

Mr Adams' prophecy that the Union could not emerge from the talks stronger that it entered into them will be fulfilled, and the ratchet of Irish unity will have been advanced by several notches. On a wider scale, the curse of international terrorism will have received a boost; the principles of democracy will have been debased; and, within the United Kingdom, the blight of terrorism will remain. The message to Mr Major must be this: either you enforce the rule of law or, like Mr Chamberlain, make way for someone who will.

Eighteen

Why the UK/Unionists are not at the Talks[1]

INTRODUCTION

The powers that be in Northern Ireland have opted for a policy of the appeasement of violence. Their strategy is to buy peace by offering republicans more through negotiation than the latter could ever achieve through war. No one is permitted to dissent from this chosen political path. With the media fully signed up to the strategy, an appearance of unanimity is carefully created. Anyone who disagrees is pilloried as a crank and a bigot.

Despite this careful manicuring of events, the government and its followers in the media, business and churches have failed to persuade large numbers of Unionists of the merits of their approach. In last week's *Belfast News Letter* telephone poll of 13,000 readers, the majority declared support for Unionist leaders who have withdrawn from the current talks. It is true that the majority of active UUP members still support their party's presence at the talks, even though a substantial minority, including several MPs, are opposed. Even this support is entirely cynical. A huge majority of delegates to the UUP annual conference in Newcastle were shown, in a *Sunday Times* poll, to expect that the talks will fail.

Ulster Unionist Party supporters apparently want their leader to remain in talks which they are convinced will fail. Why is this? The explanation is cynicism. They do not want their party leader to be seen to wreck a so-called 'peace process' in which the current government has invested so much prestige. In other words, they wish to avoid the torrent of criticism which has been poured on the heads of those who, like the leader of the UK/Unionist Party, oppose the talks.

UK/UNIONIST OPPOSITION

Why, then, has the UK/Unionist Party chosen to withdraw from talks which so many of the middle classes in Ulster believe are the only way forward? There are two main reasons. One is a matter of deep principle. It is wrong, absolutely and always, to negotiate with armed and unrepentant terrorists in a democracy. Northern Ireland is not South Africa, where the great majority had no vote. Democracy always has to be defended, and violence must never be rewarded, either while that violence is being perpetrated or after its perpetrators have ceased. Difficulties in defeating violence are no excuse. A failure to eradicate

---

[1]*Spectator*, 6 November 1997.

the Mafia or to prevent the activities of drug dealers does not lead to offers to negotiate with the godfathers.

The lesson of history through the centuries is that appeasement does not work. Attempts to reward violence lead only to more violence until the terrorists achieve their aims. It is embarrassment at their blindness to this obvious fact that causes the supporters of appeasement to become so aggressive towards those who disagree with them. We are told, in whispers, that the republicans want peace and that they can be bought off with minor rewards falling far short of a united Ireland. This unlikely proposition appears to be widely, perhaps even genuinely, believed in government circles. Yet it defies the known facts. The IRA insists on keeping its weapons and killed ten people between ceasefires, merely to improve its negotiating position. Martin McGuinness tells his supporters that Sinn Fein is in the talks to smash the Union.

It is these considerations that form the second reason for the UK/Unionist Party withdrawing from the talks. The UK/Unionist Party refuses to adopt the cynicism of other parties. Since the UK/Unionist Party is convinced that the talks cannot be successful without substantially weakening the Union to buy peace, the Party cannot, in all conscience, join in. To do so would be to attempt to fool our supporters and many others as to the true beliefs and intentions of the UK/Unionist Party.

Many well meaning people will say that there is no harm in trying, you never know what you may achieve. The UK/Unionist Party recognises that these views may be sincerely meant. Careful thought teaches us, however, that there are dangers. Concessions will be offered by Unionists, as in the 1991-92 talks. These will be rejected by nationalists, but will form a baseline for new demands. This is what happened in the 1991-92 talks, with Unionist concessions forming a new baseline for the 1995 Framework Documents. The Framework Documents then became the minimum demand for nationalism in the current talks. And so it goes on.

If the UK/Unionist Party thought for a minute that an honourable peace could be achieved, it would have remained in the Talks. The UK/Unionist Party does not think this is possible, because we have been able to read the transcripts of the 1991-92 talks, copies of which have recently been placed on the Internet. Five years after those talks, their contents are still officially secret and too revealing to be released to Ulster's electorate. The contents of those talks show that the SDLP demanded the presence of Dublin ministers not only in a cross-border Council of Ministers, but also in the internal government of Northern

Ireland itself. Despite not being elected by one single person in Northern Ireland, and contributing nothing to the cost of running Northern Ireland, these ministers were to take part in governing us. Despite opposition from the UUP, DUP, Alliance and the British government, the SDLP did not move or compromise on these, their minimum demands, to recognise the Irish identity of Northern nationalists. Hence the failure of those talks.

These were the non-negotiable demands of nationalism five years ago, with no IRA offer at that time to cease violence. Five years on, the demands will increase, because the presence of Sinn Fein, with their implicit threats of renewed violence if their demands are not met. The UK/Unionist Party refuses to go through the cynical charade of attempting to negotiate the non-negotiable—out of a sense of honesty and principle.

A DEMOCRATIC ALTERNATIVE

But what, people will ask, has the UK/Unionist Party got to offer in its place? The answer is that the UK/Unionist Party believes in solving Northern Ireland's difficulties according to well established international principles applied in almost all similar territorial disputes. First, existing boundaries must be respected. It is the right of majorities to determine the political and national identity of the state of which they form part. Second, the rights of minorities to full and equal respect within the law must be upheld. Majority communities cannot be allowed to exploit minorities in any way. Northern Ireland must be a completely just and non-sectarian state. It is no accident that these are the principles of international justice. They have been adopted to minimise conflict. The attempts of British governments to make the Northern Ireland boundaries vulnerable to minority pressure and IRA violence causes instability. It raises the expectations of minorities and reduces the confidence of majorities in a democracy.

Appeasement and constitutional flexibility will appeal to the soft hearted, and international principle will appear tough. But it is only on the basis of these principles that a just settlement can be secured. A settlement obtained through coercive pressure and a withholding of all relevant facts is a recipe for ongoing instability that may render the true peace which all desire impossible to achieve.

Nineteen

The Union and the Economic Future of Northern Ireland[1]

INTRODUCTION

The prevailing view of the leaders of commerce and industry in Northern Ireland is that an end to terrorist violence is an absolute imperative. Yet it is an imperative which appears to be divorced from any concomitant public pledge to maintain the Union. What's more, the government of the United Kingdom has a shared understanding with pan-nationalism—arising out of the Hume-Adams dialogue of 1988-93—regarding the long-term aims of the peace process: first, establish all-Ireland political institutions, which are based on the Framework Documents of 1995 and are reflected in the recent political settlement; assign to them ever-greater cross-border responsibilities; and, finally, manage the gradual transition to Irish unity.

The leaders of the major business organisations in Northern Ireland have enhanced the credibility of this political strategy by supporting the development of a single-island economy. Since this economic model would ultimately require the formation of Ireland-wide macroeconomic planning committees and industrial policy institutions, it would eventually give rise to a functionally united Ireland. In fact, this Irish blueprint is largely predicated on the European plan for creating a politically united Europe. The distinction, however, is that while a substantial economic case can be made for a united Europe, a similar one cannot be formulated to justify a united Ireland. Nevertheless, business organisations in Northern Ireland have aligned themselves with a peace process that has discounted the economic benefits of the Union in favour of the economics of Irish unity and may, in effect, end the Union. The overriding question, therefore, is whether such a policy will ensure the future economic viability of Northern Ireland.

ECONOMIC INTERESTS AND POLITICAL PRIORITIES

Is the political role sought by commerce to be confined to serving business and commercial interests alone? Colin Anderson, the president of the Northern Ireland Chamber of Commerce, seems to think so: several months before the Belfast Agreement was signed he declared that 'whatever settlement is reached (if any), the constitutional resolution

---

[1]This chapter is based upon an address to the Northern Ireland Chamber of Commerce on 20 March 1998. It was first published in Richard English and Joseph Morrison Skelly (eds.), *Ideas Matter: Essays in Honour of Conor Cruise O'Brien* (Dublin: Poolbeg Press, 1998).

must fit with the economic one'.[2] The clear implication of this statement is that is that economic considerations must be paramount. Such interests, however, are not always compatible with the political wishes and values of Northern Ireland's citizens. In my view, if such a policy is pursued in the long-run it will alienate wide sections of the electorate and will paint the wrong picture of a business community dedicated to its own commercial interests. Moreover, when the policy seemingly adopted by business is questionable—not only on political, but even on economic grounds—the very influence which the business community seeks to exercise will become marginalised.

Only the foolish would deny the importance of commerce to the prosperity of ordinary people, but to subordinate other equally important issues, such as political allegiance, cultural identity and democracy, would be a mistake of major consequence. Men do not live by bread alone, nor do the essential welfare and liberty of a people depend only upon economic considerations—something which Rupurt Murdoch and Bill Gates have been made to remember in recent weeks.

Problems of commerce and politics are often very different and they do not easily lend themselves to the same solutions. The object of business is profit and, within the context of commerce, this is a very legitimate one. The businessman's bottom line is the size of the credit balance on the profit and loss account. He is answerable only to himself and to his shareholders. His only constraints are fiscal and social legislation tempered to his subjective view of commercial morality. His judgements are based upon an analysis of competitors, markets, cost efficiency and sales. His political concerns focus, for the most part, on policies that affect his business, whether they apply to investment opportunities, taxes, currency variations, interest rates or markets, to name but a few.

The rise of multinational corporations, economies of scale and global markets—all dedicated to greater commercial efficiency—have brought commerce and its interests into conflict with other principles and values considered important by the great majority of the electorate—and with which its elected representatives must be concerned. The BSE crisis is a case in point. A balance must be struck between the economic distress of the beef industry and the safeguarding of public health, and this is, ultimately, not an economic decision, but a political one.

By the same token, the debate about European Monetary Union (EMU) is not solely about the economic benefits of entry. The main

---

[2]*Belfast Newsletter*, 24 February 1998.

issue, which the British people will have to decide in a referendum, is whether the economic benefits to be gained by monetary union—even if they can, on balance, be proved—are worth the loss of national sovereignty and independent control of the national economy. The surrender of such control to a superior political institution will, in turn, result in the transfer of political sovereignty to a federated European superstate. Still, there are many in the upper reaches of industry and the world of finance who argue that whatever settlement is reached in Europe, the constitutional arrangement must fit the economic one. What is far from clear, however, is whether the supposed economic advantages of entry are worth the risks. It is in this general context that I wish to review some of the economic and political aspects of the settlement in Northern Ireland.

FUNCTIONALISM IN EUROPE AND IN IRELAND
The terms of the Framework Documents of February 1995 and the Northern Ireland peace plan reveal the true aims of the British and Irish governments and the Social Democratic and Labour Party (SDLP). Their goals are similar to those of Europhiles who wish to see not only trade and economic union, but political union as well. In pursuit of their agenda they rely on the theory and method of functionalism. This process promotes the centralisation and unification of two or more independent sovereign states by situating them in an interlocking web of economic and financial institutions whose functions escalate from consultation to harmonisation to, finally, the executive administration of common policies in the cooperating states (often by anonymous officials unaccountable to the electorates in those states). The ultimate, albeit disguised, objective is that once effective functional and economic union have been completed, considerations of national sovereignty will become irrelevant, and political union will follow of its own accord.

In Ireland, as in Europe, an allegedly utilitarian economic programme—largely led by the two governments and the SDLP, and given substance by certain elements in the business community—is masking a concealed agenda for political union. This project, however, has little or no support from professional economists; indeed, almost all of them, including the politically neutral, offer it little, if any, comfort.

The arguments against the economic viability of Irish unity ought to be well known, but have been suppressed, to a degree, for purposes of political expediency. Simply put, the Republic could not afford unity if it was required to maintain the social standards Northern

Ireland now enjoys as part of the United Kingdom. Suggestions that the British fiscal transfer could be replaced by support from Europe or the Irish Diaspora are the stuff of fairy tales. Equally improbable is the proposal for joint political authority, whereby each government contributes in proportion to its respective GDP, with Britain paying 95% of the cost for sharing 50% of the governance of Northern Ireland.[3] This is a very Irish solution to an Irish political problem. Realistically speaking, a thirty-two county Ireland offers no resolution to the problem of getting rid of the British while keeping their cash.

Of more immediate relevance to this gathering and, in particular, to the members of G7 (a local self-styled group of business leaders and trade union officials), is the case being made for economic integration at an all-Ireland level. The call for the creation of an island economy encapsulates this view. Sir George Quigley, chairman of the Ulster Bank, championed this blueprint in an influential paper, 'Ireland: an Island Economy', delivered at the Annual Conference of the Confederation of Irish Industry on 28 February 1992. No sound economic interpretation, however, supports the conclusion that such a model will yield a significant material advantage, even when its alleged benefits are maximised. The argument that the border has led to the reduction of intra-island economic linkages (e.g., trade, financial services or company ownership and control) is highly questionable. Certainly, claims that greater North-South trade, anchored by the creation of a Belfast-Dublin business corridor, will generate 75,000 additional jobs have been proved to be gross exaggerations: the true figure may be a tenth of that.[4] North-South trade, after all, accounts for only 4-6% of Northern Ireland's GDP and has remained virtually static as a proportion of external sales from Northern Ireland during the 1990s.[5] There is no evidence, in short, that the benefits of an island economy would make any real difference to Northern Ireland's aggregate economic performance. Besides, the market mechanism itself should be

---

[3]The case for joint, or shared, authority is made in Brendan O'Leary, et al, *Northern Ireland: Sharing Authority* (London: Institute of Public Policy Research, 1993). Arguments against joint authority are lucidly stated in the Cadogan Group's *Blurred Vision: Joint Authority and the Northern Ireland Problem* (Belfast: Cadogan Group, 1994).

[4]See Patrick J Roche and J Esmond Birnie, *An Economic Lesson for Irish Nationalists* (Belfast, 1995), pp. 35-6.

[5]*Northern Ireland Sales and Exports, 1994/95-1995/96* (Belfast: Industrial Development Board, May, 1997), p. 17.

capable of generating a greater level of all-Ireland economic cooperation: most of the potential gains can be exploited by links forged for purely commercial reasons. Political integration, or the imposition of institutional political structures, are therefore superfluous. Indeed, the insistence on such systems is politically motivated. Yet as Sir Charles Carter, former chairman of the Northern Ireland Economic Council, told the New Ireland Forum in 1984, the effects of island-wide political institutions 'on unemployment would be equivalent to the products of nine bean rows on the Isle of Innisfree when set against a requirement of new jobs in the North by 2004 in the order of 200,000'.

     The simple truth is that neither the current level of trade between Northern Ireland and the Republic, nor whatever level may be reached in the future, can sustain the hype regularly appearing in the *CBI/IBEC Joint Business Council News* about the putative benefits that economic harmonisation and a Belfast-Dublin trade corridor will bring to Northern Ireland's economy. For example, between 1991 and 1996 sales from Northern Ireland to the Republic accounted for only 7-8% of the province's total sales and approximately 11% of its external sales.[6] It will be impossible to generate significant economic development in the future from such a low starting point. Moreover, between 1991 and 1996 there was no significant growth in export trade with the Republic as a proportion of either total external sales or total exports. The claim by the *CBI/IBEC Joint Business Council News* that exports from Northern Ireland to the Republic grew by 62% between 1991 and 1996 ignores the fact that this increase involves a component still equal to only 7-8% of Northern Ireland's total sales, which themselves increased by over 60% in the same period.[7]

*   *   *

One of the attractions of the Republic for some Northern entrepreneurs is the Southern economic miracle, the so-called Celtic Tiger. While one cannot be dismissive of the substantial improvement in the Republic's economy in recent years, bust can follow boom, and all that glitters is certainly not gold. While economic growth has been very high, it has been growth from a very low level. Until recently, the Irish economy was one of the worst performers in Western Europe this century. The reasons for the recent growth surge are not entirely clear, but the experts offer

---

[6]*Ibid.*
[7]*Ibid.*

four possible explanations. First, it is suggested that the recovery is export-led, based on the 1993 devaluation of the punt. Second, it is claimed that the Social Contract, which extends to the year 2,000, secured industrial peace, led to wage restraint in the private sector, increased competitiveness and attracted inward investment. Third, it is European Union funding that has launched the Celtic Tiger into economic orbit. Fourth, the recovery has been driven by foreign capital from the multinational corporations, rather than the strength of indigenous Irish industry, which remains very weak.

Those among you wedded to the idea of an island economy should give thought to the disturbing common factor linking these explanations. None of them possess any real durability or permanence, and the Irish government lacks control over most of them. Once the Republic joins EMU, devaluation as a means to aiding economic recovery is finished. The inflation rate, which must be less than 3% in order to meet the convergence criteria, may become a significant macroeconomic issue for the Republic within EMU due to an anticipated downward pressure on interest rates. Partnership 2000, by which wages in the private sector were restrained at the expense of government spending on public sector services, is unlikely to survive the millennium. Reliance on the foreign capital of multinationals, which themselves owe no national allegiance, is an uncertain foundation for the future. This is especially so in the context of the enlargement of the European Union, which will mean that foreign corporations can draw on low-paid, highly skilled workers in the Czech Republic, Poland and Hungary. Enlargement also poses a serious threat to the current high levels of EU funding. Begging bowls for special economic assistance do not sit easily with claims that a country seeking such assistance is experiencing a raging economic miracle. To sum up, if Ireland's economy stumbles, the government's hands are tied: it cannot devalue the punt; it will not be able to count on substantial EU funding (even if a soft landing to ease withdrawal symptoms has been guaranteed); the restraints of the Social Contract may have disappeared and, with them, the multinationals, in search of cheaper labour and a skilled work force in other parts of an enlarged EU.

The above may represent a worst case scenario, but closer all-Ireland integration, with the Republic in EMU and the UK outside of it, would be risk-taking of proportions unacceptable to a prudent businessman, particularly when the likely gains are relatively marginal. Indeed, Samuel Brittan of the *Financial Times*, one of the world's most respected commentators, has warned of the dangers of Ireland's rapid growth and doubts whether such high rates of expansion can be maintained: 'The pressures are already showing up in asset price inflation, especially in the Dublin property market. Yet far from being able to raise interest rates in a preemptive move, the Irish Central Bank is having to prepare to reduce them as EMU membership looms.' It is, of course, not just a matter of keeping inflation under 3% to meet the convergence criteria, but of holding it down thereafter to meet the stability requirements.

IRREDENTIST ECONOMICS
Let me now turn to a serious analysis of the absurd economic arguments advanced in this forum several weeks ago by John Hume, the leader of the SDLP.[8] On this occasion, economic proposals devoid of reality and substance were used to disguise a political agenda in favour of Irish unity. The economic myth of the island economy shared by some members of G7 was crystallised by Mr Hume. He offered two imperatives for Northern Ireland's economic future. First, that Northern Ireland must enter EMU as quickly as possible. Second, that Northern Ireland must associate with, or integrate into, the economy of the Republic.

Northern Ireland is a region of the United Kingdom, and there is simply no provision for a region being admitted into EMU while the sovereign state of which it is a part remains out of EMU. In any event, for Northern Ireland to enter EMU with the Republic would simply be buying into all of the problems which the Republic is going to face in the very near future. The key point here is that as a region within the EMU, and with the euro as its currency, the Republic, because of its significant trade with the United Kingdom (in the range of 30-40% of its GDP) will be vulnerable to both the depreciation and the appreciation of sterling against the euro within European Monetary Union. Why saddle Northern Ireland with this unnecessary economic burden? Further, Mr Hume's suggestion that Northern Ireland's position outside of EMU will affect trade relations with the rest of Europe or Ireland is groundless. The February issue of *Eurolink* clearly states that 'the effects on cross-border trade and economic integration may be managed easily, since a two-currency island, whether sterling-punt or sterling-euro, is already a reality'.

---

[8]*Belfast Telegraph*, 7 March 1998.

Mr. Hume's second point—Northern Ireland must associate or integrate with the economy of the Republic—is based on two assertions. First, that there is no other economy with whom we have more in common; second, that there is no other economy which is so willing to share with us. Neither of these arguments bear close scrutiny.

At present, trade links with the UK represent approximately 50% of Northern Ireland's external sales, while those with the Republic total 11%.[9] The fiscal transfer from Westminster ranges from £3.5 to £4 billion per year. Northern Ireland shares with the United Kingdom all of its institutional economic machinery. What the Northern Ireland economy shares with the Republic of Ireland is minuscule by comparison. With regard to the assertion that there is no other economy which is so willing to share with us, where is the evidence? We share with the rest of the United Kingdom its economic fortunes because we are an essential part of that sovereign state and as such enjoy all of the economic linkages and fiscal benefits that such a constitutional relationship naturally entails.

Those members of G7 who have bought into the island economy concept seem to have accepted the political thinking of Irish nationalism, that is to say, that a discrete geographical entity such as an island must have one economy, constitute one nation and be ruled by one government. It is the economics of map imaging and natural frontiers. The concept is as equally illogical and absurd as is its political counterpart. Mr Bertie Ahern, in a recent statement, declared that 'any new settlement has to recognise the logic of Ireland as an economic entity'. This statement is as devoid of economic validity as claims to natural frontiers are devoid of political realism.

THE UNION AND PROSPERITY
In his paper, 'Ireland: an Island Economy', Sir George Quigley firmly placed the idea of developing an all-Ireland economy on the political agenda. The Quigley economic perspective fitted into the political strategies of the so-called peace process and it has been especially employed to lend economic credibility to cross-border executive bodies, which are central to the recent political settlement. The use of economics to underpin a unificationist strategy has never been publicly challenged or repudiated by Sir George Quigley or by the leadership of the local Confederation of British Industry (CBI), the Institute of Directors or the

---

[9]*Northern Ireland Sales and Exports, 1994/95-1995/96* (Belfast: Industrial Development Board, May, 1997), p. 17.

Northern Ireland Chamber of Commerce, whose leaders are all in the vanguard of change. This represents, in my opinion, a combination of political naïveté and gro ss economic miscalculation, because the realisation of the unity objectives of the peace process and the settlement may destroy what is necessary for the viability of the business sector in Northern Ireland, namely, the Union.

Why do I say that the Union is the absolute basis for our future economic prosperity? I say so because there is no context outside of the United Kingdom within which Northern Ireland can sustain the robust rates of growth and the high levels of economic activity that its citizens desire. The island economy project envisages a range of economic harmonisation measures between Northern Ireland and the Republic in areas such as job promotion, tourism and farming and is underpinned by the development of the Belfast-Dublin corridor. The case for the latter is based on a gross exaggeration of anticipated trade and employment benefits that I have already mentioned. Nevertheless, nationalist politicians, particularly Albert Reynolds and the economic pundits of the SDLP, have employed the CBI's incredible claim that 75,000 new jobs will be created to underpin their political agendas, despite it being totally discredited by competent economic researchers. The use of the CBI's statistics by nationalist politicians is not merely a characteristic flight from economic reality, it also testifies to the high degree of intellectual dishonesty required by the lack of supporting evidence for the nationalist case. All of this was reflected in the empty economics of Mr. Hume's address, which provided a thin veneer for a very strong argument for political unification.

The economic future of Northern Ireland lies, as it always has, in its association with Britain as an integral part of the United Kingdom. For Northern Ireland's captains of industry to buy into the economics of Irish unity on the back of the uncertainties of European Monetary Union would be to risk the prosperity of one and a half million people for the financial gambles of a few. It would be to equate the possibilities of marginal gain with the probabilities of economic disaster and would, in the process, prejudice the constitutional wishes of the majority of our people.

VIII

THE MCCARTNEY REPORTS

Twenty

The McCartney Report on Consent[1]

INTRODUCTION

The vast majority of those citizens living in Northern Ireland who are dedicated to the maintenance of the Union take some comfort from the belief that the constitutional position of Northern Ireland as an integral part of the United Kingdom is guaranteed by the principle that there will be no change in the status of Northern Ireland as part of the United Kingdom without the consent of a majority of the people living there.

Few are fully aware of the ongoing process for modifying and diluting that principle to the point where it will present no obstacle to the unification of Ireland. The present policy of the British government is to disengage from Northern Ireland by creating and putting in place institutions of government agreed jointly with the Irish government. These institutions will gradually evolve into a factually and economically united Ireland that will render the final consent to the transfer of legal constitutional sovereignty a mere formality. The leadership of the SDLP and the Irish government have repeatedly stated that the consent of the majority is required only for the transfer of nominal sovereignty, and this accords entirely with the declared policy of the present British government that the institutions of government and the relationship of Britain and the Republic are matters for the two sovereign powers alone and require no consent from the majority in Northern Ireland.

The principle of majority consent as understood by Unionists is very different from that accepted by pan-nationalism and the British government. The statement by the Secretary of State, Dr Mowlam, published in the *Belfast Telegraph* on 28 August 1997 rightly sent alarm and anxiety through the pro-Union community. She stated that she did not define consent necessarily in terms of numbers or in a functional geographical sense, but rather in terms of a willing accommodation. Despite her retraction, this pamphlet will demonstrate that what the British and Irish governments, in concert with the SDLP, mean by consent is the agreement, or at least the acquiescence, of the pro-Union majority to an accommodation which will spell the end of the Union. The terms of such a scheme have already been established and put in place in the form of the Joint Declaration of December, 1993 (the Downing Street Declaration), which set out the principles to be

---

[1] *The McCartney Report on Consent* (Belfast: UK/Unionist Party, 1997).

followed, and the Framework Documents, which provided blueprints of the institutions of government for giving effect to those principles.

The parameters of the present talks process have been definitively set out in the joint government 'ground rules', which, though they pay lip service to the possibility of other outcomes, make it perfectly plain that all real negotiations must be within the Framework Documents format. Pro-Union negotiators may be allowed some minor tinkering with the detail, but neither the Irish government nor the SDLP will permit any significant deviation from a commitment to both the Joint Declaration and the Framework proposals. The effect of both of these documents is to guarantee to Sinn Fein/IRA a minimum outcome of unity by instalments and participation in a process which they openly declare to be transitional on the way to a united socialist republic, an objective whose attainment they intend to accelerate by whatever means, and at whatever time, they choose as appropriate.

*   *   *

Mr Blair has revealed (*Sunday Times*, 31 August 1997) that he has a plan for the future government of Northern Ireland already in place and has stated that only the details remain to be finalised in the all-party talks. So much for the value of talks, since all that Mr Blair requires is that Unionists acquiesce in what, apparently, has been decided already, except for the details. Mr Blair can, of course, give an assurance that the constitutional status of Northern Ireland will be maintained while a majority so desire, but only until such times as the proposed institutions of government provide the consent necessary for his party's ultimate objective of Irish unity.

The purposes of this pamphlet are to set out the true realities of what the consent principle now means both for pan-nationalism and the British government and to alert the pro-Union people of Northern Ireland that their simple faith in the bulwark of majority consent could prove to be wholly misplaced. Misplaced because, while the principle is being presently accepted, the means of subverting it are about to be put into position. Pro-Union consent is now being sought to an accommodation which will contain the means by which real consent to a change in Northern Ireland's constitutional position will be obliterated.

The present threat to the Union is, if anything, greater than that which faced our forefathers in 1912. Unionists no longer enjoy the unqualified support of any major part of the British political or media establishment. Today the political cohesion and sense of purpose present in 1912 is absent. But perhaps the greatest weakness is the failure of the pro-Union people at all levels to appreciate the nature and extent of the

British government's policy to disengage from Northern Ireland, a policy which that government will make effective by creating, in partnership with the Irish Republic, institutions of government which will achieve majority consent to Irish unity as an inevitable outcome of such provisions.

THE RETREAT FROM THE PRINCIPLE OF CONSENT

Any analysis of successive British government statements on the principle of consent since the proroguing of Stormont in 1972 demonstrates an ongoing weakening of the constitutional guarantee.

The Sunningdale Communiqué of December 1973 declared that 'the present status of Northern Ireland is that it is part of the United Kingdom. If, in the future, the majority of the people of Northern Ireland should indicate a wish to become part of a united Ireland, the British government would support that wish'. In 1973 there was no suggestion that the internal affairs of Northern Ireland were a matter for anyone but the British government, and a number of ministerial statements made it clear that no such interference in the internal affairs of a part of the United Kingdom would be tolerated.

By November 1985, when the Anglo-Irish Agreement was signed, the Brighton bomb and the murder of Airey Neave had already weakened British resolve. Article 1 (a) of the Agreement provided: 'the two governments affirm that any change in the status of Northern Ireland would only come about with the consent of the majority of the people of Northern Ireland'. It was significant that while the Agreement spoke of no change in the status of Northern Ireland, it neither confirmed nor declared what that status was. Had the British government openly stated its definition of Northern Ireland as part of the United Kingdom, almost certainly the Irish government would not have signed the document. Even the title of the Agreement was required to be different in the Irish and British versions. The Irish copy declared that the Agreement was made between the government of the Republic of Ireland and the government of the United Kingdom, while the British version stated the Agreement be made between the government of the Republic of Ireland and the government of the United Kingdom and Northern Ireland.

While Northern Ireland as part of the United Kingdom remained nominally within the sovereignty of that state, the effect of the Agreement was to seriously undermine the quality of Britain's independent sovereignty over Northern Ireland and to reduce the value and nature of the British citizenship of the people living there by permitting another independent foreign state to exercise substantial powers of interference and influence over their governance.

*　　　*　　　*

The Joint Declaration of December 1993 represented a further dilution of the consent principle, both in its language and tone.[2] While in paragraph four the British Prime Minister reaffirmed that his government would uphold the democratic wish of a greater number of the people of Northern Ireland on the issue of whether they preferred to support the Union or a sovereign united Ireland, this weaker language was accompanied by what can only be described as a 'Declaration of Disinterest in the Union'. The British government stated that it had no selfish strategic or economic interest in remaining in Northern Ireland. The entire document was redolent with overtones of withdrawal and, in essence, offered the principles for British disengagement. Not once were the pro-Union people referred to as British citizens, but merely as either a tradition in Ireland or as part of the people of Ireland. The British government had now divorced itself from any responsibility to act positively in the maintenance of the Union, stating that 'it is for the people of the island of Ireland alone, by agreement between the two parts respectively, to exercise their right of self-determination on the basis of consent freely and concurrently given'. The necessity for the consent of the people of the Republic to any matter affecting the constitutional future of Northern Ireland remained unexplained.

In paragraph five the Taoiseach accepted that it would be wrong to impose a united Ireland in the absence of a freely given consent of the majority of the people of Northern Ireland. In this he was merely accepting as wrong and, therefore, to be virtuously resisted, that which he knew to be impossible until the groundwork had been laid. It is paragraph seven, however, which provides the clue to what is presently being pursued, which is a policy of positively engineering, if not actively coercing, Unionist consent to Irish unity. Paragraph seven reads:

> Both governments accept that Irish unity would be achieved only by those who favour this outcome persuading those who do not, peacefully and without coercion or violence, and that if, in the future, a majority of the people of Northern Ireland are so persuaded, both governments will support and give legislative effect to their wish.

---

[2] See Apprendix.

The fundamental question then arises as to who are the persuaders for majority consent to a united Ireland? What is the form which such persuasion is to take, and what are the reasons for certain parties being persuaders?

WHO ARE THE PERSUADERS?

The British government, under the terms of the Joint Declaration, has undoubtedly agreed to be a facilitator for a settlement of the Northern Ireland problem. It is impossible to discover within the terms of that document any solution being postulated other than that of Irish unity. The difference between one anxious to facilitate, and one willing to persuade, is difficult to discern within the context of British policy. In essence, there is no distinction whatever. Paragraph nine of the Declaration clearly forecasts the institutional arrangements that were to be formulated in the Framework Documents. Institutions which would provide the means for achieving a factual and economically united Ireland which would render consent for a transfer of legal sovereignty either inevitable or unnecessary.

THE BRITISH GOVERNMENT

The events preceding the signing of the Joint Declaration in December 1993, the subsequent publication of the Framework Documents of February 1995, followed by the setting up of the talks in May 1996 provide the evidence for counting the British government among the ranks of the persuaders. The Brooke-Mayhew talks of May 1991-92 confirmed that the British strategy of wooing the nationalist community with economic preference, social engineering and legislative measures had failed either to marginalise Sinn Fein or stop IRA terror. The talks had, however, enabled both governments to assess the terms upon which pro-Union acquiescence to a settlement might be gained.

The time was ripe, therefore, for a policy shift towards the appeasement of republican extremism and a graduated move to the Irish unity solution. This policy shift was accelerated by the IRA's mainland bombing campaign of early 1993. Indeed, the IRA claim that British officials established contact with them within one week of the Warrington bomb. The bombs at Warrington and the Baltic Exchange, though different in character, were both of decisive political effect. The wanton murder of children on the mainland and the threat to the financial heart of the City of London made the security of the British mainland the government's overriding priority—to which the constitutional future of Northern Ireland's British citizens became, and has remained, entirely subordinate. London was now entirely responsive to the calls of John Hume and Albert Reynolds for a new policy oriented towards Irish unity.

*   *   *

At this point, the British government bought into the Irish unity solution, which its officials had already been gearing up to for some time. However, if the Unionists were to be kept on board, a ceasefire of some kind would be necessary, with the attendant promise of a peace dividend in social and economic terms. Throughout the remaining months of 1993, secret negotiations with the IRA continued, although vigorously denied publicly. The Joint Declaration of 16 December 1993 was the result. The Declaration was as far as Britain could openly go to satisfy the Sinn Fein demand for 'Brits Out' without alienating moderate Unionist opinion, whose support at the time was vital. Sinn Fein's demand for clarification was an effort to gain public acknowledgement of the Declaration's real, but somewhat veiled, intent. The political importance of the Declaration was the transfer of the ambit of any future settlement from a London-Dublin axis to a Belfast-Dublin one. This transfer of the search for a solution to an all-Ireland basis has since been fleshed out in the Framework Documents, which have, in broad terms, received Sinn Fein's approval. This approval was based on Sinn Fein's appreciation that the provisions of the Framework Documents were, essentially, intended to be transitional and not final. It offers not the immediate granting of Irish unity, but the machinery that will ultimately secure it. It is beyond belief that any Unionist could accept that Sinn Fein/IRA would forego, even on a temporary basis, their only effective weapon of violence, unless they felt assured that the peace process will yield their objective by other means. The real conclusion must be that they consider that the detailed political strategy of the two governments will achieve Irish unity, although economic and political restraints may require a phased accomplishment. In the meantime, Sinn Fein/IRA will retain its weaponry to ensure British good faith and to accelerate the process—by either action or threat, as and when they deem it necessary. The ending of the first ceasefire with the explosion at Canary Wharf in February 1996, and the catalogue of subsequent outrages, from Manchester to Thiepval Barracks, illustrate the point. Indeed, they have merely underlined the priority of mainland security as the overriding factor driving London's objective of conflict resolution with republican terror, regardless of the constitutional rights of Unionists.

LABOUR POLICY AND THE BIPARTISAN APPROACH

The policy shift of the Conservative government towards Irish unity was masked under the title 'peace process', but it represented not only a change of direction, but a close approximation to what was already established Labour Party policy, the so-called 'Irish unity by consent principle'. In September 1988 Neil Kinnock, as party leader, wrote the introduction to the Labour Party policy document on Northern Ireland, which was entitled *Towards a United Ireland: Reform and Harmonisation: A Dual Strategy for Irish Unification.* The document was issued by the Labour Party's front bench Northern Ireland team in the House of Commons—Kevin McNamara, MP, Jim Marshal, MP, and Marjorie Mowlam, MP—and claimed to outline front bench strategy for implementation of party policy on Northern Ireland.

Mr Kinnock described the report as a carefully thought out and coherent strategy to implement the Labour Party's policy of unity by consent. The Anglo-Irish Agreement was, in his opinion, a positive step in that direction, but not sufficient by itself. For Mr Kinnock the party document spelled out a practical basis for harmonisation which would help progress towards gaining a united Ireland by consent. While that consent must be freely given, no group or party could be allowed to veto advance in that direction (Irish unity), for it is the course of peace for the people of Ireland, north and south of the border.

The document declares the Labour Party to be at one with the constitutional nationalist parties of Ireland, which together enjoy the electoral support of almost 95% of nationalists on the island as a whole. It continues with a series of statements of which the following are but examples: 'Whilst the logic and thrust of Labour's policy involves a British withdrawal preceded by a progressive process of disengagement, this would be an integral part of the progress towards unification . . . whilst unification must involve withdrawal, precipitate withdrawal might preclude unification.'

Since precipitate withdrawal might, undoubtedly, have caused problems for the Irish government, the Labour Party was anxious to avoid this and said such a withdrawal would be an abdication of responsibility and would ignore the wishes of the Irish government and political parties. The Labour Party, it declared, was not in the business of imposing solutions on the Irish government or people. The question of whether or not it was in the business of imposing solutions on the majority population of Northern Ireland was quite a different matter.

*　　*　　*

Paragraph five of the document stated that unlike the Conservative government, the Labour Party did not believe that it was responsible or adequate to await passively the dawning of consent. To the contrary, it was committed to working actively to build that consent. Paragraph eight of the document declared:

> In this document we will elaborate a dual strategy involving the reform of Northern Ireland and harmonisation with the Republic. The two parts, while separate in principle, are strongly connected in practice. Our strategy will from the basis of a Labour Party action in government that is central to our arguments in opposition. It is a path which we commend to all political parties in Britain and Ireland as the most viable strategy for political change and reform.

Perhaps more important, paragraph sixteen dealt with the issue of consent, and it is appropriate that it should be set out in full:

> What then is the meaning of consent as it is used in party policy? No democratic sovereign government would yield to a minority of its citizens a veto over its relations with other sovereign states or over the negotiation of cooperative agreements, or the signing of international accords, with such states. No government would allow vociferous minorities to veto policies which it believed to be in the general interest and which were compatible with the rule of law and the civil rights of its citizens. But any democratic government should accept that where a change in sovereignty was in prospect which would affect directly the interests and citizenship of a part of its population, those thus affected should have a determining say in the question.

And paragraph seventeen:

> These are the tenets central to the concept of consent. Its application turns on the distinction between the exceptional circumstances of a prospective constitutional change involving a transfer of sovereignty, when it will apply, and the normal operation of the process of government, when it will not. It will not, for instance, be applicable to the day-to-day work of government or to the regular relations between London and Dublin. It will not be a factor where steps are being taken simply to harmonise policies and practices north and south of the border. No Labour administration will allow its commitment to consent to be transformed into a veto on political progress towards unification. But consent will be required before any change is made in the sovereign status of Northern Ireland. The constitutional step of unification will

only be taken with the consent of majority of the people of Northern Ireland.

The above paragraphs vividly illustrate the trap into which pro-Union negotiators will be led. While acknowledging that consent will be required before any transfer of sovereignty occurs, it is blindingly clear that the government will utilise every means to ensure that consent cannot be withheld. The programme of reform as set out in paragraph twelve will require:

* the erosion of historically and culturally entrenched communal antagonisms to enable a united Ireland to function harmoniously;

* the establishment of institutions of state, law and justice which demand widespread support and legitimacy;

* the successful experience of mutual political cooperation and coalition between the different traditions and their political representatives with Northern Ireland; and

* the ending of social and economic inequalities which have contributed to instability. The unification of Ireland by consent, it follows, presupposes the reform of Northern Ireland.

When all the verbiage is cleared away, what it amounts to is an organised and systematised plan to remove the cultural and historical Britishness of the majority and to ensure, by means of institutionalised discrimination against the majority, that its sense of identity and its belief in its Britishness are so broken and reduced by means of these institutions that, ultimately, the giving of its consent will be inevitable.

Dr Mowlam may suggest that this document no longer represents Labour policy, but its detail, its consistency with the past, its endorsement by their party leader and her own signature would make such protestations unbelievable. Moreover, its contents are entirely compatible with her own recent definition of consent in the *Belfast Telegraph*. While the Conservative government was moving along a similar path, its progress was dictated by that party's cynical pragmatism of how best to ensure mainland security, a policy which, in some events, it may have changed. The present government is driven not only by that requirement, but also by a settled and determined doctrinaire policy for achieving Irish unity. It has openly and explicitly declared itself to be a persuader for Irish unity. It is politically dedicated to establishing and implementing policies directed solely to the manufacturing of consent for unification.

THE IRISH GOVERNMENT AS PERSUADER

It is a self evident truth that the Irish government is a persuader for Irish unity. Article Two of the Republic's constitution provides that 'the national territory consists of the whole island of Ireland, its islands and the territorial seas'. Article Three provides:

> pending the reintegration of the national territory, and without prejudice to the right of the Parliament and government established by this constitution to exercise jurisdiction over the whole of that territory, the laws enacted by the Parliament shall have the like area and extent of application as the laws of Saorstat Eireann and the like extra-territorial effect.

In the run up to the 1985 Anglo-Irish Agreement both the British government and the then Taoiseach, Dr Garrett FitzGerald, were peddling the patently erroneous line that Article Two was purely declaratory of the Irish political aspiration for unity and was not a legal claim, in a true sense, to the territory of Northern Ireland. Both governments were well aware that this was false, but the deception was necessary to avoid the embarrassing fact, among others, that one member state of the European Community was refusing to recognise the borders and territorial integrity of another member state as required by the treaties which created that community.

The truth eventually emerged when the Republic's Supreme Court decided in 1990 that Article Two consists of a declaration of the extent of the national territory as a legal claim of right and that the reintegration (unification) of the national territory is a constitutional imperative. In plain terms, the Irish Republic, by its constitution, makes a legal claim to the territory of Northern Ireland and, by implication, governments of the Republic must, by their political efforts, seek to achieve that objective. Chief Justice Finlay, in his written judgement, made it clear that in his view the government of the Republic, by signing the Anglo-Irish Agreement, was not in any way derogating from the legal claim in Article Two of the constitution, but was, in effect, attempting to resolve it by means of the machinery and consultative processes made available to it by the terms of the Anglo-Irish Agreement itself.

Not only are the Irish government political persuaders, they are obliged by their constitution to be such.

*   *   *

While the Framework Proposals provide the blueprint for creating Irish unity and manufacturing pro-Union consent, both governments are agreed that this must occur only when a number of preconditions have been satisfied. First, as the Labour Party document makes clear, the pro-Union majority must be culturally and economically conditioned, or harmonised, and, secondly, British withdrawal must be phased in over a period to avoid the chaos and instability which a precipitate withdrawal without proper preparation would entail.

While Irish unity remains the enduring policy of the Republic, its economy is only kept afloat by massive subventions from Europe and is totally incapable of accommodating the cost of any immediate unification. A joint strategy was necessary to address these problems and objectives and, after years of negotiation, it crystallised in the Framework proposals. The Framework would have the effect of offering Sinn Fein Irish unity by phased instalments, which their threat of violence would ensure were paid on time. The period over which the Joint Executive Bodies would move through consultation, harmonisation, to full executive powers would enable the Unionists to be sedated by the social and economic benefits of peace so that they would ultimately accept the fact of unification and give their consent to the final transfer of sovereignty. The Irish government, on the other hand, would work out during this period the terms upon which Europe and Britain would pay for the exercise.

The claim of the Republic under Articles Two and Three has legitimised the activities of the IRA, who can say with justification that 'the Republic claims as of right that for which we fight'. Indeed, there can be no doubt that the claim of the Republic to Irish unification has been advanced by the activities of violent republicanism.

The objective of the Republic's constitution is a united Ireland, that of the SDLP led by John Hume is a united Ireland, and the clear goal of Sinn Fein/IRA is a united Ireland. All efforts to achieve a fair and just internal settlement within the United Kingdom are doomed to failure, because of the opposition of these three groupings. None of them will permit a solution to the problems of Northern Ireland other than by way of Irish unity. Their combined opposition has forced weak and vacillating British governments to enter into agreements in respect of part of their territory which no other sovereign democratic state would have tolerated. The democratic and constitutional rights of a clear majority are being sacrificed not just to satisfy the demands of Sinn Fein/IRA's terror machine, but to satisfy the demands of the irredentist nationalism of the Irish Republic and the SDLP. For these constitutional nationalists and persuaders, the achievement of Irish unity has a far greater priority than the restoration of peace and fair government which a settlement within a pluralist United Kingdom could produce.

THE SDLP AND SINN FEIN/IRA
Whatever apparent differences in methodology, both the SDLP and Sinn Fein share the same basic objectives: Irish unity and the destruction of the majority's right to withhold their consent to any change in Northern Ireland's constitutional status within the United Kingdom.

On 19 September 1988 the *Irish Times* published the full text of the Hume-Adams dialogue. Even a cursory reading of this statement will confirm that the entire programme for the so-called 'peace process', ranging from the Joint Declaration to the first ceasefire, was laid out in the Hume proposals and response. John Hume confirmed that politically the positions of Sinn Fein and the SDLP were not unduly removed from one another and were bridgeable. Hume's objective was to persuade Sinn Fein's leadership that its terrorist gains could only be fully exploited via democratic activity and that the goal of Irish unity could be best served through the mechanism of a pan-nationalist front. A declaration of a ceasefire would give Sinn Fein political credibility, and association with the SDLP, the Irish government and Irish America would complete the process, rendering Sinn Fein democratically respectable. Significantly, this development was almost contemporaneous with the thinking in the Labour Party policy document, which was published at the same time. Joint SDLP and Sinn Fein policy coalesced in the Hume-Adams document of mid-1993, which was central to the negotiations which produced the Joint Declaration in December of that year.

*   *   *

John Hume and the SDLP have repeatedly declared that Irish unity is the policy objective of the party. The right of the majority to withhold its consent to that goal is contemptuously dismissed as the 'Unionist veto'. Northern Ireland has been described by Mr Hume as 'an unnatural enclave', created to give two Protestants to every Catholic. British policy of upholding the consent principle is the subject of scathing disapproval, of which he writes: 'as I see it, the two greatest problems in Ireland are the British guarantee and the Unionist dependence on it'.

The SDLP, in its policy document *Strategy for Peace*, published in November 1989, stated: 'the SDLP believe that the British and Irish governments should jointly set aside the present unilateral guarantee'. Sinn Fein, for its part, wholly endorsed Hume's strategy, which was entirely aimed at the removal of the consent principle. Hume's task was to persuade Adams that Sinn Fein/IRA should declare a ceasefire, at which time negotiations could be set up that would ensure that the machinery was put in place for the dismantling of the consent principle and which placed the constitution on the table for negotiation, with Sinn Fein present.

In January 1996 Sinn Fein, in its submission to Senator Mitchell's International Body on Decommissioning, stated:

> the Irish Peace Initiative of 1993 was based on the clearly established fact that there can be no internal settlement within the six counties, that any settlement must be based on the right of the Irish people to national self-determination exercised by agreement and that a lasting settlement could only be achieved through all-party peace talks led by both governments.

Both Hume and Adams were well aware that if Unionists could be lured into negotiations effectively controlled by the two governments as persuaders, and with a fixed agenda based on the Framework Documents, any agreement based on them would render ultimate Unionist consent to a united Ireland inevitable. The only difference between Sinn Fein/IRA and the SDLP is about the speed with which these mechanisms might bring about the result. It is for that reason, among others, that Sinn Fein/IRA will not decommission. They require their weapons in order to accelerate the process when necessary—a tactic they have already successfully employed once by their return to violence post-Canary Wharf.

Nationalists believe that all the people of Ireland constitute a single distinct nation with a collective right of self determination. Unionists are merely a 'tradition' within that nation who have no separate right to self determination. Therefore, as a minority, they have no 'democratic' right to claim a veto over the exercise of self-determination by the Irish nation as a whole. Partition, they argue, is therefore the root cause of violence in Northern Ireland, because it does not have the *de facto* consent of the nationalist majority in the whole of the island. The implication of all this is that the 'peace process' must be liberated from a 'Unionist veto', which effectively prevents the implementation of the 'shared understanding of the two governments' set out in the Framework

Documents —documents whose machinery is specifically designed to bypass Unionist consent.

THE FRAMEWORK DOCUMENTS
Within twenty-four hours of the publication of the Framework Documents in February 1995, this author stated his criticism in a lengthy article commissioned by the *Belfast Newsletter* and later republished by the *Daily Telegraph*. The Framework was, allegedly, offered as one for discussion, but it was patently a declaration of policy, and policy which had already been agreed with the Irish government. It offered none of the alternatives of a discussion paper. Its length was due entirely to the detail of how its single theme for the factual unification of Ireland was to be implemented. My article stated:

> Discussion or negotiation by Unionists in these circumstances can never be about anything more than the extent or speed with which this process will evolve and their participation in negotiations would be an implied acceptance of the process which is designed for one purpose only, that of Irish unity . . . The entire direction of the Framework Documents is not towards the issue of fair and equal government within Northern Ireland, but to ensuring that a minority is given, over an intermediate time span, the guarantee that it will be able to choose, not how, but who will govern Northern Ireland . . . The people of Northern Ireland do not have to make a choice between negotiation within the terms of the Framework Documents or a resumption of violence. To postulate the "peace process" in these terms is to equate that process with the single solution theory of the Framework Documents.

What was clear then, and has subsequently been emphasised time and again, is that the present talks are limited entirely within the four walls of the Framework Documents.[3] Even if the British government was willing (which it is not), neither the Irish government nor the SDLP will permit the current talks to be about anything outside the Framework and the Joint Declaration. These form the basis by which Unionist consent to Irish unity is to be manufactured. The single theme is Irish unity, for nothing less will appease Sinn Fein/IRA and their fellow travellers. No matter how it is dressed up, the ultimate question is this: what concessions are necessary to satisfy the IRA so that they will not use their retained weaponry to renew their campaign of violence? There can be only one answer: Irish unity, the destruction of the Union

---

[3] See Appendix.

and the creation of political institutions that will make both certain. Since the Framework Documents fulfill all these requirements, one simply cannot be a Unionist and negotiate within their terms.

*   *   *

The above view of the UK/Unionist Party is shared by the Ulster Unionists and the Democratic Unionist Party. Indeed, the executive committee of the Ulster Unionist Council issued a statement in 1995 rejecting in the strongest possible terms the government's Framework proposals as offering any basis for negotiations. The executive committee stated that the Framework was designed to render the consent of a majority to any change unnecessary and rightly claimed that Mr Major's assertion that the consent of the majority is a guarantee of Northern Ireland remaining within the United Kingdom is made meaningless. It described the proposed Northern Ireland Assembly as one that would be paralysed and ineffective. It declared that the proposed North-South Body would be an embryonic all-Ireland government and claimed that the Northern Ireland Assembly would become subservient to Dublin. The final conclusion of the Ulster Unionist Party statement deserves quotation in full, for it is one which all Unionists would endorse:

> The Framework Document is not a true framework, rather a full treaty between the two governments. It seeks to deny the will of the greater number in Northern Ireland to remain firmly in the United Kingdom. It proposes the transfer of power to a joint body dominated by the Dublin government. The empty boast that sovereignty is unaffected means nothing, for what use is sovereignty when the functions of government are centred in a foreign state?

The question now is: how can the Ulster Unionist Party contemplate participating in the present talks when the parameters of those talks are confined, in real terms, to the Framework Documents, which they have rejected entirely as a basis for discussion? Both governments and the SDLP held tenaciously to this position throughout the months of debate on procedure. Both claimed that the 'negotiations' referred to in the Act of Parliament setting up the talks were the negotiations described in Command Paper 3232 presented to Parliament on 16 April 1996 and could not deviate from it. Paragraph four of the Command Paper stated:

> Both governments, as signatories of the Anglo-Irish Agreement, reaffirm that they would be prepared to consider a new and more

broadly based agreement if that can be achieved through direct discussion and negotiation between all the parties concerned. The two governments, for their part, have described a shared understanding of the parameters of a possible outcome of the negotiations in A New Framework for Agreement.

All the parties to the talks process know that the negotiations are entirely within the control of the two governments and the SDLP, who are all persuaders. There is not the slightest possibility that anything but the most minor adjustments to the Framework will be permitted. There is no length to which the governments will not go to ensure that its shared understanding will be put into effect. The conception which the general public share as to the free nature and scope of the negotiations could not be more wrong. The governments are determined that the Framework Proposals will form the central core of any final agreement. If the Unionists participate in what amounts to a 'political killing field', the pressure that they are presently under to participate with a fully armed Sinn Fein/IRA will be nothing to the pressure that will be experienced in April-May 1998. Any suggestion of their unwillingness, at the time, to sign up to an agreement endorsed by the two governments, the SDLP and Sinn Fein will be met with overwhelming pressure from both sides of the Atlantic.

*   *   *

For those who take any comfort from Tony Blair's speech at the Royal Ulster Agricultural Society on 16 May 1997, some words of caution:

> * He is committed to the principle of consent, but this is only, as the Labour policy document points out, consent to the final transfer of sovereignty. He is equally committed to the creation of political institutions that will obtain that consent, as in the Framework Documents.
>
> * Devolution proposals for Scotland and Wales and the English regions are designed to bring government closer to the people, but the devolved assembly under the Framework is for the purpose of moving Northern Ireland out of the United Kingdom.
>
> * The consent principle which he claimed was now universally accepted was not understood as such by any brand of Irish nationalism.
>
> * He is committed to the approach set out in the Downing Street Declaration and believes the Joint Framework Documents offer a reasonable basis for future negotiation. In this regard, his claim that

new institutions which fairly represent the interests and aspirations of both communities will be negotiated bears close examination.

* His claims that the Irish government offers strong support for the consent principle is, at best, misinformed error.

When the rhetoric of Tony Blair's speech writers is cleared away, the Framework Document proposals are still the basis of the two governments' solution. The determination of both governments to drive their proposals through is clearly evident in their treatment of the decommissioning issue. From being a requirement of democratic procedure as the basis for participation in negotiations, decommissioning will now be an end product of a negotiated settlement. Similarly, consent will no longer be required to a change in the constitutional position, but, when an agreement providing for the ultimate removal of the right to consent is reached, consent to that agreement is all that is required.

On the basis of views expressed by Unionists of all parties, it is clear that they uniformly reject the Framework Document proposals as offering any basis for a future settlement. All are agreed that within those proposals are arrangements that would, effectively, remove the majority's right to withhold their consent to anything but the final and formal transfer of legal sovereignty. If that is the case, then all Unionists, whatever their other differences, must refuse to participate further in negotiations over which they can exercise no significant control and over whose already predetermined outcome they can affect no significant change.

*   *   *

All men and women of decency and goodwill desire peace. But peace, like everything else, comes at a price. Those of evil and violent intent will always offer peace when their demands are met. What the British government and the other persuaders are diligently working at is the convincing of the pro-Union majority that there is no other alternative than a process whose inevitable result is Irish unity. No matter how that unpleasant fact is sugared, such an outcome is the only possible conclusion. It is up to the pro-Union majority, while rejecting the Framework Documents, to uniformly and positively offer an alternative. Scarcely anyone dissents from the principle that everyone, regardless of race or religion, is entitled to equality of treatment in every sphere of human activity. Few would object to the widest and most comprehensive cooperation with the Republic of Ireland in all areas of mutual benefit. Little or no opposition would be offered to the fullest expression of a joint cultural heritage in the fields of sport, culture and the arts. But all of these are fully capable of achievement within the pluralism that already exists in the United Kingdom, where currently almost one million citizens born in the Republic work and live as the country of their choice. A settlement within the United Kingdom is not only possible, but desirable. It requires, however, the British government to offer equal citizenship to all those in Northern Ireland and to actively suppress violent terrorism, rather than reward it.

Twenty-One

The McCartney Report on the Framework Documents[1]

INTRODUCTION
In the coming months, the British and Irish governments, with the aid of the Irish American lobby, will seek by a massive propaganda campaign to persuade the pro-Union people that the benefits of a terrorist-controlled ceasefire are a fair price to pay for the sacrifice of the Union and their British identity. But a ceasefire controlled by terrorists, who have been permitted to retain their weaponry for use as and when they decide, is not peace.

When the Framework Documents[2] were published in February 1995, Dick Spring, the Foreign Minister of Ireland at the time, stated that they had been two years in the making, thus confirming that the strategy for the political settlement they contained pre-dated the August 1994 ceasefire. A suspension of violence was a necessary precondition for marketing an otherwise unsaleable peace package. A ceasefire was to be the lever used to break Unionist resistance. The whole policy contained in the Joint Declaration of December 1993 (the Downing Street Declaration) and the Framework Documents of February 1995 is the product of the Hume-Adams discussions, suitably sanitised for general consumption. The entire strategy was identified by this author as early as September 1988. Writing in the *Belfast Newsletter* at the time, I stated:

> Tactically, a deal with Sinn Fein to form a pan-nationalist front and suspend the terror would have produced tremendous political dividends for Hume and the SDLP. [Hume's] hope was surely that the British government, aided by the exhortations of the great and the good, would exert such pressure on the poor leaderless and policyless Unionists that they would accept almost any political humiliation and dishonour as the price of the suspension of murder and mutilation.

Never were words more prophetic, when the present situation is considered. The Unionist leadership is now sitting down negotiating with armed terrorists, while the British government, aided by the great and the good, is exhorting them to accept the ultimate humiliation in the form of the Framework Documents. If the Union is to be preserved and maintained, it is vital that the pro-Union community fully understands

---

[1]*The McCartney Report on the Framework Documents* (Belfast: UK/Unionist Party, 1997).

[2] See Appendix.

the consequences that the acceptance of these documents will entail. It is the purpose of this publication to provide that understanding.

POLICY OBJECTIVES OF THE BRITISH AND IRISH GOVERNMENTS

Any serious student of Anglo-Irish politics and history will recognise that British strategic policy since 1921 has been one of disengagement from all parts of Ireland. This policy, while dormant for lengthy periods, always surfaces when the mainland's interests are threatened. In 1940 Eamon de Valera was offered a British push for Irish unity in return for British access to ports in Ireland to defend the North Atlantic: an offer he refused. While the Cold War continued, Northern Ireland remained strategically important as the Russian submarine fleet continued to expand. With the end of the Cold War, this interest ceased. Britain no longer had any selfish economic or strategic reasons for remaining in Northern Ireland, but, by 1992, she had developed very selfish economic and strategic reasons for leaving. The bomb at the Baltic Exchange in the City of London is said to have cost more than the entire compensation paid out for terrorist destruction in Northern Ireland between 1969 and 1992. Any ongoing threat to the financial institutions of the City of London had, necessarily, to be contained. Conflict resolution between the British state and Sinn Fein/IRA became the primary objective of government policy and energised the long-denied contacts between British officials and the IRA, which continued right up to the date of the Joint Declaration on 15 December 1993.

*   *   *

Sinn Fein/IRA's terms for the end of the conflict were explicit: Brits out and self determination for the Irish people on an all-Ireland basis. The only obstacles that remained were the determination of the pro-Union majority to remain within the United Kingdom and the chaos and constitutional instability which precipitate withdrawal might cause in the Irish Republic. The Republic's vulnerable economy, coupled with the uncertainty of continuing subventions from Europe, rendered it totally incapable of accommodating any precipitate unification. In addition, the pro-Union majority would first need to be sedated and its security services 'reformed' in such a way as to exclude any source of lawful resistance to the proposed constitutional handover of sovereignty.

Any future political union, therefore, would require a period of gradual harmonisation and interlocking of all economic, social, educational and cultural functions. The policy objective of both governments was to establish the administration and institutions which would give effect to this strategy over an appropriate time span. Agreement between the two governments on this broad agenda probably offered little difficulty and was quickly disposed of. The real problems were in presenting it in terms which Sinn Fein/IRA would at least accept as the down payment for a ceasefire and which would obtain Ulster Unionist acquiescence. The ultimate product, after lengthy negotiations with Sinn Fein/IRA and after exploring the limits of Unionist weakness in the Brooke/Mayhew talks, was the Framework Documents as the basis for a settlement. They represented the maximum the Unionists could hope to achieve and the minimum Sinn Fein/IRA might, for the time being, accept as the price of England's peace.

THE PEAÇE PROCESS
At all times during the secret negotiations to put the government's strategy in place, the SDLP and Sinn Fein/IRA were kept fully briefed. Clearly, Sinn Fein/IRA would not have suspended their only effective weapon of violence unless they had been convinced that their policy objectives could be more efficiently achieved by other means. Though persuaded that the detailed political plan of the two governments would, indeed, move in the direction of Irish unity, they refused to declare their initial ceasefire permanent and retained their weaponry in order to accelerate the process when necessary. When it appeared to them that British insistence on the Unionist requirement for at least a parallel system of decommissioning would block their entry into negotiations, they simply abandoned the ceasefire and renewed their attack on Britain's mainland with massive bombs at Canary Wharf and Manchester. The renewed attack on the mainland justified their strategy. Legislation to set up a talks process was rushed through Parliament in May 1996 and the talks themselves commenced on June 10 of that year. The Mitchell Report had never required Sinn Fein/IRA to do anything more than consider decommissioning and, when the IRA brutally murdered two community policemen in Lurgan, the government offered them terms for admission within four days. Those terms provided that if Sinn Fein/IRA simply restored their original tactical and fraudulent ceasefire of August 1994, and maintained it for a period of only six weeks, they would gain entry to the talks without decommissioning a single gun or ounce of semtex.

*   *   *

This second ceasefire, obtained upon the government accepting even weaker terms than those required for the first, enabled both governments, aided by the United States, to persuade pro-Union opinion formers that even more concessions must be made in order to maintain it. The governments pressurised the Ulster Unionist Party and its loyalist allies to stay in the talks. The threat of being viewed by world opinion as negative and intransigent proved too much for the Ulster Unionists and, despite all their pre-election undertakings, they remained in the talks alongside the representatives of armed republican terror, who had declared that their objective was to smash the Union. At present, Sinn Fein/IRA continue their campaign to dismantle the security infrastructure and remove the continuing symbols of British sovereignty. Confident in the power of their retained weaponry and explosives, they reject with contempt the democratic principle of consent accepted by other parties.

The Irish government, unrestrained by Unionist sensitivities, continues to make the pace. Irish officials vet lists of vacant public appointments and dictate the suitability of those chosen to fill them. A host of subsidiary items, ranging from the transfer and release of convicted terrorist to a restructuring and renaming of the RUC form part of an ongoing agenda. The threat of a return to violence by the representatives of terror in the talks is sufficient to make their demands a political requirement, and the principles of democracy are daily sacrificed upon the altar of what is politically expedient. Confidence building measures abound, but only those which build up the confidence of terrorist organisations, while the belief of ordinary citizens in the democratic process continues to be destroyed. All of this is justified as 'risks for peace'. It is against this background that the theory, nature and purpose of the Framework Documents must be examined, if they are to be understood.

THE FOUNDATION OF THE FRAMEWORK DOCUMENTS
Prior to 1993, the accepted basis for a political settlement was founded on democratic principles. Such principles embraced all those parties who, despite their profound differences, rejected violence as a means of achieving political ends. Commitment to democratic values was the one thing they shared in common. After the Downing Street Declaration of 15 December 1993, all of this changed. The Hume-Adams dialogue and the discussions between Northern Ireland Office officials and Sinn Fein/IRA produced a strategy for peace based on an IRA-controlled ceasefire. A pan-nationalist consensus, founded on a shared goal of Irish unity, was established between constitutional nationalism and Sinn Fein/IRA. Constitutional nationalism exchanged the shared principles of

democrats for inclusion in a pan-nationalist front that encompassed republican terrorists pledged to violence.

The plan was simple. In return for an IRA ceasefire, constitutional nationalists would obtain from Britain sufficient concessions to satisfy their violent partners, and Adams and McGuinness would sell the plan to the IRA Army Council. John Major, in a broadcast to the nation immediately after the Downing Street Declaration, acknowledged that the entire peace process was completely within the control of violent terrorists. It is that control which has dictated every step in the process to date and will, undoubtedly, determine an outcome to which the provisions of the Framework Documents will be central.

*   *   *

The Joint Declaration was, and remains, the foundation upon which the joint government solution of the Framework Documents is to be erected. When the Declaration was published in December 1993, the Framework Documents had already been under discussion for some years, and both governments, therefore, had a clear picture of what was to be built upon it. The Declaration's objectives were to obtain a ceasefire and to create the platform upon which the means of delivering to Sinn Fein/IRA their price for the ceasefire. Its real goal was to shift the axis of Northern Ireland's administration from London-Dublin to Belfast-Dublin and to distance that administration as far away from the United Kingdom as possible. That principle, having been established, the next step was to set out in the Framework Documents the detailed mechanisms and institutions of government by which it would be accomplished. Two central institutions were required for this purpose. First, an expanding and dynamic all-Ireland Body with the broadest possible remit and, secondly, a paralysed and ineffective Northern Ireland Assembly incapable of expressing the democratic wishes of the majority. To make absolutely certain that this neutered Assembly could in no way obstruct the development of the strategy for Irish unity, provision was made whereby, first, it would be brought into line if it dissented and, secondly, for the all-Ireland body to continue to function even if the majority representatives withdrew from the Assembly and it ceased to operate. In other terms, if the pro-Union people refused to work for the furtherance of Irish unity, the process would go on anyway without them.

THE THEORY OF THE FRAMEWORK DOCUMENTS
The essential questions which underlie the purpose of the Framework Documents are these: how does one obtain the political union of the

Republic of Ireland and Northern Ireland, presently part of the United Kingdom, without infringing the latter's sovereignty? And how does one ultimately transfer sovereignty without the true consent of the majority of the British citizens of Northern Ireland? The answer to these questions can be sourced to those within the European Community whose real objective is a single, politically federated state of Europe. Those Europhiles who wish to see not only trade and cooperative economic union, but also political union, rely on the theory of functionalism. Functionalism is the centralisation of two or more independent sovereign states via an interlocking web of practical and financial institutions that results in common consultation on the harmonisation and, ultimately, executive control of the administration of the relevant states. The process is well documented in the writings of political scientists and theorists familiar with the topic. The dictates of a centralised bureaucracy and its effect on the internal laws and administration of member states is already one of the great issues in the politics of Europe. The plan is that once effective functional and economic union has been completed, theoretical considerations of national sovereignty become irrelevant and political union will follow inevitably of its own accord.

Whatever the merits or demerits of the case for a politically federated Europe, the electorate of each member state will decide the issue for themselves. This is not the case in Northern Ireland, where the democratic procedures for deciding such an issue are being denied to the majority, and the process is not being used to determine their future within Europe as part of the United Kingdom, but for the purpose of expelling them from the United Kingdom into a united Ireland. Yet such has been the hypocrisy of the present British government and its predecessor that they have been prepared, for narrow political expediency, to expose the people of Northern Ireland to a process for Irish unity which they would find unacceptable as a means of ensuring the political unification of Europe.

THE NATURE OF THE FRAMEWORK DOCUMENTS

Both governments contend that the Framework Documents are discussion documents. Any documents, even an ultimatum, may be discussed if only to accept or reject the terms on offer. A discussion document properly so-called admits of a variety of options and reflects a spectrum of different views and opinions. The most fundamental objection to the Framework Documents as being documents for discussion is the total absence of any alternative and the singular nature of their only core principle. The length of the documents are not due to the number of options available for discussion, but are wholly attributable to the wealth of detail as to how their single theme of functional unification will be implemented. Indeed, it was because the documents contained only that single theme that they were impossible to amend. Removal of their only feature would have literally left nothing else to discuss. As a consequence, discussions or negotiations by Unionists in the talks process will be limited to the extent and speed with which a functionally unified Ireland will evolve.

The two governments have not spent years of detailed discussion with each other and with the SDLP and Sinn Fein in carefully crafting their proposals in order that pro-Union representatives may cherry pick through them, selecting what they want and discarding what they don't. Time and again, not only the elected representatives of pan-nationalism, but those of the wider nationalist community, both clerical and lay, have stated that they will not allow the British government to resile from its commitments to the Downing Street Declaration and the Framework Documents. Unionist involvement in these negotiations within the terms of the Framework Documents would be a tacit acceptance of a process designed and predetermined to result in Irish unity. How anyone can equate Dick Spring's statement that the Framework Documents are not 'an *á la carte* menu' with any degree of choice beggars belief. Both John Major and John Bruton, in launching the Framework Documents, stated, without reservation, that the contents of the Framework proposals represented the agreed terms which both their governments wished to implement. To that extent, the Framework Documents are a declaration of the political objectives of them both. If there was any doubt as to whether or not the Conservative government had adopted the role of persuader, rather than that of facilitator, that doubt has been clearly laid to rest by the present Labour administration, whose publicly available policy documents afford no doubt that they will be persuaders for Irish unity.

Despite all efforts by the UK/Unionist Party and the Democratic Unionist Party to have the Framework proposals removed from their dominating central position in the talks, the two governments and the SDLP vetoed any such suggestion. Indeed, the British government argued that since the negotiations referred to in the enabling legislation were those based on the Framework Documents, as set out in the Command Paper of 16 April 1996, no such change was possible. It is now certain beyond doubt that, whether any Unionists sign up to an agreement or not, the government will offer in a referendum a settlement package containing the Framework Documents as its central core.

THE NORTH-SOUTH BODY: A SWORD FOR THE REPUBLIC OF IRELAND

The provisions in the Framework Documents for a North-South all-Ireland body put a sword in the hands of the Republic that will enable it to carve a dynamic and expanding role for itself over every area and aspect of the governance and administration of Northern Ireland. It is the key element in the strategy to produce factual, economic and administrative unification of Ireland. The role of this body is stated to be dynamic. From whence will this dynamic come? It will surely not come from Britain, which has published a 'Declaration of Disinterest in Northern Ireland', but it will come from a Republic whose very constitution charges the Irish government with a constitutional imperative to seek the reunification of Ireland.

Paragraph twenty-four of the Framework Documents provides: 'Both governments consider that new institutions should be created to cater adequately for present and future political, social and economic inter-connections on the island of Ireland, enabling representatives of the main traditions, North and South, to enter agreed dynamic, new, cooperative and constructive relationships'. These words provide not only for institutions to cover existing relationships, but also for the dynamic and expanded linkages of the future on 'the island of Ireland'. Not only the substance, but the very language, of the paragraph show their real intent. It is to be a dynamic body infused with the energy and structures to ensure its growth and development. The purpose of this provision is illustrated not only in its stated principles, but in the detail of its proposed institutions and remit. The body will be granted immediate executive functions over a number of broad categories whose limits will, doubtless, prove to be elastic. These executive powers will enable the body not only to take decisions affecting Northern Ireland, but to execute and put them into effect in various sectors involving a natural or physical all-Ireland framework, EU programmes and initiatives, marketing and promotion activities abroad and cultural and heritage initiatives

*   *   *

These sectors have been chosen with care. Their appearance, at one level, seems innocent, but, in reality, they are the most dangerous of all, for their purpose is to promote the basic self—and public—image of Ireland as a single unit. Political scientists have repeatedly emphasised that the map image of a country is of central importance. As KD Boulding puts it in his study *National Images and International Systems*, 'the shape of the map that symbolises "the nation" is constantly drilled into the minds of both young and old, both through formal teaching in schools and through constant repetition in newspapers, advertisements, cartoons and so on'. This message is already imprinted in the mind of every nationalist, but the purpose of the initial executive functions listed above is to achieve the same in the minds of Unionists, so that they begin to see themselves not as British, but as a 'tradition in Ireland'. On this basis, the education, culture and heritage of the pro-Union people will be reshaped and redefined. All marketing and promotional activities abroad will reinforce, on an international basis, the image of Ireland as a single unit. The natural, or physical, all-Ireland framework will, doubtless, be interlocked with EU programmes and initiatives, once again on an all-Ireland basis. What the pro-Union people must now realise is that the strategy for Irish unity is being organised at a level of political sophistication which many of their leaders are inadequately equipped to cope with.

Apart from those functions over which the North-South body would be given immediate executive powers, a more extensive range of functions will be subjected to a process of harmonisation. These include almost every aspect of daily life upon which government impinges: health, education, social welfare, transport, consumer affairs, industrial development, agriculture, energy, trade and economic policy. Having first imprinted Irish unity in the minds of the pro-Union people, a detailed programme for provision is made for a gradual escalation of the North-South body's control. Matters originally categorised for consultation can be elevated into areas for harmonisation, and those initially bracketed for harmonisation can move into the range where the body exercises its executive powers. The entire scheme is designed to both progress and expand dynamically the input and control of the Republic over every detail of Northern Ireland's governance.

Paragraph thirty-five of the Framework provides that all decisions within the North-South body should be by agreement between the two sides. The nature of such agreement remains undefined, but the Heads of Departments from the Northern Ireland Assembly, who will be legally obliged to participate, will have to act within rules laid down by Westminster. On one side will be the Irish representatives, backed by the entire resources of the Irish government and its civil service and operating to a single, well defined agenda, and on the other side, the

Assembly representatives, composed of many who will share the Republic's objectives and the pro-Union members who will be a distinct minority, ill-equipped and under resourced to meet the relentless pressure of the Republic's dynamic exploitation of the Frameworks' strategy and structures.

THE NORTHERN IRELAND ASSEMBLY: A PAPER SHIELD FOR UNIONISTS

A devolved administration which distances Northern Ireland from the politics of the rest of the United Kingdom and leaves it available for absorption into a united Ireland has always served a policy strategy for future disengagement. The Labour Party's policy, aimed at Irish unity, refuses, for this reason, even to accept any British citizen living in Northern Ireland as a party member. It is not surprising, therefore, that provision for a Northern Ireland Assembly is included within the Framework Document proposals. Such an Assembly offers both the illusion of democratic control and the lure of remunerated office. It is the bait which British governments have traditionally offered as the means of forwarding their own policy throughout their colonial history. Unlike devolved assemblies currently proposed for other parts of the United Kingdom, it is not intended to offer the people more efficient and accessible government. Its real purpose in Northern Ireland is, and always has been, to provide a vehicle for the ultimate easing of Northern Ireland out of the United Kingdom. The creation of the Stormont parliament in 1921 owed more to the political requirements of solving the Irish problem than to any theory of good government, and that principle remains the case today.

The Ulster Unionist Party, in its policy document of March 1995 on the Framework Documents, rejected them in their entirety as offering any basis for discussion. It described the proposed Assembly as one that would be paralysed and ineffective. That is a view with which most Unionists would concur. Yet this paralysed and ineffective body is offered to the pro-Union community as one that would protect their interests. In truth, it is designed not as a shield to defend them, but as a conduit pipe for the gradual transfer of all effective power to the all-Ireland body.

*   *   *

While the detailed proposals for the Northern Ireland Assembly appear complex, their general purpose is clear. They are specifically designed to completely nullify any genuine wish or aspiration of the democratic majority. The system of checks and balances intended to sustain confidence in the institution, i.e., to obtain SDLP and Sinn Fein support, is a negation of basic democratic principles. Weighted majority voting to ensure that the minority can exercise an effective veto are proposed in the region of 65% to 75%. The Assembly itself would be under a wide degree of control by a Panel of Three which would act by consensus which, in this context, means unanimity. This panel would be elected by proportional representation from a single Northern Ireland constituency. The very appointment of the Heads of Departments who would be required to serve on the North-South body would be subject to the approval of the Panel and the Assembly, and even the Assembly's approval would require that of a weighted majority. Nationalists would thus be given a stranglehold on even which pro-Union Heads of Departments were politically acceptable to serve on the North-South body.

It should be borne in mind that when the Stormont government was set up, it comprised some members who had held office in the Westminster government and others who were experienced administrators. All were supported in government by a Northern Ireland Civil Service of quality, which was itself committed to Northern Ireland. Any proposed Assembly would be unlikely to have anyone of equal experience serving as a Head of Department nor could such Heads of Departments count upon the unqualified support of officials dedicated to the preservation of the Union. In the context of the North-South body, pro-Union Heads of Department would constitute a minority, opposed by the representatives of Northern nationalism and the experienced political administrators from the Republic who would, in turn, be backed by all the resources of an Irish civil service totally dedicated to a united Ireland agenda.

How any pro-Union politician could contemplate participating in such an arrangement defies not only logic, but the imagination. The proposed Assembly offers nothing to the pro-Union people other than a possible yardstick with which to judge the loyalty and integrity of those of their elected representatives who would choose to participate upon such terms.

THE FALL BACK PROVISION: THE CLOSING OF THE TRAP
Not content with affording to the Republic a dynamic institution for Irish unity and fobbing off the pro-Union people with a worthless Assembly, the two governments had to provide measures that would ensure that when Unionists entered the trap there could be no escape.

Paragraph forty provides that the Inter-Governmental Conference will be maintained with its respective government ministers continuing to be supported by a permanent secretariat of civil servants from both governments. Paragraph forty-two declares that the Inter-Governmental Conference will be the principle instrument for the intensification of the Agreement. Specifically, if either government feels that any institution, perhaps even the worthless Assembly, is not properly functioning within the Agreement, either government may make proposals for remedy, and adequate measures to redress the situation shall be taken. So it appears if Unionist are not behaving as the Irish government would wish them to behave, the British government has undertaken to bring them into line.

While the above paragraphs provide measures for dealing with Unionists who are participating, but not behaving, paragraph forty-seven deals with the situation which might arise when even the foolish and naïve Unionists who agreed to play their part in the Assembly are finally brought face to face with its awful reality and decide to abandon it in disillusion. Paragraph forty-seven states:

> In the event that devolved institutions in Northern Ireland cease to operate, and direct rule from Westminster was reintroduced, the British government agree that other arrangements would be made to implement the commitment to promote cooperation at all levels between the people, North and South, representing both traditions in Ireland, as agreed by the two governments in the Joint Declaration, and to ensure that the cooperation that had been developed through the North-South body be maintained.

So, even if the Northern Ireland Assembly collapses as unworkable, the dynamic and expanding North-South body will remain, in essence, alive and kicking. The British government has actually agreed to continue to implement promotion of North-South cooperation at all levels and to ensure that the cooperation developed through the North-South body be maintained. The message for pro-Union politicians is clear. Once they get themselves committed to any part of the Framework Documents, there will be no escape from their ultimate consequences. The trap will have been well and truly sprung.

THE CONSTITUTIONAL EXCHANGE: THE REPUBLIC'S CLAIM MADE REAL

In keeping with the general policy for the withdrawal of Britain's sovereign authority over Northern Ireland, Paragraph twenty of the

Framework Documents contains proposals for the amendment of section seventy-five of the Government of Ireland Act (1920). This section provides that the Parliament of the United Kingdom shall remain the supreme authority, unaffected and undiminished, over all persons and matters and things in Northern Ireland. In effect, it asserts the supreme authority and sovereignty of the Westminster Parliament over a part of its own Kingdom. Paragraph twenty, however, infers that this declaration of single sovereign control may be amended and diluted in a trade-off for some undefined amendment of the Republic's wholly unjustified claim made in Articles 2 and 3 of its constitution. In reality, the powers already given to the Republic of Ireland under the Anglo-Irish Agreement of 1985 represent an existing breach of the principle of the United Kingdom's single sovereignty over Northern Ireland.

Paragraph twenty-one of the Framework only obliges the Irish government to introduce and support proposals for a change in the Irish constitution to implement that government's alleged commitments in the Joint declaration. Those commitments, however, are couched in the vaguest possible terms. Indeed, such an amendment may not even be approved in any referendum in the Republic. This trade-off can only be described as ludicrously one-sided and could only have been agreed by a British government that had clearly lost all interest in exercising independent sovereignty over a part of its own Kingdom. In return for, at best, the hope of a possible softening, not removal, of an unlawful claim, the Republic would be given the institutional machinery to make that claim good in fact. In exchange for its claim, the Republic would be given expanding and dynamic executive power over every aspect of Northern Ireland's government and internal administration.

Any referendum in the Republic will only be held when its government is satisfied that it has struck a deal which enables it to exchange a claimed right to govern Northern Ireland for the reality of extensive executive powers enabling it to do so.

CONCLUSION
Within twenty-four hours of the launch of the Framework Documents in February 1995 by John Major and John Bruton, this author, who then held no political office and was a member of no political party, wrote a commentary on the Framework Documents at the request of the *Belfast Newsletter*. The conclusion which he arrived at then remains the one which he holds today and is repeated here:

The British government has, at the least, offered a conditional surrender to the IRA. Peace on these terms could have been obtained at any time over the past twenty-five years. In the interim, the dead have died in vain and the maimed remain mutilated for nothing. In an attempt to stand truth upon its head, the Unionist people, who have suffered largely in silence, will be castigated by the propaganda machines of both governments as negative obstacles to peace. Those who have bombed, murdered and maimed will be presented as peacemakers, while the victims will be blackmailed with the resumption of violence if they do not acquiesce in the destruction of the Union. The good and the great, both lay and clerical, will be called in aid by the British political establishment to lend their voices to a constitutional conspiracy. Those who believe in the Union must stand firm by their own convictions and conscience, for one thing is clear: one simply cannot be a Unionist and negotiate within the terms of the Framework Documents or accept them as the central framework for negotiations.

All which the author forecast has now taken place. He and those who share his views are being castigated by the propaganda machines of both governments as obstacles to peace. But he and they, in opposing a 'yes' vote in a referendum which will offer a peace package with the Framework Documents as their central core, are standing firm by their convictions and conscience, for they believed then, as they do now, that one cannot be a Unionist and negotiate within the terms of these proposals.

IX

DECOMMISSIONING AND DEMOCRACY

Twenty-two

Decommissioning and Democracy[1]

INTRODUCTION

In this submission, presented during an early phase of the Stormont negotiations (autumn 1996) to Senator George Mitchell, the chair of the proceedings, the UK/Unionist Party sets out its approach to the issue of paramilitary decommissioning within the context of the peace process. The UK/Unionist Party asserts that decommissioning cannot be considered in isolation from the political objectives of the major participants or their strategies and tactics for achieving them. Regardless of the denials of the British and Irish governments that their policies are unshaped by terrorist activity, no one believes this to be true. The reality is that they simply cannot publicly admit that political violence pays.

Methods apart, constitutional nationalism and violent republicanism have a common goal: the unification of Ireland. For the Irish government, unification is a constitutional imperative. For the SDLP, the satisfaction of the minority's civil rights claims has left it to compete more openly with Sinn Fein on the common objective of Irish unity. On major constitutional issues, the position of both parties is barely distinguishable.

The 1985 Anglo-Irish Agreement formed the last major effort by the British government to accommodate nationalist requirements for a political settlement within the United Kingdom. The undemocratic manner of its inception, and the powers which it afforded a foreign government over the internal affairs of what is part of the United Kingdom, created a degree of distrust within the Unionist community, which still informs its relationship with the British government. Between 1985 and 1991 a clearly discernible pro-nationalist emphasis was evident in terms of the government's economic preferences, social engineering and legislative measures. The virtually unfounded assertion that high Catholic unemployment was the result of discrimination was embodied in legislative measures, although independent research has clearly established that such discrimination as a cause of this effect was negligible.

All these efforts, while enjoying positive results among the minority population as a whole, found no favour with the SDLP. Sinn Fein/IRA remained as uncompromising as ever, but became increasingly aware that personal and property violence in Northern Ireland itself was,

---

[1] UK/Unionist Party Submission to Senator George Mitchell, Chair of the Stormont Talks, November 1996.

within certain limits, both politically acceptable and economically tolerable by the British government. Real political pressure upon the government could best be achieved by attacks on the mainland that were both politically and economically spectacular.

The Brooke-Mayhew Talks of 1991-92 merely confirmed that the strategy of nationalist accommodation had failed to either marginalise Sinn Fein or stop IRA terror. The SDLP remained committed to the idea of joint authority with a strengthening and expansion of the powers given to the Republic under the Anglo-Irish Agreement. Pro-Union parties, on the other hand, continued to reject the terms of an agreement that had been undemocratically imposed, so that although a settlement proved impossible both governments had been able to assess the terms upon which some degree of pro-Union acquiescence might be obtained.

APPEASEMENT AND IRREDENTISM

The failure of the Brooke-Mayhew Talks broadly coincided with the emergence of other factors which were to turn the direction of joint government policy away from the accommodation of nationalists within the United Kingdom towards the appeasement of republican extremism by a policy aimed primarily at Irish unity, but for which at least a degree of pro-Union acquiescence was necessary.

On 19 September 1988, the *Irish Times* published the full text of the Hume-Adams talks. Even a cursory perusal of this statement will confirm that the entire peace process agenda, from the Downing Street Declaration to the IRA ceasefire of 1994, is adumbrated in the Hume proposals and response. Mr Hume confirmed that the political positions of Sinn Fein and the SDLP were not unduly removed from one another and were bridgeable. The objective was to create some form of political control over the terrorist arm. Achieving this aim depended upon persuading Sinn Fein/IRA that terror had maximised its political effect and further gains could only be exploited through democratic activity; indeed, the goal of Irish unity could best be served through the mechanism of a pan-nationalist front. The declaration of a ceasefire would afford Sinn Fein political credibility and association with the SDLP, the Irish government and Irish America would complete the process of democratic acceptability. There seems little doubt that this strategy was being considered by both governments before and during the Brooke-Mayhew talks. In fact, Mr Brooke's statement, since embodied in the Downing Street Declaration of December 1993, that Britain had no strategic, economic or selfish reasons for remaining in

Northern Ireland is an almost straight adaptation of Mr Hume's stated belief in September 1988 that 'Britain has no interest of her own in remaining in Ireland, that she has no strategic, military or economic interests and that if the Irish people reached agreement among themselves on, for example, Irish unity, that Britain would facilitate it, legislate for it and leave the Irish to govern themselves'.

*   *   *

Central to the effectiveness of such a grouping is the political leverage which can be claimed by the constitutional element arising out of its real, or perceived, control over its violent component. Political concessions may be the reward for those who can allegedly elicit the declaration of a cessation of violence from those threatening violence or avert the breakdown of an existing cessation. Demonstrations of these forms of political leverage have been evident throughout the peace process. A prerequisite to the use of this political muscle is the retention within the particular grouping of a terrorist capacity. Just as the retention of weapons afford Sinn Fein both a prominence and influence beyond any electoral mandate it possesses, so the retention of Sinn Fein within the pan-nationalist camp by proxy affords that grouping increased bargaining power. In this situation, a distinction must be drawn between the desire to see all arms ultimately removed from the political ethos of the state once a group's political objectives have been realised and a process which requires all arms to be removed from the equation in order that the democratic process alone may determine the validity of any participants' objectives. Paragraph twenty-three of the Mitchell Report states that an agreed political settlement, and the total verifiable disarmament of all paramilitary organisations, are ultimately essential if the gun is to be taken out of Irish politics. That may be a self-evident truth, but it does not answer the question as to whether an agreed political settlement is possible while the guns remain. Commitments to the Mitchell principles do not remove the influence of the gun while it continues to remain in circulation.

The UK/Unionist Party considers that whether the Irish government or the SDLP desire or intend it, progress towards the political goal which they share with Sinn Fein/IRA has been advanced by violence, and that the retention of weaponry by Sinn Fein/IRA is of less significance to them than it is to the pro-Union parties, who, if democratic principles alone are observed, can attempt to preserve their electorate's position within the United Kingdom as equal British citizens.

Another significant factor in the shift in policy from accommodation to appeasement is the IRA's mainland bombing campaign. The bombs at Warrington and the Baltic Exchange, though different in character, were both of great political effect. The wanton murder of children and the attack upon the commercial heart of the city of London rendered the British government more responsive to the calls of Mr Hume and Mr Reynolds for a new strategic policy departure. The formation of the pan-nationalist front and the sanitising of Sinn Fein enabled the British government to appeal directly to the latter via secret negotiations along the lines of a ground plan already laid out by the SDLP and the Irish government. Indeed, the persistent theme of the SDLP—that the two governments can take decisions over the heads of other participants—still echoes in these current talks and confirms that in 1992 the stage was being set not for a search among democrats for an agreement in accordance with democratic procedures, but the holding of a peace conference between the representatives of violent and extreme nationalism and the British state.

*   *   *

The aim of Sinn Fein/IRA has always been their involvement in an exercise in conflict resolution to end hostilities between two sides who have been pursuing their aims by the use of arms legitimately held. In this context, the presence of the democratic representatives of Northern Ireland's parties are viewed by Sinn Fein as an irrelevance. The attitude of both governments and the SDLP has lent credence to this position. Many of the participants in the present talks do not appreciate that their presence constitutes nothing more than a democratic veneer necessary to lend credibility to arrangements originally designed to be a peace conference between the British government and the plenipotentiaries of terrorism called to determine the latter's terms for peace. The presence of the Irish government and the SDLP within the talks would not only strengthen Sinn Fein's position, but would advance progress towards their own common objective. For this reason it is evident that the constitutional element of the pan-nationalist front is anxious to have Sinn Fein at the talks at any price. What this front requires from the pro-Union parties is not their consent, but their acquiescence.

Since the presence of Sinn Fein is essential, nothing, including any requirement for decommissioning, will be permitted to obstruct their entry. This entire process has, to a degree, legitimised the political terrorism of the IRA and elevated it from the role of a ruthless, anti-social and anti-democratic organisation to that of an essential participant without whom the process 'is not worth a penny candle'. This view, expressed by Mr Fergus Finlay, one-time special advisor to Mr Dick Spring, underlines the real function and purpose of the present talks, which are not about finding a basis for democratic agreement, but about eliciting the terms upon which the IRA will make peace with the British government.

The determination of both governments and the SDLP to overcome all obstacles which would form a constraint on the participation of Sinn Fein provides further evidence for the above analysis. In any negotiations the political leverage available to nationalist groupings by the use or threat of violence is manifest. Any negotiations which take place against such a background are bound to prejudice the pro-Union position. While the pro-Union parties can do little to limit such prejudice while Sinn Fein/IRA remain outside the talks, they are most definitely in a position to decide the terms upon which they will participate with Sinn Fein in accordance with democratic procedures inside the talks. The UK/Unionist Party will not remain in the talks process if Sinn Fein are admitted at any stage without the IRA declaring a complete and permanent ceasefire upon such conditions as offer real confidence in their *bona fides* and which would include providing an earnest of good faith for that declaration by the immediate handing over of a significant quantity of guns and semtex. Thereafter, detailed arrangements and modalities for the destruction of the remainder could be put in place. Such ongoing arrangements for decommissioning would be completely independent of any political progress that might be made in contemporaneous political discussions. Any arrangement which involves the principle of the decommissioning of guns and semtex in exchange for political progress as determined by Sinn Fein/IRA is wholly unacceptable.

THE REPORT OF THE INTERNATIONAL BODY ON DECOMMISSIONING

Both governments, the SDLP and a number of the minority parties have indicated their willingness and, indeed, their intention to approach the issue of decommissioning by a complete implementation of the report of the International Body on Decommissioning (the Mitchell Report).[2] The UK/Unionist Party, while acknowledging and accepting the six principles set out in paragraph twenty of the report, does not accept the report in its entirety and cannot agree to implement it on that basis.

In particular, paragraphs thirty-four and thirty-five offer no foundation for an acceptable form of decommissioning. Paragraph thirty-four is nothing more than a suggested compromise between a pro-Union

---

[2] See Appendix.

requirement that some decommissioning occur prior to all-party negotiations beginning and Sinn Fein's declared position that there would be no decommissioning of any kind until an agreed settlement which they could endorse had been reached. The suggested compromise in paragraph thirty-four offers some decommissioning during the process rather than before or after. The reasoning behind this suggested compromise is flawed in its basic premise that each party is starting off from an equi-distant point and compromise represents a midway position. The pro-Union parties, whatever their political objectives, are starting from the position of accepting democratic procedures as the only means of obtaining these. Sinn Fein/IRA are beginning from the totally anti-democratic position of using violence for political ends regardless of the principles of democracy. The decommissioning of weapons is not, in the opinion of this party, to be viewed as a surrender by anyone to anyone, but as a mere acceptance of democratic principles and procedures as the basis for the settlement of disputes and the attainment of political objectives.

The flaw in the reasoning in paragraph thirty-four is further illustrated by the terms of paragraph thirty-five. The suggestion in the former is said to offer an opportunity to use the process on political issues as the price for modest mutual steps on decommissioning. Stripped of its political padding, paragraph thirty-five suggests decommissioning in return for political concessions. In any event, the real question would be who will determine, and upon what criteria, what is political progress and assess its value in terms of quantities of guns and semtex? The answer can only be that those who have weaponry will determine both questions. Nothing more vividly illustrates the general principle stated above, namely, that the object of the talks is not the determination of a democratic settlement, but the assessment of the IRA's price for a permanent cessation of violence.

*   *   *

If one accepts Prime Minister Major's declaration on 16 December 1993 that only the men of violence can give peace, then the British and Irish governments' terms for such a peace are manifest in paragraphs thirty-four and thirty-five and become clearer with any detailed analysis of the joint government scenario document published on 6 June 1996, especially paragraphs nine to fourteen. Paragraph nine promised an agenda that would provide all the participants (presumably to include Sinn Fein/IRA) with reassurance that an inclusive process of negotiation was genuinely being offered to address the legitimate concerns of their traditions and the need for new political arrangements with which all can identify. Pared to its essentials, Sinn Fein/IRA were being told that the Union was up for negotiation, despite the principle of consent.

Paragraph ten confirmed the commitment of both governments to paragraphs thirty-four and thirty-five of the Mitchell Report and to the implementation of all aspects of that document. It was, however, paragraphs eleven to fourteen that revealed the true intentions of both governments to ensure that Sinn Fein/IRA were not required to decommission at all during the negotiations. It was evident that the governments had accepted, as had Senator Mitchell, that there was absolutely no prospect of Sinn Fein/IRA decommissioning before, during or after the negotiations unless an outcome which they could endorse was concluded. Paragraph twenty-six of the Mitchell Report merely reiterated part of this conclusion to the effect that the paramilitary organisations would not decommission any arms prior to all party negotiations. The truth was that the Commission was given no indication at all by Sinn Fein/IRA that they would decommission any arms during the process of negotiations, a position that Sinn Fein spokesmen have reiterated on many occasions since the report was published.

Paragraph eleven of the scenario document proposed that Senator Mitchell should satisfy himself of the good intent of all participants to show good faith regarding the implementation of the report in the context of an inclusive and dynamic process which builds trust and confidence as progress is made on the issues. Paragraph twelve then proposed that when Senator Mitchell had so satisfied himself, a sub-committee would be formed with the Senator in the chair. A composite whereby Senator Mitchell would be the litmus test for good intent, the arbiter of good faith, and the establishment of what was, effectively, a fourth strand of the talks in the form of a sub-committee on decommissioning, would have constituted 'addressing the decommissioning issue'.

Paragraph thirteen provided that once the issue of decommissioning had been addressed in this way, the opening plenary would be convened and, essentially, negotiations in what would now be four strands would proceed alongside each other. Until this scenario document had been produced, the British government had failed completely to give any understandable explanation or definition of what the term 'addressing decommissioning' actually meant. The strenuous pro-Union objection to this scenario for addressing the decommissioning issue is a matter of record, and both governments withdrew the proposal. It is the contention of the UK/Unionist Party that the rejection of the above proposals, which would have invested Senator Mitchell with extraordinary powers, was fully justified by post-report events. These events, beginning with the Canary Wharf bomb in February 1996, confirmed that the International Commission had either been misled by the provision of inaccurate data or had been guilty of errors of judgement in concluding, in paragraph twenty-five of the Mitchell Report, that there was a clear commitment on the part of those in possession of arms to work constructively to achieve full and verifiable decommissioning as part of the process of all-party negotiations. Not only did such commitment not extend to decommissioning prior to such negotiations, it did not extend to the cessation of active planning and preparation for outrages such as Canary Wharf and those that followed it.

*   *   *

For both governments to attempt to invest Senator Mitchell with the proposed powers post-Canary Wharf confirms, more than anything else, their determination to arrange a peace conference including terrorists rather than to prepare for a democratic round of negotiations with parties abiding by democratic procedures. This conclusion is strengthened by the continued insistence of both governments in keeping contacts with Sinn Fein open even after the bomb at Thiepval Barracks. The basic assumption underpinning the Mitchell report was the Commission's conclusion 'that there is a clear commitment on the part of those in possession of such illegal arms to work constructively to achieve full and verifiable decommissioning as part of the process of all party negotiations'. This determination was founded upon what the report described as 'the sustained observance of the ceasefires', which had then existed for more than a year. This factor, according to the report, was of such significance that it had to be given weight in assessing the commitment of the paramilitaries to work constructively to achieve full and verifiable decommissioning.

        Since the report was published in January 1996, however, the IRA ceasefire has been terminated by a series of appalling atrocities which have resulted both in the loss of life and billions of pounds worth of damage. The IRA has also publicly declared that it will never decommission its arms until it has achieved its final objective. In these circumstances, it is impossible not to conclude that the whole basis of the Mitchell Report has been destroyed. Despite this, as indicated above, both governments, the SDLP and a number of the minority parties continue to base their policy towards Sinn Fein/IRA on the implementation of this report. Moreover, they insisted that Senator Mitchell be appointed chairman of the talks.

The UK/Unionist Party has concluded that in these circumstances a renewed IRA ceasefire no more permanent than its predecessor is all that will be required by both governments to admit Sinn Fein to the talks process so that the original strategy of both governments and the SDLP can be achieved. There can be no foundation in the present circumstances for Senator Mitchell and his colleagues to assume that there was any commitment of any kind on the part of Sinn Fein/IRA to a full and verifiable process of decommissioning.

PROPOSALS ON DECOMMISSIONING: THE BRITISH AND IRISH GOVERNMENTS AND THE SDLP

The proposals of the above participants, though displaying some variation in language, essentially advocate the implementation of all aspects of the Mitchell Report, particularly paragraphs thirty-four and thirty-five. These paragraphs constitute a recurrent feature of all joint-governmental documents and reflect the political strategies of these participants for the ultimate solution of Irish unity as the eventual outcome of the Framework Proposals. These proposals offer a strategy for the erosion of the principle of consent by a process of functional unification of the institutions of government and the economy and by confining the principle of consent to the issue of nominal sovereignty. It was this strategy that made the integrity of the Ground Rules Document of 16 April 1996 a vital requirement for these participants.

The requirements of any party, particularly Sinn Fein, to undertake to abide by the principles set out in paragraph twenty is in no way inconsistent with the IRA retaining all its weaponry right up until the conclusion of any talks process. In particular, the language of paragraph twenty-three requires careful study. This paragraph states that commitment to the six principles, if made and honoured, would remove the threat of force before, during and after all-party negotiations. With respect to the draftsman, this does not follow. The object of the principles is to focus all those concerned on what is ultimately essential if the gun is to be taken out of Irish politics, namely, an agreed political settlement and the total and verifiable disarmament of all paramilitary organisations. Senator Mitchell could rightly claim as a self-evident truth that an agreed political settlement would bring about a willingness to have total and verifiable disarmament. However, what is really required to obtain that ultimate agreed political settlement is a prior agreement to bring that ultimate conclusion about by democratic means only and some real evidence of the good faith of those presently committee to violence.

SINN FEIN/IRA

Few neutral observes would disagree with the conclusion that Sinn Fein and the Provisional IRA are so inextricably bound together in political objectives and the shared experience of their personnel that they cannot be considered separate entities. The British government has repeatedly claimed the organisation to be two sides of the same coin. It is hardly open to dispute that if Sinn Fein was bereft of its present terrorist associations, it would, as a party with only a 15% share of the vote in Northern Ireland, be no more than a minority party with a proportionate political influence. Once, however, Sinn Fein is admitted to any stage of the talks it will insist that its representation is on the basis of its electoral mandate as a political party and that it has no responsibility for, or control over, the IRA other than the political advice, mediation or directional influence it may offer. Sinn Fein will contend that it has no difficulty in undertaking to abide by the Mitchell Principles or any agreements on decommissioning, since it is not involved in anything but democratic politics and, as a political party, has no weapons to decommission. It is vital, therefore, that before Sinn Fein is admitted into negotiations appropriate terms and safeguards are obtained not just from them, but from the IRA as well.

The terms of admission for Sinn Fein must relate not only to the nature and duration of any new cessation of violence, but must also relate to the issue of decommissioning. The anxiety among the pro-Union parties is that the governments, in their determination to include Sinn Fein, will accept a ceasefire whose durability is as fragile as that of August 1994 and will enter into decommissioning arrangements that will not require any real or effective handing over of weapons. Arguments that the IRA can withhold weapons or re-arm miss the point. The terms of decommissioning and of an acceptable ceasefire are about the conditions which democrats themselves set for the entry of those previously committed to violence into discussions with those wedded to democracy. Of course, people of bad faith can break conditions upon which they have agreed to enter democratic discussions, but such violations after agreement would relate to the circumstances of their ejection from the talks rather than their initial admission. Allegations by both Sinn Fein/IRA and representatives of the Irish government, such as Mr Albert Reynolds, that decommissioning was never a precondition of entry into the talks just do not stand up to even a cursory examination of the public record.

A NEW CEASEFIRE AND DECOMMISSIONING

The permanence of a cessation of any IRA violence has a direct bearing upon the issue of decommissioning and the modalities for its implementation. The language used to describe any new cessation of violence must deal with not just the nature of the ceasefire, but its duration. If a ceasefire is declared to be both complete and permanent there can be no logical basis either for the retention of weapons or for objections to agreements providing for an immediate commencement of a process of decommissioning. Conversely, a failure to declare that a ceasefire is of permanent duration, coupled with a reluctance to decommission either before, during or after negotiations, must be construed both as a very strong indicator of the rejection of an absolute commitment to democratic procedures and a reservation that if such procedures do not generate an acceptable outcome, there will be a return to violence. The British government reiterates, in its speaking note of 30 October 1996, that under the legislation there must be an unequivocal restoration of the IRA ceasefire before Sinn Fein can be invited to nominate a negotiating team.

The UK/Unionist Party finds this requirement wholly inadequate. The original terms for an IRA ceasefire required it to be permanent. This was a reflection of paragraph ten of the Dowining Street Declaration to the effect that the achievement of peace must involve a permanent end to the use of, or support for, paramilitary violence. The passage of time has dimmed the concentration of political attention on the importance attaching to the use of the word permanent in the period between 16 December 1993 and 31 August 1994. Both the Irish government and the SDLP accepted the requirement of permanence and were vocal in their claims that the IRA's use of the word 'complete' was synonymous with the word 'permanent'. This ignored entirely that the term 'complete' was a description of the nature of the alleged ceasefire, but was no indication of its duration or permanence. The British government, on the other hand, refused to accept that 'complete' meant 'permanent', but side-stepped the issue by adopting a working assumption of permanence after the ceasefire had held for a period of three months. In the event, this ceasefire proved to be nothing more than a temporary and tactical respite, with all subsequent available evidence indicating that the gains which the IRA obtained in terms of the relaxation of security measures and surveillance were used for the purposes of training, monitoring targets, testing weapons and putting in place logistical arrangements for the outrages commencing with Canary Wharf. To suggest, therefore, that the unequivocal restoration of such an arrangement would be a passport for Sinn Fein's entry into the talks does nothing but confirm the general thesis of this paper, namely, that the purpose of the negotiations is primarily peace with terrorists rather than a settlement of differences on the basis of democratic procedures. The definition of the ceasefire required is the institution of a cessation of all violence which is both complete in its nature and permanent in its duration. An end to violence on these terms would, on any logical basis, obviate the need for the retention of any weapons. Conversely, anything less than such terms would merely strengthen the need for more stringent decommissioning requirements.

*   *   *

As page two of the British government's speaking note states, a start to decommissioning of illegal arms would demonstrate a practical commitment to exclusively peaceful methods. On this basis alone, decommissioning cannot be separated from the terms of any declaration of a cessation of violence. An immediate handing over of significant arms and semtex must accompany any declaration that violence has terminated both completely and permanently. Conversely, any verbal declarations, no matter how strongly worded, cannot be accepted without a practical demonstration of good faith. The breach of the August 1994 cessation, and the evidence of activity during it for the preparation of its breach, demands more stringent rather than reduced evidence of both the good intentions and the good faith which other parties dedicated to the principles of democracy are entitled to demand.

The suggestion that the enormity of Sinn Fein/IRA's current activity, the flexibility of their political demands and their stated refusal to decommission all make the likelihood of their entry so improbable as to render, for the present, decommissioning a less immediate issue can only be described as absurd. The flexibility of Sinn Fein's opportunist policies on tactical issues, coupled with the anxiety of both governments and the SDLP to have them admitted upon any terms, means that a declaration of a ceasefire on almost any basis would see them included. John Major informed the leader of this party that a permanent ceasefire was not being required from Sinn Fein/IRA since it was plain that it would never be given. The terms of any ceasefire which the IRA decides to offer will almost certainly be accepted by both governments. Moreover, it is the governments, not the other participants, who will determine whether the requisite terms have been met by Sinn Fein/IRA for entry into the talks process. It is, therefore, absolutely essential if the other participants are to exercise any control whatsoever that they clearly lay down in advance the decommissioning principles and requirements that they will insist be implemented before they participate with Sinn Fein in democratic negotiations.

THE PRINCIPLE OF MUTUALITY
Paragraph thirty-five of the Mitchell Report states, *inter alia*, 'as progress is made on political issues, even modest mutual steps in decommissioning could help create the atmosphere needed for further steps in a progressive pattern of mounting trust and confidence'. This reference can only be to mutuality as between republican and loyalist paramilitaries through the medium of the political parties fronting them. This interpretation is confirmed by the language of paragraph fifty: 'decommissioning would take place on the basis of the mutual commitment and participation of the paramilitary organisations. This offers the parties another opportunity to use the process of decommissioning to rebuild confidence one step at a time during negotiations'. Here again the emphasis is on progress on political issues being the *quid pro quo* for modest mutual decommissioning. Not only does this imply that the front parties for the paramilitary organisations will be the subjective arbiters of political progress, but that the paramilitary organisations will, in turn, determine if such progress merits the handing in of some weapons. The whole direction of these talks will be determined by the demands of anti-democratic terrorists, which might be a valid consideration if the talks constitute a peace conference between combatants, but totally unacceptable in the context of democratic negotiations.

The absurdity of the mutuality principle is highlighted by the fact that the political objective of Sinn Fein/IRA is the total opposite of the PUP/UDP/CLMC aspirations. One group is inflexible on the goal of Irish unity, the other declared itself absolutely committed to the preservation of the Union. Political progress for one is, by definition, defeat for the other. If Sinn Fein decided that there had been sufficient progress towards its goal to warrant a modest decommissioning on the basis of a mutual degree of loyalist compliance, the whole scheme would founder immediately. This is typical of the difficulties that arise when political expediency is substituted for democratic principle.

The loyalist fringe parties have been admitted on the basis of a continuing loyalist ceasefire and their own acknowledgement of the Mitchell principles. The CLMC still retains its weaponry and, on the basis of the mutuality principle, will not be required to decommission as the price of its political representatives remaining within the talks. The presence of the loyalist parties is an absolute requirement for both governments if Sinn Fein is ever to be admitted and the governments' real objective of a peace conference implemented. The loyalist parties are, in fact, the beneficiaries of the threat of violence, for rewards may be offered not only for restoring or renewing ceasefires, but also for maintaining them. Only upon these terms can some loyalist prisoners convicted of the most serious crimes against humanity known to society be described by national politicians as 'the unsung heroes of the peace process'.

MACHINERY AND MECHANISMS FOR ACTUAL DECOMMISSIONING

The UK/Unionist Party endorses the importance of agreeing the legislation—both primary and subsidiary—necessary to implement compliance with the principles upon which actual decommissioning will take place. These considerations, however, can be treated as ancillary to the fundamental requirements. The principles should set out what the parties fronting paramilitary organisations are required to do in order to participate in democratic negotiations. The modalities and machinery for decommissioning relate in their essence as to how and in what manner compliance with the agreed principles will be effected. Mr Adams and others fronting paramilitary organisations have indicated their willingness to discuss at length the nature and application of the machinery for decommissioning. Indeed, this very possibility is a cause for pro-Union concern as to what would happen if decommissioning was consigned to a fourth strand. Political negotiations might, in these circumstances, be accelerated down one track within a fixed time table (favoured by both the SDLP and Sinn Fein), while endless discussions about legislation modalities, possible amnesties and procedures for delivery of weaponry ensured that the timetable for the decommissioning train were never ever agreed, let alone the train set in motion, until the political considerations in Strands One, Two and Three were dealt with on the allegedly parallel track. Endless debate as to whether there was such political progress as would warrant any decommissioning would effectively ensure that no decommissioning occurred before or during the talks process.

It is, therefore, an imperative for the UK/Unionist Party that at this stage, and before any negotiations are commenced in any of the three strands, that the issue of decommissioning is not only addressed, but determined in the sense that a set of clear and positive principles are agreed to which all participating parties must comply, not only as their passport to the negotiations themselves, but as governing their participation in any discussions about the modalities or mechanisms for actual decommissioning.

CONCLUSIONS AND PROPOSALS
The UK/Unionist Party considers that it is the primary objective of both governments to obtain the presence of Sinn Fein within the present talks. The party believes that the equivocation of the British government on the use of clear and explicit terms for the nature and duration of any new ceasefire is indicative of a willingness on the part of the government to accept virtually any ceasefire as sufficient to justify Sinn Fein's entry. The current terminology—'the unequivocal restoration of the August 1994 ceasefire'—as the definition of acceptability is worthless. The language used indicates that what is deemed unequivocal is not the ceasefire, but the restoration. In any event, what is required is not the restoration of an impermanent, failed, tactical ceasefire, but a new, total cessation of violence of all kinds that is both complete in its nature and permanent in its duration. The current efforts to negotiate some form of ceasefire with Sinn Fein/IRA which the British and Irish governments can endorse as acceptable for entry to the talks has done nothing to lessen pro-Union mistrust of their intentions. Their present denials of such involvement do nothing in the light of experience to lessen pro-Union suspicions.

    In conclusion, the UK/Unionist Party asserts that before entering into negotiations regarding the future of Northern Ireland, political parties fronting paramilitary organisations, and the organisations themselves, must adhere to the following decommissioning principles :

1. Political parties fronting paramilitary organisations, and the organisations themselves, must issue a declaration of a cessation of violence that is complete, in the sense that it encompasses violence of any kind against anyone, and is permanent in its duration.

2. Any such declaration to be accompanied by a handing over of a credible quantity of weapons and explosives as a demonstration of the maker's good faith that the cessation of violence is both complete and permanent.

3. A public declaration that the relevant party, and the organisation it is said to front, subscribe to the six Mitchell principles.

4. An acceptance by the relevant party that the democratic process of negotiations can in no way be related to, or made dependent upon, any process of decommissioning and that decommissioning will progress to completion whether or not a political agreement acceptable to that party or its related organisation is achieved.

*   *   *

In addition to the above requirements for relevant parties, and in order that pro-Union confidence can be restored in the truly democratic nature of the present talks, both the Irish and British governments should declare:

1. That acceptance of Sinn Fein's entry into the talks at any stage must be preceded by the declaration of a complete and permanent ceasefire. Since both governments either claimed or assumed that the August 1994 ceasefire was both complete and permanent, it is difficult to see how there could be any objection on their part to this requirement.

2. Acceptance of Sinn Fein's entry into the substantive Three Stand negotiations will not take place until both governments have enacted all enabling legislation and passed all necessary regulations for the practical processing of decommissioning.

Twenty-three

Democracy Will Die Without Decommissioning[1]

INTRODUCTION

The requirement for all paramilitary groups to decommission their weaponry as a prerequisite for their political wings taking part in government is not a precondition imposed by other parties, it is a fundamental demand of democracy itself. This basic principle is recognised in every state where representative democratic government is practised. No agreement can set this principle aside and at the same time claim that the institutions it creates are democratic.

The initiative recently announced by Seamus Mallon at the SDLP conference fails utterly to recognise this basic tenet of democratic procedure. To equate the demand of the pro-Union parties that this principle be implemented with the repeated assertion of Sinn Fein/IRA that the latter will not give up its capacity for political violence is utterly fallacious. No democratic institution worthy of the name can exist if it contains representatives of a party backed by a private army which declares 'if the objectives of those who speak for us politically are not met, we reserve the right to achieve those aims by violent means and to retain the weaponry we currently possess to enable us to do so'.

Seamus Mallon and his party need to be reminded that the declared purpose of the agreement is to bring peace through democratic institutions, not to supplant or supersede the central principle of democracy itself. Paragraph ten of the Downing Street Declaration recognised this principle by stating that peace must involve a permanent end to violence and that only such parties as have shown that they abide by the democratic process are free to participate fully in democratic politics. In an attempt to circumvent this principle both governments, while repeatedly accepting that Sinn Fein and the IRA are 'inextricably linked', have at the same time permitted Sinn Fein to participate in negotiations and, perhaps, even to enter government on the basis that it is a distinct political party with an electoral mandate which entitles it to take part in the democratic process of government. Despite the total inconsistency of these two positions, this 'doublethink' has been stamped all over the government's dealings with Sinn Fein, not least in the terms of the agreement itself.

---

[1] *Irish Times*, 17 November 1998.

POLITICAL FRONTS AND PARAMILITARY ORGANISATIONS
By treating Sinn Fein within the agreement as a democratic party like all the others, the government has permitted it to shed its IRA connections and to falsely offer all sorts of commitments to exclusively peaceful means for the resolution of differences. As long as Sinn Fein is permitted to maintain the fiction that it is separate and distinct from the IRA, it has no more difficulty in giving such affirmations than it had when signing up to the Mitchell Principles.

By the same token, while Sinn Fein is placed on the same standing as other democratic parties it can happily affirm its commitment to the total disarmament of all paramilitary organisations. It simply has to claim that it is a political party with an electoral mandate and no weapons to decommission. In such circumstances, once recognised as a party similar to the others, it can happily agree 'to use such influence as it may have' to achieve the decommissioning of all weapons by those like the IRA who do have weapons, but from whom it claims to be separate.

The reality, as opposed to the total fiction encapsulated in the agreement, is that Sinn Fein, the PUP and the UDP are not at all the same as the other parties. These three are the political fronts for terrorist organisations responsible for thousands of deaths, countless hideous injuries and the mass destruction of property—organisations which to the present day are engaged in murder, shootings, brutal beatings, intimidation and criminality of every kind, from drug peddling to extortion and racketeering. Of these activities no one wants to know, for they are 'unhelpful to the peace process'. For our government to support an agreement which on the face of it treats such parties as normal and democratic, while the Prime Minister, Tony Blair, continues to claim that Sinn Fein is 'inextricably linked' with the IRA, is not only politically shameful, but morally wrong.

Almost every informed political scientist and experienced political journalist who has written about Sinn Fein and the IRA has stated, or inferred, that many of the highest offices in both are occupied by the same people. The Prime Minister and the Secretary of State, Mo Mowlam, as well as their security advisers, are well aware of these connections. Indeed, such information is the very basis for their repeated assertions that the two are inextricably linked; and inextricably means they can never be separated.

Despite all this, Sinn Fein was treated in the negotiations and the agreement as if it were merely a democratic party which could do no more than exert such influence as it might have. But by what means or criteria can the discharge of even that worthless obligation be proved? On any interpretation of the clause which imposes that duty, even if the IRA does not hand over a single bullet Sinn Fein would still retain all its rights under the agreement unless, by some miracle, there was acceptable proof that it had not used its influence.

Seamus Mallon thunders at the SDLP party conference that his party will throw Sinn Fein out of government if decommissioning is not delivered within two years. For a man who treats the agreement as written in stone this is mere empty rhetoric—and he knows it. Provided Sinn Fein complies with paragraph three of the decommissioning section of the Belfast Agreement, neither he nor anyone else can throw it out of government.

The UK/Unionist Party left the talks and supported the 'no' campaign on the basis that the decommissioning of weapons prior to inclusion in the democratic process was an inescapable inference of paragraph ten of the Joint Declaration, and was recognised as such by both governments at that time. However, both governments, the Ulster Unionists and the SDLP accepted a weakening of that principle during the talks by agreeing with Senator Mitchell's proposal that political negotiations towards an agreement and the process of decommissioning should proceed towards completion on parallel tracks. Although this political agreement was reached on 10 April 1998, the decommissioning train never left the station. Did Seamus Mallon or Dr Mowlam complain about this breach of a twin-track approach which they had both been repeating with nauseating regularity? They uttered not a word, yet Mr Mallon would have Unionists embark on another journey into Never Never Land on the basis of his valueless assurance.

CONCLUSION

The desire of the British government to obtain an agreement that would not only secure the mainland against attack, but bolster Mr Blair's relationship with an American president-under-fire dominated all other considerations, including those of democratic principle. The Ulster Unionist leadership allowed itself to be pressured into an agreement that perpetuated the fiction of the separateness of Sinn Fein and the IRA, an agreement that contained no clear and express terms that the IRA must decommission its armaments before Sinn Fein and the IRA's prisoners could benefit from the agreement's terms! By this failure they have permitted both Sinn Fein and the SDLP to use the terms of the agreement itself to subvert the principles of democratic government.

Decommissioning is a necessary requirement, because without it real democracy is dead.

What the agreement does do, as its forebear the Framework Document intended, is to provide political institutions for transporting Northern Ireland out of the United Kingdom and into the Republic of Ireland. Sinn Fein's view of the agreement as a transitional phase has been used to persuade the IRA to maintain what passes for a ceasefire. Once the Ulster Unionists begin to recognise where the agreement is taking them, they will protest and even try to inhibit progress in that direction. But one factor will ensure that the process continues to its planned destination: the capacity of the IRA to threaten the City of London and the British economy. And that is the real reason why there will never be any effective decommissioning by the IRA until Sinn Fein's political objective of Irish unity is achieved.

Twenty-four

Democracy and Terror[1]

INTRODUCTION

Mr Speaker Designate, I rise to propose the motion standing in my name on behalf of the UK/Unionist Party. I hope that the motion will command support from every democrat in this Assembly, regardless of party. The Assembly aspires to create democratic institutions of government for the benefit of every citizen, regardless of creed or political loyalties. No democratic institution worthy of the name can exist if it contains the political representatives of an unlawfully armed organisation which is committed to bringing about change by either the use or threat of acts of terrorism. An organisation which states that if the aims of those who speak for it politically, and with whom it is inextricably linked, are not met it reserves the right to achieve those aims by the use of violence, and to retain the weapons it currently possesses to make that threat good, is inherently undemocratic.

The Belfast Agreement has the avowed purpose of bringing peace through democratic institutions of government and is alleged to contain the recognition of the principle that any change in Northern Ireland's constitutional position within the United Kingdom can be brought about only with the consent of the majority. Sinn Fein/IRA have never subscribed to these principles, however. What is more important is that no agreement can set aside the fundamental principles of democratic procedure. No agreement can override or supersede the central principles of democracy itself. Nor can any political party within a democracy claim that it has an electoral mandate to substitute violence for peaceful persuasion and threaten democratic institutions with violence if its demands are not met. There is no historical record of a minority grouping ceasing to use violence for political ends before its objectives have been achieved or the lawful forces of democratic government have defeated it. The IRA will be no exception.

ABANDONING DEMOCRATIC PRINCIPLES

At the very beginning of the peace process the fundamental principles of the democratic process were emphasised. It was made clear that the

---

[1]Remarks introducing a motion into the Northern Ireland Assembly on 15 December 1998 calling on the Assembly to exclude any political party inextricably linked with a terrorist organisation still retaining arms. The resolution received the unanimous support of the pro-Union parties in the Assembly, but did not pass because the SDLP failed to give it the cross-community support it required under the Assembly's rules of procedure.

requirements for participation were not the demands of parties, or conditions imposed by them, but were the essential demands of democracy itself. To use or threaten to use violence are violations of democracy, and a determination to retain the weapons and means of violence constitutes a threat in itself.

The Downing Street Declaration of 15 December 1993 made it clear that a permanent end to the use of, or support for, paramilitary violence, an established commitment to exclusively peaceful methods and adherence to the democratic process were the criteria necessary to establish entitlement to participate in democratic politics and enter into dialogue. Soon after the declaration was announced, Dick Spring, the Foreign Minister of Ireland, told Dail Eireann what his government's understanding was: 'We are talking about the handing up of arms and are insisting that it would not simply be a temporary cessation to see what the political process had to offer. There can no equivocation in relation to the determination of both governments in this regard.' In truth, from that moment the history of both governments on this issue has been exactly the opposite. Far from witnessing unequivocal determination, it has been one of temporising, vacillation and weakness. Successive positions have been taken up only be resiled from in the face of threat. The IRA, like Hitler, must have been astonished at the weakness of its adversaries.

On 1 June 1994, again in the Dail, Mr. Spring repeated: 'There is little point in bringing people into political dialogue if they are doing so on the basis of giving it a try and, if it does not work, returning to the bomb and the bullet.' But that is exactly what Assemblyman Francie Molloy told a Sinn Fein audience they would do if the political process did not yield the required results: Sinn Fein/IRA 'would go back to doing what they do best'. In order to do so, they must necessarily retain their weapons and their semtex. It is that threat, and the capacity to make the threat good, that has produced in successive British governments a craven policy of appeasement, of surrender to every threat of renewed mainland violence, of concession to every fresh and increasing demand from a criminal conspiracy.

*   *   *

Throughout the talks, the government's line was one of a twin-track policy of decommissioning in parallel with political progress towards an agreement. Who did not hear this twin-track policy being repeated with nauseating regularity by the Secretary of State, Dr Mowlam? During the talks not a single bullet or ounce of semtex was delivered. An agreement was reached at the end of those talks on 10 April 1998. The talks train left the station and reached its destination, but the decommissioning train never left at all. Since 10 April 1998 not one single bullet has been handed up nor, according to the IRA, will one ever be handed over until their objective of a united Irish socialist republic is achieved.

At every point Unionists who trusted the government were deceived by promises and pledges never intended to be fulfilled. How has the principle been observed that only those abiding by the democratic process would be free, not just to participate in democratic politics, but to participate as ministers in government? How could the Prime Minister and the Secretary of State contemplate having as ministers in government members of a party which they both claim is inextricably linked not only with an armed terrorist organisation, but one that publicly declares its intention to remain armed until its political objectives are achieved?

FACT AND FICTION

The proposal to place Sinn Fein in government under these circumstances is so outrageous and does such violence to the principles of democracy as to make it only possible if the people have been brainwashed into oblivion. Is there anyone with the remotest interest in political life who does not know that the highest offices in both Sinn Fein and the IRA are occupied by the same people? They are inextricably linked; they are welded together.

While General Pinochet is threatened with extradition, while Saddam Hussein is threatened with extinction, Mr Adams and Mr McGuinness are welcomed through the front door of Number Ten Downing Street. Why? Because they, unlike Pinochet and Hussein, have the capacity to threaten the financial heart of the City of London with destruction. For this reason, while declaring Sinn Fein and the IRA to be inextricably linked, Sinn Fein was accepted in the Belfast Agreement to be separate and distinct from the IRA. This fiction enabled Sinn Fein to confirm a commitment to the total disarmament of all paramilitary organisations—and the same fiction enabled it to sign up to the Mitchell Principles.

The reality, as opposed to the fiction, is that neither Sinn Fein fronting the IRA nor the PUP fronting loyalist terrorists have any connection with democracy or its principles. They are the political masks for organisations who have murdered, mutilated and destroyed; organisations which, to the present day, are engaged in murder, shootings, beatings, intimidation, forced exile and every form of criminality. The ceasefire is a macabre fraud. Since the beginning of

1998 nearly 500 reported acts or threats of violence, from murder to forced exile, have been recorded by FAIT and authenticated by the RUC. Brutal beatings and shootings are a daily occurrence. From 1-25 November the following occurred:

IRA Outrages	Loyalist Outrages
Exiles 9	Exiles 9
Intimidations 67	Intimidations 48
Shootings 2	Shootings 5
Beatings 7	Beatings 7
TOTAL 85	TOTAL 69

The Secretary of State, Dr Mowlam, and the Security Minister, Adam Ingram, simply ignore these acts as being unhelpful to the peace process. It is no excuse to say, as the Secretary of State responded to me in Parliament, there is no evidence against the perpetrators. Of course there is no evidence, because those who are beaten are threatened with murder, and those who are exiled are threatened with death if they remain. But these fully authenticated brutalities are not simply the work of individual perpetrators. The indictment is not against individuals; the indictment is lodged against the organisations and their political parties who front them and mask them. These fully authenticated brutalities are being carried out in areas which the police, indeed the Chief Constable of the RUC, Sir Ronnie Flanagan, admit are dominated by paramilitary groups—the IRA and the UVF—that are fronted by parties in this Assembly.

CONCLUSION

Let me finish by saying this: no mandate, no agreement, no government, no parties can supersede or set aside the fundamental and immutable principles of democracy, morality and justice. I may have very different political aims and objectives from the SDLP and from others in the Assembly. However, I share with the SDLP and most of the other parties here a belief in democracy. Violence has no part to play in a political party. A party that claims to be democratic cannot be inextricably linked with terror, murder, mutilation and death.

There is a way forward—and I say this without malice or political gain, but as a democrat. It will entail every party, both nationalist and Unionist, recognising that the common bonds of democracy are infinitely preferable in the long run to the bonds of an

Irish nationalism that yokes people to a party inextricably linked with the forces of republican terror. I call upon all democrats, all people of good will, all people who are revolted by political violence and terror, to join with me, regardless of party, to support this motion.

X

DEFENDING DEMOCRACY, SUSTAINING THE UNION

Twenty-five

Defending Democracy, Sustaining the Union[1]

INTRODUCTION

Surveying the political landscape in early 1999, just over a year since the UK/Unionist Party's last conference, it becomes clear that the cause of the Union has suffered a number of serious misfortunes, and most of them have been self-inflicted by those claiming to be Unionists. The divisions within Unionism, including those within our own party, have contributed more to the ongoing success of Irish republicanism than its own efforts. The British government, by the use of its purse and its patronage, as well as a relentless propaganda machine, has sown discord and difference amongst Unionists.

THE PRINCIPLES OF GOVERNMENT POLICY

To fully appreciate the current political situation, and to forecast where it could lead us, it is necessary to understand certain fundamental principles of government policy. For starters, the Belfast Agreement, crafted and controlled by the British government, is not designed primarily to achieve a peaceful and stable Northern Ireland, for on that basis it is a manifest failure. The Agreement's real purposes are to further the government's policy of disengagement from Northern Ireland and to protect the lives and property of its 'first class' British citizens on the mainland. It represents the terms of a conflict resolution treaty between Sinn Fein/IRA and Britain. Under the Agreement's real agenda, Sinn Fein/IRA are offered the terms for transitional arrangements to a united Ireland in return for their agreement not to kill security personnel, not to endanger the lives of British citizens on the mainland and to refrain from bombing mainland economic targets. In essence, all the other parties to the Agreement are merely stage props to be moved about as required to suit the current scene.

Nothing establishes the truth of this analysis more clearly than the government's attitude to the shootings, beatings, intimidation, exiling and criminality which are presently destroying the social infrastructure of this province. The Chief Constable of the Royal Ulster Constabulary, Sir Ronnie Flanagan, has unequivocally stated that these activities are largely the work of paramilitary organisations represented by parties that assented to the Belfast Agreement—including Sinn Fein and the Progressive Unionist Party—have members in the Northern Ireland Assembly and shortly hope to have ministers in government. Sir

---

[1] Address to the UK/Unionist Party Annual Conference, Belfast, 6 February 1999.

Flanagan has confirmed that these barbarities are centrally controlled and authorised by the IRA and the UVF. These organisations are known to be engaged in the profits of drug pushing and other crimes. The Chief Constable declares that this form of terrorist violence is being used to effect social control and to create a law enforcement vacuum which terrorists will then claim to fill with 'community policing' and 'restorative justice'.

POLITICAL DISHONESTY
Both Mo Mowlam, the Secretary of State, and Tony Blair, the Prime Minister, dishonestly avoid the political issue by suggesting that it is a legal one which requires evidence to be produced against individual criminals upon which they may be convicted. I repeat the word 'dishonest' for two reasons. First, because they know that such is the terror inspired by the people committing these crimes that it is almost impossible to get the victims to denounce them in a court of law. Second, because the crimes are being committed for political reasons by groups that the Chief Constable has identified, and the sanctions which ought to be applied are political in nature and directed not to individuals, but to groups. These sanctions have to be imposed by the Secretary of State and not the courts. What are the sanctions which the Secretary of State could impose, and why does she not do so? It is clear that the Secretary of State, upon any reasonable basis, should conclude that the shootings and beatings which are now a daily occurrence are a breach of the paramilitary ceasefires as understood by the overwhelming majority of those who voted 'yes'—primarily on the basis of Mr Blair's handwritten pledges—in the referendum on the Belfast Agreement. An end to these barbarities was one of the requirements of the Mitchell Principles, which both Sinn Fein and the PUP supposedly signed up to. These activities are also a breach of the Belfast Agreement itself. The first page of the Agreement contains a Declaration of Support. Paragraph four requires the participants, who included Sinn Fein and the PUP, to affirm not only their total and absolute commitment to exclusively democratic and peaceful means, but their opposition to any use, or threat, of force by others for any political purpose, whether with regard to the Agreement or otherwise. These terms are, broadly speaking, repeated in the legislation relating to the release of prisoners.

COURAGE AND COWARDICE
No less a person that the Right Reverend Monsignor Dennis Faul, in a recent letter to the *Irish Times*, states that 'IRA beatings and expulsions

have political purposes'. Father Faul lists these political purposes as being to exclude the RUC and replace them, or any new force, with none other than themselves; to intimidate the community; to prevent the return of normality and community life; and to stifle cross-community based solutions to problems across Northern Ireland.

The Secretary of State's response, and that of the Security Minister, Adam Ingram, is that viewed in the round this tidal wave of politically motivated criminality does not amount to a breach of the ceasefires. In the early part of last year, however, both Sinn Fein and the PUP were temporarily excluded from the talks process, because their paramilitary associates had breached the ceasefires by killing, respectively, Protestants and Catholics. It now seems that republicans may kill, maim and mutilate any number of Catholics, as can Loyalists in relation to Protestants, but such activities do not amount to a breach of the ceasefires. What sort of morality is this? What sort of peace is this? What sort of democracy is this? What sort of worthwhile society can be built upon conduct such as this?

Dr Mowlam should declare that the present barbarities are breaches of the ceasefires and, on the basis of the Chief Constable's advice and intelligence, exclude both Sinn Fein and the PUP from the democratic process, because they are clearly in breach of both the Mitchell principles and the terms of the Agreement itself. She should also determine that because the IRA and its loyalist counterparts have broken the Agreement, no further prisoner releases will be allowed. No less a person than Lord Mayhew, a former Secretary of State for Northern Ireland, has written in the *Daily Telegraph* to this effect. He brings to his statement both political and legal authority. Political, because for five years he was Secretary of State for Northern Ireland, and legal, because he was formerly the Attorney General. Dr Mowlam, however, will do none of these things, because the destruction of Northern Ireland's social and community infrastructure is of far less importance than the security of mainland citizens and the City of London. To impose any such sanctions might cause the IRA to go back to bombing the mainland, and, therefore, Sinn Fein/IRA must be appeased at all costs. The Prime Minister himself has openly stated this in the House of Commons when he suggested that to impose any restrictions on the release of prisoners might bring the peace process to an end. Since the object of the process was never to bring peace to Northern Ireland, but to ensure the safety of the mainland, the end of a process designed to protect the mainland must never be allowed to happen.

*   *   *

In truth, the British government is actually blackmailing its own law-abiding citizens by declaring that if such citizens do not agree to a policy of appeasing those who are terrorising them, such citizens will once again bring the full weight of terrorist violence down upon their heads. The government ignores its primary duty to its own citizens, namely, protecting their lives and property, and says to them that unless they agree to the demands of their tormentors being met, the government cannot protect them.

The government has forgotten that decommissioning was originally insisted upon as a necessary prerequisite for democratic dialogue. It accepted that a primary demand of democracy was that in order to be included in that process the use of violence and terror had to be abandoned. Now the government is saying to its law-abiding citizens that they must not insist upon weapons of violence and the threat of violence being decommissioned, because if they do there will be a return to violence, the very thing that decommissioning was required to prevent.

THE ULSTER UNIONIST PARTY AND DECOMMISSIONING

On the issue of decommissioning, like almost everything else, the leadership of the Ulster Unionist Party has been utterly weak. It has resiled from virtually every position it has taken up. David Trimble's record is one of capitulation after capitulation. Very soon he will have absolutely no cards left and will be forced to accept unconditional surrender.

On 7 June 1996, three days before the negotiations began, he announced in the *Belfast Telegraph* that 'if decommissioning does not begin right away, I will stop the talks'. One year later, in June 1997, he told the *News Letter* that decommissioning could be parked. In September 1997 he agreed to Sinn Fein entering the talks without any agreement to decommissioning occurring during the course of them. Despite the fact that no decommissioning did take place during that period, on 10 April 1998 he signed up to the Belfast Agreement, with the votes of the PUP and the Ulster Democratic Party assisting him in making up the majority of the Unionist representatives.

David Trimble signed up to that Agreement without a single bullet or an ounce of semtex being handed over. Nor did this law lecturer insist upon any specific term that would have barred Sinn Fein from executive positions in government unless decommissioning had actually commenced and a schedule for its completion agreed. On the other hand,

Sinn Fein, like all the other participants, were merely required to use any 'influence' they might have to achieve decommissioning within two years. No sanctions of any kind were imposed upon participants known to be inextricably linked with armed terrorist groups. It was clear to everyone that had David Trimble insisted on such a term, Sinn Fein would simply not have signed up. Thus circumstances revealed the very core of British policy. The British government was not concerned that decommissioning was necessary to secure the restoration of peace and stability to Northern Ireland. Its primary concern was getting an agreement that Sinn Fein/IRA would sign up to which would prevent them returning to mainland bombing.

Absolutely no one but David Trimble and his close political cronies believes that the Agreement imposes any legal requirement upon Sinn Fein. David Trimble cannot afford to accept that this is the case, because it would expose his pathetic incompetence as a negotiator. He, therefore, clings to an untenable requirement for decommissioning within the Agreement, when a far greater and more fundamental argument is available to him, namely, that decommissioning is a fundamental demand of democracy itself.

THE BETRAYAL OF DEMOCRACY

The Belfast Agreement was, and is, a disaster for the pro-Union people and for democracy. The leader of the Ulster Unionist Party allowed himself to be coerced into an Agreement that served the interests of Irish republicanism and mainland Britain. But, if this negotiating disaster is bad, the Ulster Unionist Party's present policy is even worse.

The Ulster Unionist leadership, by endorsing the Belfast Agreement, accepted the release of the most infamous criminals. It agreed to the representatives of violent republicanism being in government. It conceded the right of the Irish government to have a share in the governance of Northern Ireland. It consented to the reform of a criminal justice system necessary to combat terrorism. It acquiesced in the proposed reform of the RUC to placate those terrorists and criminals whom that force had given lives and limbs to apprehend. It allowed Sinn Fein/IRA the legal, though not the moral, democratic right to demand the fulfilment of every concession before any actual decommissioning of their weapons was required.

On 18 January of this year, the Ulster Unionist Assembly Party, with one notable and courageous exception, voted to approve a report which, on 15 February, will become, by their vote, a 'determination' as required by the 1998 Northern Ireland Act. Mr Trimble has given a pledge to Mr Mallon that all the contents of the report of 18 January will be embodied in the determination which his party will endorse on February 15. This gives the Secretary of State time to put in place all the necessary machinery and arrangements for putting Sinn Fein/IRA into government. After 15 February, the Secretary of State will be able to set the D'Hondt machinery in motion, and Sinn Fein will be placed in shadow ministries. Mr Trimble has, in fact, agreed that there will be ten ministries. He has allocated the functions to be attributed to each of those ten ministries. He is aware that when the machinery for allocating the ministers to those Ministries is put in place, Sinn Fein will have two.

At that stage, having surrendered almost every negotiating card to his nationalist opponents, and given them almost everything they have demanded, the Ulster Unionists are then going to make complete and utter fools of themselves by refusing to participate in the Executive until the IRA decommissions. Sinn Fein/IRA will clap their hands at the prospect of Trimble's abstentionism. Should the Assembly flop at that point, they will have achieved everything they wanted in this phase of their transitional programme. The North-South Council of Ministers will continue in place, enshrined in treaty, as will the cross-border bodies. The Ulster Unionists, having consented to both the ministries and the cross-border bodies prior to the actual transfer of power, will be in no position to withdraw their consent. If they themselves do not occupy the positions allotted to them, the government may provide for alternative arrangements.

*   *   *

A more likely scenario is that when Mr Trimble is brought under pressure he will, once again, capitulate. However, as in the past he will have to be provided with a fig leaf to cover his abandonment of almost the last possible position on decommissioning. John Hume is already pointing the way, as is Seamus Mallon, by describing the role of General De Chastelain as pivotal. Efforts will be made to persuade the General to propose a time table for decommissioning to commence at some date after Sinn Fein are actually seated in the Executive. Initially, Sinn Fein/IRA will not refuse to consider this possibility, and protracted negotiations will ensure that no decommissioning has, in fact, taken place before September 1999, when the Patten Commission reports on the reform of the RUC. At that point, the IRA will declare themselves dissatisfied unless the RUC has been disarmed or, to use its term, demilitarised. As a result, no decommissioning will have taken place, but, by then Sinn Fein will have held ministerial posts for some months and, once again, the Unionist leadership will be pressurised to continue as long as Mo Mowlam's brand of ceasefire is being observed, i.e., the British mainland is not being bombed.

On 15 February next, a crucial vote will take place in the Assembly. It is a vote to formally approve what David Trimble has already pledged his party to accept and it will pass. The Secretary of State will then be in a position to operate the mechanism for allotting the government ministries and Sinn Fein will become entitled to two. The cross-border bodies with all-Ireland executive powers will be put in place and the North-South Ministerial Council established. The principle that the government of the Irish Republic has a right to interfere in the governance and administration of Northern Ireland will have become a reality. The defence of the Union will become increasingly difficult, and the IRA will remain fully armed. One Sinn Fein/IRA objective, however, will still remain unfulfilled: the reform of the Royal Ulster Constabulary.

THE ROYAL ULSTER CONSTABULARY

No words of mine can do justice to the debt which the entire community of Northern Ireland owes to the Royal Ulster Constabulary. That police force has been the bulwark against a total descent into chaos and anarchy. That it is the primary obstacle to the success of terrorism in its attempt to destroy democracy is only too well recognised by the terrorists themselves. If the British government, however, is to ensure that Sinn Fein/IRA do not return to mainland bombing, it may have to sacrifice the RUC in order to placate the terrorists. The government realises that this may be a bridge too far for Unionists and will attempt to persuade Sinn Fein that, like the deal on Irish unity, the reform of the RUC must be a 'transitional phase'. The RUC may, therefore, not face immediate execution, but only receive, at this time, wounds that will ultimately prove fatal. One thing is clear: there is little possibility of any effective decommissioning until there is an understood agenda between Sinn Fein/IRA and the British government for the fatal weakening of the RUC. It must be a central objective of all Unionist parties, and their policies, to ensure that this does not happen. Without the RUC to protect the entire community, opposition to terrorism and its agenda for government will be impossible.

THE ROLE OF THE UK/UNIONIST PARTY

What, you are entitled to ask, is the purpose and future of the UK/Unionist Party in these circumstances? What can one small David do against the Goliaths of government and the large parties? We can serve perhaps the most important task of continuing to be the guide, guardian and conscience of the ordinary pro-Union people, whatever their party. We can continue to provide the truth and insight about the conduct, objectives and interests of those who would otherwise deceive and mislead. We can ensure that the ideas, analyses and principles of democracy and the rule of law are used to confront those who would cast them aside. We can demonstrate that support for the cause of the Union can be effectively made without resort to bigotry or sectarianism. We can advocate the benefits of a pluralist society that protects the interests and equality of minorities while respecting the democratic right of a majority to determine the national and political identity of the state in which they constitute that majority. We can, in summary, provide the yeast for the bread of democratic principles upon which the entire community may be nourished.

This party has influenced the political life of Northern Ireland out of all proportion to its size, though that is growing on a daily basis. Increasingly, many of those who voted 'yes' in the referendum are stating that they were deceived and the voice of the UK/Unionist Party was the one to which they should have listened.

Oliver Wendell Holmes, an American Supreme Court Judge and one of the world's greatest jurists, once said that real power lay in the command of ideas. In that sense, this small party is a powerful party with an influence on events out of all proportion to its numbers. Let me give but two examples. In November 1998, the *Irish Times* published an article which stated that 'without decommissioning democracy is dead'. It claimed that decommissioning is a demand not of the Belfast Agreement, but of democracy itself. Not only is Mr Trimble now using that idea, but the government of the Republic now realises that in the North-South Ministerial Council its Ministers may be required to sit down with Sinn Fein Ministers who are inextricably linked with the organisation that took the life of Garda Gerry McCabe and which may, ultimately, threaten its own democratic institutions.

In January of this year, both the *Belfast Telegraph* and the *Irish Times* printed an article relating to the beatings, murders, exiles and criminal activities of those organisations represented by Sinn Fein and the PUP in the Northern Ireland Assembly. The UK/Unionist Party believes that the article, and the concepts and ideas it contained, detonated the tidal wave of condemnation which is presently engulfing the Secretary of State and the Prime Minister and which has exposed the immorality of the government's present policies. Last Sunday, the *Irish Independent* published the results of an opinion poll which showed that over 80% of those who responded considered that these barbarities constituted a breach of the ceasefire, and some 60% thought that decommissioning was a necessary requirement to Sinn Fein being seated in government.

* * *

The UK/Unionist Party has a pivotal and powerful role to play in alerting all decent people to the realities of the peace process, the Belfast Agreement and the sort of future for the entire community that they will entail. This party, more than any other, has the task of exposing the truth of what is being suppressed by an unthinking and government-controlled media. Ideas take time to percolate down into the minds of ordinary people whose lives are filled with the necessities of earning a living and raising their children. But the task of alerting them to the future in which those children will live is the real business and purpose of this party.

Whatever abilities I have been granted will be used in the service of our people, but unless I enjoy the confidence, trust and support of those within this party, such abilities will not alone ensure success. The function of a leader is to lead, to take decisions after canvassing opinion. The ultimate exercise of judgement must be his until such time as the party should choose otherwise. I believe that I have not only your trust and support, but also your affection and that, acting together and in harmony, we will ensure that truth and integrity will win the day.

Twenty-six

Placating Terror Will Cost Dearly[1]

INTRODUCTION

This writer may currently stand alone in terms of Assembly representation, but he enjoys the overwhelming support of his party and of many thousands throughout Northern Ireland who respect truth and political integrity. On the day when his former Assembly colleagues resigned to form a sixth Unionist party, and further factionalise pro-Union support, he had a lengthy consultation with the leaders of the anti-terrorist organisation Families Against Intimidation and Terror (FAIT). Their revelations made his concerns pale into relative unimportance, for they provided a grim and horrendous future for the people of Northern Ireland in the new Millennium.

Many decent and law abiding people voted 'yes' in the May 1998 referendum, not only on the basis of the Prime Minister Blair's pledges, but in the sincere belief that it would bring not only peace and social stability, but secure a future for their children and grandchildren. These were worthy and honourable aspirations and hopes, with which few would quarrel. Such people, in their desire for these objectives, were willing to swallow many things they found abhorrent. They accepted the early release of those convicted of the worst crimes against humanity. They were willing to abide the political representatives of terrorist organisations in government, in the belief that these people would abandon murder and terror in exchange for a commitment to exclusively peaceful and democratic means. They acknowledged that in such changed circumstances a reduction in security measures and a reform of the RUC might be justified. All of this they were prepared to tolerate in exchange for a peaceful and secure future for their children.

A MACABRE NIGHTMARE

What this writer's consultation with FAIT leaders confirmed was that this utopian future was fast turning into a macabre nightmare which the government, in pursuit of its own political agenda, was either ignoring or, worse, suppressing. While the newspapers and the media were flooding the electorate with largely unfounded prospects for the future, the whole social sub-structure of Northern Ireland was being systematically destroyed in an increasing tide of criminality, drug culture and violence.

---

[1]*Belfast Telegraph*, 11 January 1999; *Irish Times*, 12 January 1999.

From a government perspective, the entire peace process depended upon persuading terrorist groups to desist from violence. To obtain this goal, it was necessary not only to meet their political demands, but to refrain from antagonising them. In this, the government has been partially successful in that the current ceasefire has obtained a respite in the killing of security force personnel and the bombing, by some groups, of economic targets. The price to be paid for peace at this level was to tolerate the activity of terrorists in the disadvantaged areas which, under the relaxed security policy, they now dominate. Parties and the terrorist groups they represent now assumed social and political control over areas of Northern Ireland where the rule of law ceased to operate. This control is enforced with a callous brutality, the results of which are now a daily occurrence. The FAIT statistics, authenticated from official agencies, confirm that in 1998 more incidents of beatings, shootings, intimidations and exiles occurred than at any time in the last thirty years. The actual cost of this violence is estimated at ten million pounds, yet this is only the tip of the real cost. As a direct consequence of this breakdown of the rule of law in such areas, criminality of a non-political kind has flourished. This is particularly evident in the vast increase in drug trafficking and drug-related crime. Within the terrorist organisations there are many more criminals than political idealists, and, in many cases, these groups are now little more than mafia families whose ethos and methods they share.

The IRA, UVF and the UDA are all now main players in the trafficking and profits of drugs. The IRA operates less directly than the others. Drug dealers are licensed by them upon payment of a percentage. Direct Action Against Drugs (DAAD), which has been responsible for the murder of known drug dealers, is the IRA's enforcement agency against those who do not pay or who flout the IRA's authority, like the late Michael Mooney. The UDA, which largely controls drugs in loyalist areas such as Belfast, Ballymena, Antrim and Bangor, is much more directly involved. According to the *Sunday Times*, Johnny Adair, while still in the Maze Prison, is currently in receipt of £1,500 per week. The Mafia comparisons are startling, and the money involved runs into millions of pounds. Many of the deaths and mutilations are the product of gang warfare by enforcers, whose relation to political activity is minimal. Like many of the cities in the United States, the disadvantaged areas are becoming uncontrollable by the forces of law and order, whose authority is put in question on largely fabricated political grounds.

INTO A GLASS DARKLY

But what of the future for the children and grandchildren of the 'yes' voters? Many such voters, for the present, live in residential areas which the RUC still police, but what of the future in the Millennium? The growth industry will be that of security devices and secure private developments with patrol arrangements. The well-off may be able to retreat behind fences, but drug-related crime will hit new levels. Middle class children will have to emerge from schools, discos and concerts, and there the peddlers and the traffickers will be waiting.

The present policies of the government require a relaxed attitude towards terrorist crime. Mo Mowlam and Adam Ingram show absolutely no inclination to confront those responsible for these beatings and shootings or to acknowledge that these occurrences are breaches of the ceasefires, which would require the expulsion of those parties, like Sinn Fein and the PUP who, on Mo Mowlam's own admission are inextricably linked to the perpetrators.

The Prime Minister and the Secretary of State are not the only people who fail adequately to acknowledge these connections, for the same accusation can be laid at the door of the great, the good and the well-off. Mrs Kearney, the mother of Andrew Kearney, one of the IRA's recent victims, may pray by her lighted candle, knowing who brutally murdered her son, but the requirements of a morally bankrupt government, and policy, will ensure that she and the thousands like her will be ignored. In the Millennium, the great, the good and the well-off may not need to enquire for whom the bell tolls in the ghettos, for by then it may also be tolling for both them and their children.

Twenty-seven

The Royal Ulster Constabulary and the Future of Democracy[1]

THE POLITICAL CONTEXT OF THE RUC

The UK/Unionist Party, while a relatively small political grouping, is not wholly without influence on public opinion. This submission to the Independent Commission on Policing in Northern Ireland (the Patten Commission) is thus broadly directed at the possible political and social consequences of any proposed reform of the Royal Ulster Constabulary.[2] Many of the difficulties which the Independent Commission is required to resolve are the legacy of the past, but the ideologies and aspirations which have created them are alive and relevant in the present. The resolve of the pro-Union majority to remain within the United Kingdom, and the aspiration of the minority nationalist community to incorporate Northern Ireland within a united Ireland, represent the basis of the conflict which engenders the problems of policing.

The perception of the RUC as a force, or service, dedicated to the preservation of the Union is central to its unacceptability by the nationalist community. This view manifests itself most acutely in the form of republican political terrorism, which has been responsible for the murder of some 300 police officers and the infliction of the most serious personal injury upon thousands of others. In its benign form, as reflected in the attitude of constitutional nationalists, this interpretation amounts to an ongoing, and often unjustified, criticism of the RUC and an unwillingness to give it any demonstrable public support. The common basis for these attitudes is the shared aspiration for Irish unity and an end to partition. Both groups see the RUC, albeit in different degrees, as one of the main obstacles to their common political goal.

Unionists view the political terrorism of Sinn Fein/IRA as the cutting edge for the rapid advancement of nationalist objectives. IRA strategy has long been devoted to rendering any form of internal settlement within the United Kingdom impossible, thus ensuring that any political settlement is channelled towards a united Ireland solution. Mainland bombing campaigns, and the determination to maintain the capacity for their renewal, are seen as vital to maintaining this political direction. The concept of no internal settlement has been broadly supported by non-violent nationalists, and the formation of a pan-

---

[1]UK/Unionist Party Submission to the Independent Commission on Policing in Northern Ireland (Patten Commission), October, 1998.

[2] See Appendix.

nationalist front to maintain political momentum is central to the so-called peace process.

Few objective commentators would deny that since 1988 movement in this direction has been the policy of successive British governments, and that the Downing Street Declaration, the Framework Documents, the Stormont negotiations and the Belfast Agreement are milestones en route to British disengagement from Northern Ireland. As this becomes clearer to the Unionist majority, its attitude to a police force perceived as being utilised for the execution of such a policy may change. Despite the 71% 'yes' vote in favour of the Belfast Agreement in the May 1998 referendum, which was achieved by massive media manipulation and misinformation, there is now an increasing appreciation among Unionists that they were misled. The consequences of this political misrepresentation in terms of early prisoner releases, and the seating of Sinn Fein ministers in government while the IRA remains fully armed, are now surfacing, and the terms of the Commission's report on the reform of the RUC may prove the most potentially explosive of them all.

Sinn Fein/IRA's call for 'the root and branch destruction of the RUC', and their assertion that anything less will cause the Belfast Agreement to fail, illustrates their determination to remove, or fatally demoralise, the single organisation which can frustrate the triumph of terror. Their retention of the capacity for a renewal of mainland terror is viewed by them as the main leverage in pushing the British government in that direction, illustrating but one aspect of the importance of decommissioning, in general, and its particular relevance to the issue of future policing arrangements. The SDLP, ever conscious of the nationalist electorate, calls more softly for 'radical reform of the RUC'. The Unionist community views both with a mixture of anger and anxiety. The paradox of those fronting or benefiting from terrorism attempting to dictate the terms for the reform of those who have given their lives protecting society from it does not escape them.

*   *   *

The consent principle, which Sinn Fein has never accepted, allegedly ensures that Northern Ireland will remain part of the United Kingdom until a majority decides otherwise, but it applies only to the transfer of *de jure* sovereignty. The Belfast Agreement provides for the creation of institutions of government that will progress towards a functionally and factually united Ireland. The result of such a *de facto* united Ireland will render consent to the transfer of sovereignty either unnecessary or inevitable. To ensure that no obstruction is offered to this progression, and to accelerate it, if necessary, Sinn Fein/IRA require two things. First, the retention of their terrorist capacity either to use or to gain leverage by the threat of its use; and, second, the demoralisation of the RUC and its neutralisation as an effective anti-terrorist force. The latter objective will, of course, greatly enhance the application of the first.

It is the view of this party that any fundamental reform of the RUC in its anti-terrorist role can only take place against a background of full and effective decommissioning of all terrorist weapons and the dismantling of the terrorist organisations that have used them. That a democratic state should take any steps which would lessen the morale or operational effectiveness of anti-terrorist arrangements, while terrorist organisations retain theirs, is unthinkable—unless the hidden political agenda is, in fact, to meet in some form the political aims for which the violence was being used. In this regard, it should be noted that Sinn Fein/IRA view the Belfast Agreement as being nothing more than a 'transitional phase'. One Sinn Fein Assembly member is on record as stating that should the process fail to deliver the party's objectives, which include the root and branch destruction of the RUC, then 'the IRA will go back to doing what it does best'. The essential content of Mr Adams' statement after the Omagh outrage was that it would be the last, provided that the Agreement delivered, without obstruction, Sinn Fein's objectives. History does not record any terrorist organisation ceasing its activities until its goals were attained or it was effectively suppressed by the forces of democracy. At every point in the history of the present process, when resistance has been offered to the demands of Sinn Fein/IRA it has been resolved in their favour after they have returned to violence.

THE HISTORIC ROLE OF THE RUC

Violence as a means of achieving political goals has been endemic in Ireland for centuries. Throughout most of the nineteenth and twentieth centuries this violence has largely focused on the constitutional relationship of Ireland and Great Britain. Insofar as the United Kingdom was the sovereign power, and its policy was to keep Ireland within that Kingdom, the state was constantly being called upon to oppose those who, by violence, sought to remove Ireland from it. In order to combat political violence, the British government has utilised the police in a paramilitary role as well as expecting it, simultaneously, to discharge its normal functions in dealing with non-political crime. This dual responsibility has been the source of most of the RUC's problems in terms of acceptability by the nationalist community. The fact that the majority community wished to remain within the United Kingdom encouraged recruitment from it and fixed the RUC with the image of being both a Protestant and Unionist force. So long as the British government was determined to maintain the Union, and the RUC, in opposing republican violence, was seen to be defending it, the force continued to receive the unqualified support of the pro-Union majority. While this situation prevails, the RUC will never obtain the approval or acceptance of nationalists. This basic principle should inform the Commission's approach to reform. No amount of reform relating to symbols, names, balanced recruitment or complaints procedures will alter nationalist attitudes to the police force while it retains paramilitary functions for the suppression of political terrorism directed towards the achievement of nationalist goals. Exactly the same strategy as has been adopted to remove all political options other than Irish unity will be utilised by Sinn Fein. Sinn Fein will simply not allow any solution but their root and branch formula to work. The Commission must, therefore, exercise extreme caution in advising and recommending reforms which will prove totally ineffective in obtaining nationalist acceptance, but will inflame the anxieties of the Unionist community and demoralise the RUC.

*   *   *

While no two periods of history are entirely comparable, the Commission may obtain some valuable insights from an examination of the policies and operations of Sinn Fein/IRA towards policing in the period 1918-21. In 1920 two police forces operated in Ireland: the Royal Irish Constabulary and the Dublin Metropolitan Police. The latter, numbering some 1,100, were unarmed and operated on similar lines to comparable mainland urban police. The Royal Irish Constabulary numbered some 10,000 and were equipped with sidearms and rifles. Their organisation was paramilitary and had no counterpart in Great Britain. They, nevertheless, combined the roles—much like the RUC— of normal policing and a gendarmarie responsible for containing political and related outbreaks of violence. Its Inspector General was a Catholic, the proportion of officers was 60% Protestant to 40% Catholic and the rank and file was 70% Catholic to 30% Protestant.

By 1920 the Dublin Metropolitan Police had become totally demoralised and ineffective. Unarmed and dispersed all over Dublin, they were defenceless and totally unable to counter terrorism. From mid-1919, when the RIC was outlawed by the Dail as agents of the British, a systematic policy of murder and intimidation was executed by the IRA, with the political approval of Sinn Fein. By coercion and terror, the populace was intimidated against reporting crimes to the police or giving evidence in the courts. Total dominance of the civilian population was the key to the successful undermining and demoralisation of the RIC. While the widespread political support for Sinn Fein rendered these tactics very successful in Southern Ireland, they succeeded despite the fact that the RIC had an overwhelmingly Catholic membership.

The relevance of this historical reference is to underline the point that the attack upon the RIC, and the methods used to undermine it, were not caused by its religious composition or any significant complaint about its performance in relation to 'ordinary crime', but its perception as an agency of the British government in maintaining a constitutional status quo. The physical attacks upon RIC personnel, and the destruction of its organisation and administration, were accompanied by a highly effective propaganda campaign calculated to destroy its integrity and reputation for impartiality and its general acceptance by the electorate—propaganda which was readily accepted by the liberal media and politicians in Great Britain. All of this took place against the background of a British political establishment that broadly desired to disengage from Ireland as a whole. This desire could only be partially met due to the opposition of the pro-Union majority in Northern Ireland.

HISTORY REPEATS ITSELF

Unionists today see this situation being replicated. The policy of the present government is one of disengagement. It was most clearly set out in the Labour Party's detailed appraisal of September 1988, entitled *Towards a United Ireland: Reform and Harmonisation: A Dual Strategy for Irish Unification*. This document stated: 'Whilst the logic and thrust of Labour's policy involves a British withdrawal preceded by a progressive process of disengagement, this would be an integral part of the progress towards unification'. One of the signatories to this statement of policy was the present Secretary of State for Northern Ireland, Dr Marjorie Mowlam. If the historic role of the RUC in its anti-terrorist mode has been the preservation of the constitutional status quo in Northern Ireland against change guaranteed by political violence, this begs the question as to its role when the policy of the government itself is aimed at constitutional change, largely in accordance with the objectives of those using terror and violence to secure them?

Many pro-Union people are aware of the dilemma which has faced British governments since 1921 and, more acutely, from 1969. On the one hand, almost the entire British political establishment would wish a total disengagement from Ireland, and any strategic arguments against this virtually disappeared with the end of the Cold War. On the other hand, any strong security measures to eradicate terrorism or to politically strengthen the Union would run counter to the long-held political strategy for disengagement. Paradoxically, the ultimate aims of the British government were seen as supporting the objectives of Irish nationalism. At the same time, successive British governments had to accept the basic democratic obligations of protecting the lives and property of its Northern Irish citizens. The solution to this dilemma was expressed by the late Reginald Maudling in the term 'an acceptable level of violence in Northern Ireland'. So long as murder, injury and destruction of property were largely confined to Northern Ireland, and the economic loss was minimal in terms of the national expenditure, chronic terror in Northern Ireland was acceptable and the province would be left in a political limbo. The IRA's mainland bombing campaign, with its escalating cost to the economic well-being of the United Kingdom and the security of the financial heart of the City of London, accelerated the move towards disengagement. The peace process is seen by thinking Unionists as almost entirely the product of IRA terrorism and British policy.

THE REFORMED ROLE OF THE RUC
It is in this broad context that the provisions of the Belfast Agreement, in general, and those relating to the reform of the RUC must be assessed. Is the RUC to be reformed in such a way as to create a new perception in the minds of the Unionist majority that its reformed role will be the policing of a policy designed to protect a process aimed at removing Northern Ireland from the United Kingdom? This question is already becoming increasingly relevant in relation to Drumcree and the marching issue generally. It would be unwise to ignore the implications of the perception of the RUC by the majority community or to dismiss it as the product of the quasi-criminal.

While undoubtedly the unjustifiable attacks upon the police were the work of a criminal and terrorist minority, the overwhelming majority of people involved were law-abiding citizens committed to industry, honesty and civil society. Those supporting the right to walk the Garvaghy Road extended far beyond the ranks of the Orange Order, many of whom were conscious that most of the nationalist residents groups represented what Mr Adams, in an RTE interview, described as years of work by Sinn Fein activists with criminal convictions for terrorist offences involving violence. This development was viewed by many as the opening of a second front by Sinn Fein/IRA, that is, a means of provoking the pro-Union community into confrontation with the RUC. It placed the police in a no-win situation. If they secured the political decision to permit a march, they reinforced the perception within nationalism that they were a support group for what republicans call Unionist triumphalism. If they implemented a political decision to enforce a ban, they risked confrontation with the community from which they were largely recruited and among whom they, for the most part, resided.

Recent events and attacks upon RUC personnel, and intimidation at their homes, is evidence of this change in perception from one of support to a view that the RUC is policing a government policy which threatens expression of the majority community's political, national and cultural identity. As yet, this change in perception is restricted, but the potential for its growth is in direct proportion to the progression of a policy aimed at a united-Ireland solution and the use of the RUC to police and enforce it. The policy of the government to distance itself from its executive function by interposing a Parades Commission will fail if only because of its overt transparency.

*   *   *

In the period 1918-21 Sinn Fein/IRA was able, by reason of its widespread political support and the general consensus of the population, to exert not only its political will, but its physical dominance over what is now the Irish Republic. It succeeded in removing the RIC as a force for defending the policy of the lawful government. In 1998 the presence of the Unionist community limits the same tactics to effecting control over the nationalist enclaves. Sinn Fein/IRA's current objective is, therefore, to consolidate that control and remove the RUC, which it sees as an obstacle to that control. The strategy to achieve that end is now political, and Sinn Fein/IRA's achievement in having an RUC reform element included in the Belfast Agreement is accompanied by the threat that should a root and branch reform not take place the Agreement will fail, with the implicit threat of a resumption of violence. To all of this, the retention of its guns and explosives is essential.

THE REQUIREMENT FOR REFORM

Many Unionists believe that the sections of the Belfast Agreement relating to security, policing and justice are specifically drafted to meet the demands of nationalists generally and Sinn Fein/IRA in particular.

The requirements to reduce the security measures directed against terrorism, to reform the RUC and review the criminal justice system were almost certainly the product of Sinn Fein/IRA demands as the price of acquiescing to the Belfast Agreement and maintaining what passes for a ceasefire. The insurance against the British government resiling from any of its terms was Sinn Fein/IRA's retention of its weaponry, the maintenance of its infrastructure and ongoing training. The assumption that a prolonged ceasefire would lessen the IRA's effectiveness, and make a return to violence less likely, is both highly questionable and high risk. Small, highly trained units with considerable technical expertise are more than capable of resuming politically effective violence. Against this background, the Independent Commission has been assigned the task set out in Annex A to the Policing and Justice section of the Agreement.

Once again, just as in the example of the Parades Commission, the government, in order to further its policy, has interposed a Commission to which it has given an almost impossible remit. The reform of the police in a normal society faced with increasing crime and the need to balance effective measures for apprehension and prosecution with respect for civil liberties would, in itself, be a formidable task. But to include in the Commission's remit the responsibility for reforms necessary to secure the success of a political settlement, while one of the parties to this settlement maintains a private army capable of threatening the security of the state itself, borders on the absurd.

Since the mid-seventies, successive British governments have failed, for reasons of policy, to draw a clear line between a level of political violence requiring executive action and criminal activity capable of being dealt with by the police and the criminal justice system. The policy of criminalisation in dealing with terrorists enabled the government to claim, with a degree of justification, that there were no political prisoners in the United Kingdom, but only those convicted of crimes considered to be such in any civilised country. It also avoided the rising tide of civil liberty protests. But it did not provide the rapid solution which resolute government might have achieved. It was a policy which simply made terrorism a chronic disease. The necessary modifications to the criminal justice system to make it work, such as the abolition of juries in the Diplock Courts and the departure from established legal principles for the protection of the accused, damaged the reputations of judges and the judicial system, exposed the judiciary to terrorist violence and witnesses to intimidation. Nor did it stem the propaganda machine of Sinn Fein/IRA or the torrent of criticism from well intentioned, but often ill-advised, civil libertarians who drew little distinction between the competing values of the right to silence and the right to life.

Executive action in the form of internment, in circumstances where a new level of intelligence and cooperation between the United Kingdom and the Republic would have made it effective, would also have enabled both governments to release internees when appropriate. The provisions for prisoner release under the Agreement have dealt a further blow to accepted standards of justice which have been totally subordinated to the requirements of political expediency. The early release of terrorists, tried and convicted of the most brutal crimes upon evidence establishing their guilt beyond reasonable doubt, is an affront both to justice and morality. But such is a consequence of the policy of using the judicial process to serve political ends.

*   *   *

The recent hasty terrorist legislation following the Omagh atrocity is but another example of the baleful influence which policy has upon the administration of justice. During Prime Minister Blair's statement to the House of Commons, he appeared to draw a distinction between terrorist groups such as the Real IRA, whom he claimed to have no support, and other terrorist groups presently on ceasefire and fronted by parties such as Sinn Fein, which had significant electoral support. The new anti-terrorist legislation applies only to the 'wicked terrorists' outside the Agreement, but not to the 'good terrorists' currently within it. Yet since the signing of the Agreement the 'good terrorists' have been responsible for nine murders, almost forty punishment shootings and nearly sixty of the most brutal beatings, inflicting injuries more permanently disabling than some of the shootings. The absence of virtually any prosecutions for these offences bears the clearest evidence of the effectiveness of the terror and intimidation exercised by those responsible. Indeed, many of the victims of these 'punishments' do not even report them to the police. Moreover, they are carried out by both republican and loyalist groups represented by parties in the Assembly, some of whose members may shortly be ministers. These activities do not apparently constitute breaches of the ceasefire and, therefore, do not prejudice early release of the groups' prisoners or make the groups subject to the new legislation.

All of these disturbing trends are justified by the necessity of making the Agreement work, by describing them as necessary risks for peace, while profound questions about sacrificing principles of morality or justice are dismissed. In the above circumstances, the requirement for the reform of the police seems very secondary to the reform of standards within the political process.

CONCLUSION

It is the submission of the UK/Unionist Party that the effective reform of the police must be based upon the clearest separation of those crimes properly the subject of normal police investigation within the parameters of non-terrorist crime and crimes arising from political violence of a scale such as would warrant executive action. In the event that the RUC is charged with a continuing responsibility for counter-terrorism, there should be no diminution in the powers available to it in discharge of that function.

The UK/Unionist Party entertains the gravest concern that reforms designed to provide a police service that will service government policy for a phased withdrawal from Northern Ireland will simply shift an unfavourable perception of the RUC's role from the minority to the majority community with the attendant disastrous consequences for both the police and public order.

Twenty-eight

Patten's Flawed Vision[1]

INTRODUCTION

Destroy the morale of a police force and you remove its capacity to discharge its duties, both of combating crime and protecting society from political terrorism. The maintenance of morale is therefore a basic requirement of effective policing. Those who expose themselves to the risk of death or injury must believe that the law-abiding community values their service and honours the sacrifice they may have to make on society's behalf. Within the force itself, morale is maintained by the pride that is derived from the name, uniform, insignia and traditions that weld it together. Men may die for the honour of the regiment, but in history there is no record of a demoralised force ever succeeding, regardless of the quality of its administration or equipment.

The present policies of the government as demonstrated in the Patten Report have done much to achieve what terrorists have failed to accomplish, namely, the destruction of the morale of a police force which has upheld the rule of law for thirty years and averted a descent into chaos and civil war. When those such as Johnny 'Mad Dog' Adair are described by the Secretary of State, Mo Mowlam, as an 'unsung hero of the peace process' and are released back into the society which they terrorised, then the police who under due process of law removed them from that society must necessarily lose heart in the value of their sacrifice.

At the core of the Patten Report is the unwritten adoption of the governments' policy to solve the problem of Northern Ireland by way of a gradual process of British disengagement. This is in the hope of avoiding a resumption of IRA bombing on the mainland. It is a policy which Chris Patten, as an architect of the 1985 Anglo-Irish Agreement, well understands. Such a policy entails meeting at least some of Sinn Fein's demands for the reform of policing.

THE STATE AND THE LAW

Mr Patten claims that 'the police should not be treated as an arm of the state rather than upholders of law'. This statement shows his confusion, since the police uphold the law precisely because they *are* an arm of the state. The state makes the laws, and the law enforcement agencies uphold them on the authority of the state. In this regard, the laws relating to the constitutional integrity of the state are in some respects more vital

---

[1]*Belfast News Letter*, 18 September 1999.

to the maintenance of the rule of law than those bearing on individual crimes, for their destruction is often the object of political terrorism.

Every democracy has a duty to protect itself from subversion by terrorism, and to the extent that the police are charged with providing that protection they act as an arm of the state. Are not the FBI and the National Security Agency arms of the United States government? Who would deny that their UK counterparts perform a similar role, as do the Garda Siochona in the Republic of Ireland.

The Patten Report, in reflecting government policy as set out in the Belfast Agreement, entitles Sinn Fein to two members on the proposed police board to which the Chief Constable is accountable for operational matters. Yet both the Prime Minister and Secretary of State have repeatedly confirmed that Sinn Fein and the IRA are inextricably linked. Security heads accept that the same people occupy the highest offices in both organisations. How can a police force operate effectively when it is accountable to people whose terrorist associates it has a duty to combat?

The basic defects in the Belfast Agreement have now been reflected in the Patten Report, whose terms of reference it provided. The degree to which democratic principles were sacrificed for political expediency is now apparent. The Ulster Unionist Party, in rejecting the Patten Report, has tacitly admitted their failure to recognise the consequences of endorsing an agreement which provided Patten with his remit. Patten, in turn, has seized the opportunity to avoid a real response to their valid criticisms by pointing out that his report accords with the terms which that party agreed to. This response fails, however, to acknowledge that their agreement was induced by the unfulfilled pledges and letters of comfort with which the Prime Minister silenced their misgivings and which they foolishly accepted.

The Patten Commission was never independent in the sense that it had an unrestricted remit. It was curtailed by its limited terms of reference, which were political and designed to produce reforms that would serve the political objectives of the Agreement rather than being confined to the improvement of the RUC's operational performance. The Chief Constable, the Police Authority and the Police Federation were never opposed to reforms that might have made the RUC more efficient and acceptable, nor are they now. The proposed reforms to which they and the pro-Union electorate object are those designed to enhance political objectives rather than operational effectiveness.

Balanced recruitment, an improved complaints procedure, administration streamlining, new operational structures coupled with modern training and communications technology would all have been welcomed. Proposals for downsizing the force in circumstances of a stable and peaceful society were understood. What was, and continues to be, totally unacceptable is the stripping away of everything that associates the police with the current constitutional identity of the state of which Northern Ireland will continue to be a part until a majority agree otherwise. Mr Patten has bought completely into the nationalist definition of parity of esteem, which he confuses with the concept of pluralism. Parity of esteem entitles all citizens to equality before the law, to equal economic social and educational opportunity and to have their religious and cultural views and traditions afforded equal recognition. It does *not* entitle a minority in a democracy to have equal rights with a majority on the issue of the political and national identity of the state. Indeed, to argue otherwise would be to negate the principle of consent upon which the peace process is allegedly founded.

SYMBOLS, IDENTITIES AND THE STATE

In essence, the Patten Report would give the Northern Ireland Police Service the status of a stateless person, which conforms exactly with the Sinn Fein view of the Belfast Agreement as a transitional phase in the inevitable progress to Irish unity. As part of the process of adopting a new national identity, it is first necessary to divest a people of all the symbols of its association with the old. In the view of pan-nationalism, particularly in its most violent form, the RUC is the central obstacle to its success. It is not hated by them because of any operational shortcomings, since Patten stated that 77% of the entire population found the RUC to be both polite and helpful. It is not unacceptable because of its composition, which IRA terror has largely dictated. It is the object of their murderous activities—as was the Royal Irish Constabulary, which was over 70% Catholic—because they were both seen as defending the constitutional status of the state which violent republicanism was determined to change by terror—a terror whose scope for activity will be enlarged by Patten's naive tinkering with the Special Branch.

The Patten Report is unfortunately but a part of a political process to facilitate change as a response to, and appeasement of, political violence. As the product of an inherently flawed Agreement, it is difficult to see how the report could have been otherwise.

Twenty-nine

Devolution and Deception[1]

INTRODUCTION

As they did after the collapse of the 1974 executive, when the Ulster Worker's Council strike merely acted as Dr Death to a terminally sick institution, the spin doctors are busy turning David Trimble's seventy-two days at the head of a devolved government, which recently came to a screeching halt, into some mythical golden age when democracy flourished. Nothing could be further from the truth. The primary purpose of the Belfast Agreement, marketed as the 'Good Friday Agreement', was not to confer upon Northern Ireland the blessings of accountable local democracy, but to appease Sinn Fein/IRA and avert mainland bombings by creating transitional institutions of government leading to Irish unity, while sedating gullible and greedy Unionists with the illusion of devolved democracy. In return, Britain would offer a package of institutions that would neutralise pro-Union majority voting strength, place Sinn Fein in executive power and splice the devolved institutions into dynamic and expanding all-Ireland executive bodies.

Initially, Sinn Fein/IRA were required to declare a permanent end to violence. Unwilling to abandon its cutting edge until the thrust for Irish unity was irreversible, Sinn Fein simply upped the ante with bombs in the Docklands and Manchester. The retention of the IRA's capacity for mainland terror was its insurance that Britain would keep the process in motion. This is the real reason why Britain has abandoned its positions on decommissioning and coerced Unionists into government with the spectre of a terrorist organisation determined to remain armed. Against this background, the undemocratic and impermanent nature of the devolved institutions becomes evident.

DYSFUNCTIONAL DEVOLUTION

Devolution in Scotland and Wales rests upon the premise of the electorate being able to replace those in government. This is not the case in Northern Ireland, where the number of ministers in the executive and the number to be allocated to each party has been rigged so as to ensure that Unionists are under-represented in terms of overall electoral support. Of the one-hundred-eight seats in the Northern Ireland Assembly, ninety are held by the four major parties, which between them provide all ten ministers plus the First Minister and his deputy. The remaining seats are divided among the minority parties, which can

---

[1]*Observer*, 20 February 2000.

constitute no effective opposition. The ministers are nominated by their parties and can be removed only by them. They are not subject to any real collective responsibility. Decisions taken by the two Sinn Fein ministers (Health and Education) give no indication that they feel accountable either to the views of their relevant Assembly committees or to the Assembly itself.

Any elections in Northern Ireland following a period of patently incompetent and divisive government will almost certainly result in the return of the same parties in broadly the same ratio. These would, in turn, again nominate their ministers to the largely unchanged executive; an executive in which all of the major parties would again share power and the minor parties form an impotent opposition. Nothing is intended to change until the expanding and dynamic all-Ireland bodies have effectively assumed the powers of these stagnant institutions.

*   *   *

While devolution operates in this dysfunctional manner, Unionist and nationalist parties, whether in government or not, will continue to oppose and harass their ministerial counterparts, who each will continue to ignore the advice of the Assembly committees when they conflict with their parties' interests. The absence of any strong central authority and a sense of collective responsibility will ensure that devolution in this form is a macabre parody of real democracy. The only question will be whether such inherent defects and weaknesses will destroy the institutions before they achieve the policy aim of Irish unity for which they were designed or whether the IRA's determination to retain its weapons to ensure the attainment of its policy goal will destroy devolution before this goal is achieved.

Thirty

Unappeasable Revolutionaries[1]

INTRODUCTION

To reject the benefit of hindsight, even though it is the cheapest form of
wisdom, is to be completely foolish. Many Unionists who voted 'yes' for
the Belfast Agreement bitterly regretted their decision when its full
implications finally emerged. Many voted 'yes' on the basis of Mr Blair's
broken pledges and media propaganda. Few actually read the contents of
the Agreement itself. Now, at the time of writing (May, 2000), new
proposals to restore the suspended executive are being offered,
accompanied by largely unanalysed media comment on the actual
substance of both the Irish and British governments' statement and the
Provisional IRA's response. The latter is neither an offer nor even a
promise to disarm, except on the IRA's terms. The IRA's statement is
entirely conditional upon the achievement of a united Ireland. It makes
clear that a 'just and lasting peace' can only come about by the removal
of the 'root causes of the conflict'. These causes are the claim of the
British government to a part of Ireland; its denial of Irish national self-
determination; alleged social and economic inequalities and partition.
There cannot, therefore, even on the IRA's own statement, be any lasting
peace until the removal of these causes is obtained.

The IRA's statement also implies that full implementation of the
Agreement, as they see it, marks only one stage in an enduring process of
removing all of the causes of the conflict. The IRA clearly believes, in
other words, that the Agreement has the potential to deliver Irish unity—
as, indeed, it has been designed to do. Some media commentators have
even suggested that the IRA's latest comment—full implementation of
the Agreement will provide a political context in which Irish republicans
and Unionists can peacefully pursue their respective political objectives
as equals—is some novel concession to democracy. They are wrong. It is
simply a repetition of Sinn Fein's view of the Agreement as nothing more
than a transitional phase en route to a united Ireland. Unionists will only
be treated as equals for as long as Sinn Fein/IRA feels that the
implementation of the Agreement is removing the root causes of the
conflict as they define them—and that means Irish unity.

THE SILENT POTENTIAL OF ILLEGAL ARMS

Only in this context will the IRA initiate a process that will completely
and verifiably put its arms beyond use, a context in which its arms will

---

[1]*Belfast Telegraph*, 19 May 2000.

no longer be needed, for they will have served their purpose. While the British government continues the implementation of policies that will deliver Irish unity, the guns and bombs will remain silent, but they will never be dispensed with until the potential of these policies has been realised in full. The IRA claims that its arms will remain silent and secure and offer 'no threat to the peace process'. But this claim is also conditional on the British government facilitating the IRA's demands.

The media generally appears unaware that this tactic in itself represents an assault upon the fundamentals of democratic government, for the threat of renewed violence is implicit if Unionists do no accept the terms upon which the IRA has decreed that their arms will not be used. It has long been evident that any concession by the IRA, no matter how minimal, would be seized upon by both the British and Irish governments as an excuse for coercing Unionists into acceptance. Only the foolish will believe that both governments were not in possession of the IRA terms before they issued their recent joint statement. The contents of both statements were almost certainly agreed before the joint-government statement was issued. By making it appear that the IRA had positively responded to the governments' statement, the Unionists were placed in the position that if they, too, did not respond positively, blame would fall upon them. But blame will always fall upon Unionists if their actions in any way jeopardise the security of the mainland against a renewed IRA bombing campaign. Mainland security is a policy imperative that will override everything, including the rule of law and democratic principles.

The IRA's confidence-building measure is, in real terms, worthless. The number and contents of the designated arms dumps will be selected by the IRA, and ultimate control of them will remain with the IRA. The contents will not be 'put beyond use' and will, almost certainly, only represent a small fraction of the total arms that will remain fully available for immediate use by the IRA. The IRA has not agreed to any of the schemes for disposing of arms as set out in the legislation under which General de Chastelain is empowered to act. The IRA will have until June 2001 to agree the modalities of alternative schemes. This date, however, is not a deadline, but only a target date capable of indefinite extension.

THE POLITICAL PAYOFF

The political benefits that will accrue to Sinn Fein/IRA during this indefinite period will be enormous. The executive will be restored, giving power back to Sinn Fein ministers. This time the executive may be reviewed, but never again suspended. The Patten reforms will be implemented in full as Peter Mandelson has confirmed. The criminal justice system will be reformed in accordance with Sinn Fein's wishes. All equality and Irish language agendas will be implemented, and full impetus given to the dynamic of the all-Ireland institutions. On top of all this, there will be a full programme of substantial demilitarisation. All of this will transpire without any sanctions being levelled if the terms for putting arms verifiably beyond use are not agreed or any definite timetable for doing so arrived at. The British government has, in this final act of appeasement, abandoned even the pretence of requiring decommissioning.

If the Ulster Unionist Council approves a return to the executive upon these terms, it will have effectively signed the death warrant of the Union. Nothing will be left save the fixing of the date for execution. As for the total myth that the Agreement secured the principle of Unionist consent, this will finally be exposed. At this point Unionist defeat will already be accomplished and consent to the legal transfer of sovereignty to the Republic will be nothing more than the formal acceptance of a factual reality.

Thirty-one

The Ends Never Justify the Means[1]

INTRODUCTION

The ends never justify the means and rarely do dishonourable ones achieve them. This will almost certainly prove to be the case in relation to an immoral and unjustifiable policy which allows the early release of killers, criminals and thugs back among the people whom they terrorised, maimed and murdered. In every civilised society the prime function of government is to protect the lives, personal safety and property of its law-abiding citizens by the application of the rule of law. Those alleged to have committed crimes are tried by the judicial process and, if found guilty, sentenced according to the seriousness of their offences. The criminals recently released have been so tried and convicted of crimes of the most horrifying barbarity. Successive British governments have rightly claimed in the past that there were no political prisoners in Northern Ireland, but only criminals convicted and sentenced after due process for offences deemed to be crimes not just in Northern Ireland, but in every civilised country throughout the world.

Yet since the commencement of the alleged peace process, a developing pattern of government and media manipulation has nurtured the idea that these brutal psychopaths can have their appalling acts justified as having been performed for some political purpose. One loyalist who murdered two people in a frenzied knife attack has claimed that his subsequent meeting with a Prime Minister in Downing Street had legitimised his crime as political. Mo Mowlam, in the run up to the Belfast Agreement, when its endorsement by the inmates of the Maze was considered vital, extolled 'Johnny' and 'Michael' in the *Belfast News Letter* as 'two of the unsung heroes of the peace process'. Johnny Adair and Michael Stone were, of course, very anxious to support a policy that would dramatically shorten their time in prison. Stone was incarcerated because he had murdered six Roman Catholics and attempted to murder five others. Adopting the language of the 'freedom fighter', he now describes his behaviour as that of a soldier and his victims as 'casualties'. He expresses no regret for any of the fatalities that occurred.

NO CRIME, NO GUILT, NO REMORSE

These men have no sense of guilt, because by granting their crimes a political stamp the government has removed any requirement upon them either for guilt or repentance. The celebrations with which they have

---

[1]*Belfast Telegraph*, 2 August 2000.

been received back into their respective communities becomes the absolution for their sins, while the British government has now become the vendor of 'indulgences' for past crimes. Sean Kelly, who in 1993 placed a bomb in a Shankill Road fishmonger's shop and murdered nine people, including a pregnant woman, was sentenced in 1995 to nine life sentences; he now walks free. Michael Caraher, the Armagh sniper who fired the rifle that killed at least twelve men, including Lance Bombardier Stephen Restorick, will have served only sixteen months of sentences totalling 105 years. James McArdle and Bernard McGinn, two other members of his sniping team, were also convicted of making and delivering the bomb at Canary Wharf. McGinn's response to three life sentences and 490 years for other offences was to laugh; as well he might, for, like Caraher, he will have served less than two years in prison. The above are but a few examples of a litany of sickening crimes committed by those granted early release by a weak and cowardly government.

ABANDONING THE RULE OF LAW
There is nothing more corrosive of the human spirit than a sense of blatant injustice, and nothing more destructive of the fabric of society than the violation of the rule of law by its own government. The army of those who grieve for their innocent dead, and the vast number of those who will live maimed and mutilated, are not comforted by the emollient words of Peter Mandelson. Nor is their hurt eased by the exhortations of the economically well off that victims must put the past behind them for the sake of the financial benefits of a terrorist-controlled ceasefire that passes for peace. Few of such people were ever at the sharp end of terrorist violence.

Those men and women of the Royal Ulster Constabulary who risked life and limb in bringing to justice those whom the government now sets free must rightly question the value which not only the government, but those who supported the Belfast Agreement, put upon their sacrifice. Even the judges themselves who had to be guarded night and day, and some of whom paid with their lives, must question if the whole judicial system has not been turned into a farce. Worst of all for the future of Northern Ireland is the confidence-building effect which the current releases will have upon paramilitary criminal activity. Already many of those released display the wealth of their mafia-like involvement in drug peddling, extortion rackets, smuggling and the selling of counterfeit and stolen goods. Deals in contraband cigarettes, liquor and diesel fuel have become big business, while criminals under the guise and flags of loyalism or republicanism turn the areas they control into Mafia ghettos.

*   *   *

Why, against such a background, does the British government pursue such a policy? The answer is simple: because the appeasement of terrorism has become a political imperative to keep bombs out of the City of London. From the early seventies, a level of violence was acceptable in Northern Ireland that would not have been tolerated on the mainland. So, today, the Krays, the Hindleys, the Brixton bomber and many of their like will continue to serve life sentences commensurate with their crimes. But in Northern Ireland it is sufficient to claim association with a paramilitary group on ceasefire to escape any adequate punishment.

In July 1997 James Morgan, an innocent Catholic boy aged sixteen, was brutally beaten to death with a hammer and then flung into a pit used for the burial of diseased animals. His murderer, jailed for life eighteen months ago, has now been released. Try to justify that on any possible basis, Mr Mandelson.

XI

MEDIA MANIPULATION AND POLITICAL SPIN

Thirty-two

Politics and Public Relations[1]

INTRODUCTION

The brevity of the title of this address, 'Politics and Public Relations', gives little hint of the vastness of the subject or of the gravity and complexity of its moral and political implications. What do we mean by politics, either in the general sphere of the United Kingdom or in the more specific context of Northern Ireland? What is the difference, if any, between public relations and political propaganda? What is the role of the public relations consultant in the realm of politics? Is he or she subject to any moral duty to present, albeit in the most attractive form, an essentially true picture of a political personality or policy? Or is the PR expert simply a hired professional image maker with no responsibility other than to those who foot the bill? Since politics is ultimately about the power to govern, involving the making of decisions that may affect not only how we are to be governed, but by whom we are to be governed, the answer to such questions may have a crucial bearing upon the future of democracy itself.

The media in all its forms, from the press to radio and television broadcasting, is the instrument, or medium, for assessing, creating and manufacturing public opinion. Political leaders and their parties, in the quest for and use of power, must necessarily have the backing of public opinion, as their success is dependent upon having both the party's leader and policies endorsed by the electorate. Public relations experts, whether in the government service or in the private sector, provide the ideas and strategy for presenting their clients in the most advantageous light. While it may be argued that in a free market for such services competition may provide an adversarial atmosphere in which the public may make an objective assessment of the respective merits, this is far from being the reality, and it is certainly not true where the interests of a national minority are at stake.

Professors Curran and Seaton, in their book *Power Without Responsibility*, which is a review of the press and the broadcasting media in Britain, make a very telling point. The argument that the press and broadcasting media function as an ideological market place without an impact of their own, they assert, ignores the extent to which the weaker and less organised groups are excluded from the process altogether. Indeed, even when not totally excluded they are often effectively

---

[1] Address delivered at the University of Ulster, 13 November 1997.

marginalised. This is a point to which, in the context of Northern Ireland politics, I will return.

POLITICS, POWER AND PROPAGANDA

In the meantime, what do we mean by politics? In general terms, politics is about the acquisition of power and the uses to which it may be put when obtained. It is about not only how we are to be governed, but also about who is to govern us. In a state with defined and accepted frontiers the how and the who are internal matters. Will it be a Conservative or Labour government? In a state whose frontiers are under question from a foreign power, whether it be the Sudetenland in 1938, the Polish Corridor in 1939 or Northern Ireland in 1997, the question of who is to govern in terms of political and national identity becomes the overwhelming issue. In a state whose territorial integrity is secure, the dominant issues are socio-economic. Since the Northern Ireland electorate has been effectively excluded from the national parties in Britain who are likely to form the government and who will determine such socio-economic policy, and as the territory which they occupy is subject to a claim by another sovereign state, it is not surprising that the issues of union and unity form, in a real sense, the very core of politics in Northern Ireland. Any discussion of politics and public relations in Northern Ireland must accept this central premise.

*   *   *

There is a fine line to be drawn between public relations and propaganda. Both are essentially concerned with assessing, moulding and proselytising a person, a policy or a philosophy in terms of their application to political ends. Sir Isaiah Berlin was arguably one of the greatest of political philosophers. He had this to say about governments: 'Few governments, it has been observed, have found much difficulty in causing their subjects to generate any will that the government desired. The triumph of despotism is to force the slaves to declare themselves to be free.' In the past, such control has been associated, for the most part, with totalitarian regimes of the right or the left, in which propaganda saturation of every aspect of life—economic, social and cultural—was accompanied by terror and repression. But it would be naive to consider that governments claiming to be democratic are immune from practising more sophisticated propaganda as a means of social control for the purpose of achieving policy objectives. Where the policy objective is one which is claimed to offer a national benefit at the expense of a minority interest or a foreign interest, it is likely to be pursued more ruthlessly. The point to be made is that the enormous increase in the technology of communication and the concentration of media control in a diminishing number of hands makes the potential for misuse in the mass control of the public and their opinions a matter of crucial importance for the protection of democracy.

The role of the PR consultant is seen as that of an expert retained by a person, a party, even a government, to project to the public the best image of that person or group's activities. At one end of the scale it is seen as somewhat obvious and relatively harmless. The manner and voice of Mrs Thatcher may be softened and lowered to present a warmer and more caring image. Mary McAleese may be made over from a middle class, somewhat ethnic, Catholic mother into a thoroughly modern Millie, expertly coiffured and eager to build bridges, while Tony Blair's incessant smiles are only interspersed with bursts of tough, hard-edged compassion. At the other end of the scale, ever-increasing technology is being coupled with the detailed research of the behavioural sciences. Everything from the impulses uncovered by psychoanalysts, to the vocabulary counts of educationalists and the analyses of information polls and attitude studies is brought to bear upon creating the image that will achieve the objective. But who, if anyone, makes a value judgement upon the worth of the goal itself. In many instances, the only people who really know what is going on are those who are involved, whether as clients, providers or media. One of the biggest threats to democracy is the fact that the enormously increased capacity of the image makers and professional opinion formers coincides, certainly in the United Kingdom, with the concentration of power in the hands of fewer and fewer people.

CENTRALISED GOVERNMENT AND ONE-PARTY RULE

The domination of Parliament by the two major parties has been accompanied by a vast increase in the centralisation of government. The Prime Minister governs the country from the apex of a power pyramid composed of a highly centralised party machine and a concentrated bureaucracy. Since 1979 this trend has continued, and the present Labour government, with its huge majority and a public relations machine of great efficiency, has taken this personalised form of government to a new level—a level at which the spin doctor outside the cabinet has his portrait hung in the National Gallery before that of his Prime Minister. The term *eminence grise* has taken on a new dimension. It is becoming increasingly difficult for the public at large to distinguish real leaders from those created and packaged by the image makers from an advertising agency or a public relations firm. Today, in the age of massive opinion research, speech coaches, TV tutors, make-up artists and the powerful impact of television, it has become possible for the image makers to create frontmen who can affect the votes and other behaviour of a very large percentage of the national audience. The selling of a perception, particularly one that the public themselves wish to perceive, is more important than reality. Many believe that the public is increasingly under the control of those whom Vance Packard described thirty years ago as the 'hidden persuaders'.

As long ago as 1970, one knowledgeable expert described the process in the following terms:

> There are now four essential ingredients to a professionally managed political campaign: political polls, data processing, imagery and money. The polls discover what the voter already believes, and the data processing interprets and analyses the depths of voters' attitudes. After that, an image of the candidate is tailored to meet the voters' demands and desires, and the whole package is then sold by massive expenditures of money in the advertising media, particularly television.
>
> The candidate has become relatively unimportant as long as he can be properly managed. The candidate must be bright enough to handle the material furnished to him, but not too intelligent, because there is always the danger that an intelligent candidate may come up with unpopular or controversial ideas of his own and thereby destroy a carefully contrived campaign strategy.

Bill Clinton springs instantly to mind as the product of this philosophy, and Tony Blair and his team of advisers are said to have modelled much of their campaign strategy on ideas culled from the Clinton campaigns. But Clinton and his advisers have not only utilised PR and media techniques in order to get him elected, they have used them with remarkable success in deflecting both personal and political attack upon him when he was in office. Clinton has been described as the 'teflon man to whom nothing sticks', an attribute increasingly applied to Tony Blair. A recent article in the *Sunday Telegraph* commenced with the question: is Tony Blair teflon coated? And it suggests that he, like JFK, Ronald Reagan and Bill Clinton, has acquired a political immunity system which rubs off viruses that would kill other people's careers. The highest interest rates for five years, a tax raid on pension contributions, the abolition of student tuition fees, u-turns on policy and ministerial gaffes have done absolutely nothing, according to the writer, but add to Tony Blair's popularity. This, he contends, defies any form of rationality and he argues that, as post-Lady Diana sentimentality progresses, so

British politics is being gradually depoliticised. Elections as beauty contests are, he suggests, the sinister end to which New Labour strategists are working.

Even when allowances are made for the hyperbole of a newspaper columnist, the underlying change in the practice of politics and its relation to the media and PR is a cause for unease. Serious political commentators have noted the increasing tendency of British general elections to become more presidential in character. Television in France and the United States has been regarded as a powerful force strengthening the presidential system of government, since the President can easily appeal to a national audience over the heads of elected legislative representatives. The danger in the United Kingdom is that both the executive and legislative functions are joined in the hands of the Prime Minister. Unlike a President, a British Prime Minister does not have to submit his proposals for legislative approval in circumstances where he does not have political control of the legislature. He is Prime Minister precisely because he controls the majority in the legislative body. Power over the legislative function in Parliament is his remit in right of his party's majority, and, of course, he himself controls all executive action through the cabinet in government

*   *   *

The real fear is that increasing control of public opinion, coupled with a huge majority, could lead to an assault upon the elements of constitutional control that would tilt the balance almost permanently in favour of one party. The control of public relations and media briefing has been extended under Labour. Peter Mandelson, though not holding cabinet rank, has a supervisory role over departmental ministers in their relations with the media. Mr Alastair Campbell, the Prime Minister's press secretary, exercises a tight control over press and media briefings, while each of the ministers has his own personal adviser on the government payroll. The independence of the Information Office within the sphere of the civil service has been weakened. The entire apparatus for informing the public is now under greater government control, despite that government's pledge to create greater openness in the conduct of government business. Certainly, the present administration has not been subjected to the scrutiny and criticism by the press and media as was the lot of its predecessor.

If political power is held only with the consent of the electorate, and if the electorate can only exercise control on the basis of information and knowledge, then governments have a vested interest in shaping, planting or, indeed, withholding information which they consider detrimental to their survival. A free press and an independent media are necessary components of democratic government. The question which the public relations industry must ask itself is this: in matters of political activity, what is the industry's moral responsibility for the images of personalities and policies which it is hired to create and promote?

POLITICAL PROPAGANDA IN NORTHERN IRELAND
Let us now focus on the relationship of PR to the politics of Northern Ireland, which are, essentially, those of union and unity. I mentioned earlier that where a policy objective claims to offer a national benefit at the expense of a minority or foreign interest, it is likely to be pursued more ruthlessly. The Northern Ireland of 1997 and the Czechoslovakia of 1938 are two cases in point. The similarities and the media manipulation of government in both cases are remarkable. In each case, the marketing of peace in the face of naked violence and threatened aggression is the central consideration. The IRA's mainland bombing campaign of 1992-93 accelerated a policy shift towards appeasement of Republican violence and a graduated move towards an Irish-unity solution. The bomb at the Baltic Exchange is claimed to have cost more than the entire compensation paid in Northern Ireland from 1969 to 1992. The threat to the financial heart of the City of London made the security of the British mainland's economy the government's overriding priority, a priority to which the constitutional future of Northern Ireland's British citizens became, and has remained, subordinate. The primary goal of policy became the resolution of the conflict between the British state and Sinn Fein/IRA. In order to meet the latter's demands, it was necessary to obtain at least pro-Union acquiescence to the terms offered. Conflict resolution had to be sold as peace and the pro-Union majority had to be persuaded that an end to murder, mutilation and destruction in the form of a terrorist-controlled ceasefire was a fair price to pay for the sacrifice of what they saw as their political and national identity.

*   *   *

At this point, the propaganda, or perhaps public relations exercise, of marketing the peace process commenced. Recognised propaganda techniques identify a number of factors that must be taken into account in addition to the packaging of the policy. First, the predisposition of the reacting public must be considered, such as what they perceive as their past history. The skilled propagandist is careful to advocate only those acts which he believes the public already wishes to perform. Second is the provision of a set of economic inducements, such as increased employment, the threat of job losses or a reduction in the level of state services. Third is the set of physical benefits, including personal and family safety, security against violence and crime and freedom to socialise and enjoy leisure activities. Fourth is the array of social pressures that may either encourage or inhibit the public from doing or thinking what the propagandist advocates.

These criteria have not been invented by me nor are they referable to any particular situation, but each and every one of them has been utilised in the marketing of the peace process by the government, whether with or without the assistance of public relations experts of the public or private kind. The predisposition of the vast majority of the people of Northern Ireland, in the light of twenty-eight years of violence, is for peace. The government has blatantly offered a plethora of economic inducements, ranging from increased investment with more jobs to a peace dividend to be extracted from security savings and to be spent on health and education. The prospect of freedom from the risk of violence has been heavily emphasised in emotional advertisements like that which portrays the small boy with his father saying, 'Wouldn't it be great, Dad, if it was like this all the time?' The fact that any decent human being would agree with the boy is scarcely the point.

All of this has been underlined by a range of social pressures upon those who dare question the price at which this range of good things may be obtained. Those who query the morality of the appeasement of violent terrorists, or suggest that it is a course of action that corrupts democracy or that the price demanded is too high are pilloried as wreckers and bigots. Their values and sense of cultural and historical identity are derided as archaic traditions unsuited to a brave new world of post-nationalist Europe, consensus and political correctness. To be against the policy of the propaganda is, after all, to be against peace, and to be against peace cannot be right.

It is true that propaganda only succeeds insofar as the media allows or permits itself to be the means of its dissemination. Ironically, for the most part, the only serious questioning of either the moral or democratic validity of the peace process policy comes from the national broadsheets like the *Times* and the *Daily Telegraph*. The main focus of journalism in Northern Ireland is, almost entirely, factual news reporting, and since government agencies are the most fertile source of political facts and information, their control of news of a political kind is overwhelming. The extent of investigative and analytical journalism in Northern Ireland is limited, with the result that much of the media political content is a reflection of poorly analysed government propaganda. There are, of course, some exceptions, but in general almost all the in-depth political comment is from sources outside professional journalism in Northern Ireland.

APPEASEMENT REVISITED

As mentioned earlier, the comparison of 1938 and the search for peace affords some uncanny similarities to our current problems. A recent BBC programme celebrating the Corporation's seventy-fifth anniversary admitted that in the 1930s the BBC actively suppressed the views of those, like Churchill, who opposed the policy of appeasement. Indeed, Churchill claimed that the BBC conspired with the press and government to exclude all opponents of this policy from any access to the public. Little has changed today: many opponents of the current British policy to purchase peace by the sacrifice of pro-Union interests believe that they are deliberately excluded or marginalised in their access to the public or that the visual media present an image of them unfavourable to their case, but well disposed to the policy of the government.

In 1938 Britain sacrificed the Czechs to buy peace for England. 'What have we to do with a far away country of which we know little?' was Neville Chamberlain's justification for one of the most shameful episodes in British history. Yet because then, as now, all the criteria for a successful propaganda campaign were in place, Chamberlain's welcome on his return from Munich with 'peace in our time' was positively euphoric.

The legacy of the Great War and its consequences meant that the predisposition of the people was for peace at any price. Emergence from the Depression and the inducements of growing employment and stability which peace offered were heavily sold. Then, as now, the captains of industry were great supporters of appeasement. The threat of air warfare was deliberately heightened, and measures which induced fear, but offered scant protection, abounded everywhere. Social pressure was brought to bear by the great and the good, lay and clerical, upon those like Churchill who warned that peace at Hitler's price was not worth having. Such people were condemned as eccentric mavericks, wreckers and war mongers. Yet as in our current situation, each concession brought a fresh demand, and when evil could no longer be bought off it had become so strong that successful resistance to it hung in the balance and millions died. As Henry Kissinger has lamented, 'the tuition fee for learning about Hitler's true nature was tens of millions of graves stretching from one end of Europe to the other'.

I fear that the association of politics with public relations as presently practised, with a far greater expertise than in 1938, is one fraught with danger for democracy unless it is regulated with great care. The public relations of governments with their people is increasingly directed towards serving the interests of those who govern rather than of those who are governed. There is a growing public distrust of politics and politicians, whose place in the public esteem throughout the Western world has never been lower. This association is producing leaders whose purpose is not to lead, but to be suitable for management—by whom or what the public does not always know. In the end, perhaps, all we may have to rely upon is a paraphrase of Abraham Lincoln's maxim: 'You can fool some of the people all of the time, and all of the people some of the time, but even PR gurus may not be successful in fooling all of the people all of the time.'

Thirty-three

Media Manipulation in Northern Ireland: A Warning For Britain[1]

INTRODUCTION

I believe in the concept of an independent and sovereign United Kingdom. I also am passionately committed to the principle that Northern Ireland should remain an integral part of such a United Kingdom. What causes me some concern is the degree of indifference which many British citizens display to the plight of their fellow citizens in Northern Ireland who wish to remain British. How, one may ask, can the vast numbers of mainland British citizens who have the most basic objection to the United Kingdom losing its national, cultural and political independence within a politically federated European superstate sit idly by when exactly the same methods being used to achieve that objective are being used by the British government to take Northern Ireland out of the United Kingdom and into a united Ireland?

The essential point of my address here today is to alert those of you who live in mainland Britain to several developments underway in Northern Ireland in terms of the government's strategy for dealing with 'the Northern Ireland problem', the methodology being employed to effect that strategy and the knock-on effects which these will have on the future political and cultural integrity of Britain.

DISENGAGEMENT FROM NORTHERN IRELAND

Successive Secretaries of State for Northern Ireland have declared that their governments 'have no selfish economic or strategic interest in remaining in Northern Ireland'. At the same time, it has been necessary to pay lip service to the basic principle of democracy that the consent of the majority of the people in Northern Ireland would be required before there could be any legal transfer of sovereignty from the United Kingdom to the Republic of Ireland.

Since 1969 Irish nationalists have dedicated themselves to the removal of this principle of consent which they dismissively refer to as the Unionist veto. Since the consent principle is one firmly based on the procedures of democracy, it must necessarily be circumvented or removed by a process that is both disguised and gradual. Few people in Northern Ireland, at the date of the May 1998 referendum or even now, are fully aware of the ongoing process for modifying and diluting the

---

[1]Address delivered to the United Kingdom Independence Party, New Britain Conference, 24 October 1998.

principle of consent to the point where it will present no obstacle to the political unification of Ireland.

One of the most frequent themes used to engage support for the alleged peace process is the promised economic dividend. Although there are powerful arguments that the economies of Northern Ireland and the Republic are not complimentary but competitive, these are drowned out by an orchestrated tide of propaganda about the economic virtues of unification, for which there is scarcely any evidence. As on the mainland, financial institutions like banks, multinationals and companies with financial interests in both parts of Ireland are part of this chorus. Organizations like the Confederation of British Industry and the Institute of Directors largely mirror the attitudes of their larger and more powerful members in Great Britain. Those who challenge the views offered by the government either have their views suppressed by being effectively denied media coverage or they are subjected to character assassinations, being categorised as wreckers, political dinosaurs or, in Northern Irish terms, sectarian bigots. The government control of the media in Northern Ireland has reached quite awesome proportions and it is to the issues of propaganda, media control and the increasing use of referendums that I now turn, for the relevance of these issues not only to national independence, but to individual liberty and freedom, is crucial.

GOVERNMENT PROPAGANDA AND MEDIA CONTROL

The Northern Ireland experience in terms of the use of propaganda, media control and referendums is but a foretaste of what lies ahead for mainland Britain at the hands of the present government, in much the same way that the Spanish Civil War was a test bed for the technology and ideologies that were later to beset the whole of Europe. Northern Ireland has valuable lessons to offer to those in the United Kingdom who believe in democracy.

The late Sir Isaiah Berlin, a champion of individual liberty, has written:

> Few governments, it has been observed, have found much difficulty in causing their subjects to generate any will that the government wanted. The triumph of despotism is to force the slaves to declare themselves free. It may need no force; the slaves may proclaim their freedom quite sincerely; but they are nonetheless slaves.

The question is, 'how is this to be done?' In Hitler's Germany and Communist Russia, it was achieved by a combination of intensive propaganda, suppression of the truth and, ultimately, by brutal physical oppression. Paradoxically, while television has been a powerful agency for exposing the crudity and, therefore, the unacceptability in democracies of physical oppression, it has become the medium for an even more effective power of control, because such control is welcomed, is self-inducing and often wholly unrecognised. The slaves, while sincerely proclaiming their freedom, do not recognise their slavery.

There are two vital requirements for the preservation of democratic government and individual freedom: reason and memory. The slogan of the Party in George Orwell's *Nineteen Eighty-Four* was: 'Those who control the present, control the past. Those who control the past, control the future.' A necessary prerequisite for such control is the machinery for eradicating those parts of the past that are politically inconvenient, those facts which are required to be consigned to 'the memory hole'. More recently, the celebrated author and Czech political dissident, Milan Kundera, has put the issue succinctly. For Kundera, who experienced totalitarian oppression at first hand, 'the struggle of man against power is the struggle of memory against forgetting'. The essence of totalitarian control, by whatever methodology employed, is the destruction of the past and, therefore, the capacity of reason to use history in order to judge the present. The removal of reason and memory, which together are required to shape and control the future, becomes an absolute requirement for control.

ON THE EVE OF THE MILLENNIUM
What then, you may ask, have these speculations to do with Britain on the eve of the Millennium? The answer: everything. For today Britain is governed by a political leadership that is increasingly using modern technology to supplant democracy. Neil Postman, an American professor of communications, states that there are two ways in which the spirit of a culture may be shrivelled. In the first, the Orwellian culture becomes a prison. In the second, that of Aldous Huxley, the culture becomes a burlesque. Orwell's prison, whether in fascist Germany, communist Russia or Pol Pot's Cambodia, has had its evil face made recognisable. Huxley's theatre of burlesque warns that spiritual destruction in an age of advanced technology will come with a smiling countenance. In the Huxleyan world, Big Brother does not watch us by his choice; we watch him by ours. In these circumstances, says Professor Postman in his study *Amusing Ourselves to Death:*

There is no need for wardens or gates or Ministries of Truth. When a population becomes distracted by trivia, when cultural (including political) life is redefined as a perpetual round of entertainment, when serious public conversation becomes a form of baby talk, when, in short, a people become an audience and their public business a vaudeville act, then a nation finds itself at risk, culture death is a clear possibility.

The danger signs for Britain under Tony Blair are evident. This government is advocating a Third Way, but it is a way that has equal dangers for democrats, whether they be of the left or the right. Did Peter Mandelson support Tony Blair, rather than Gordon Brown, because of Blair's superior intellect or wiser policies? No. He supported Blair because he was simply better 'box office'. The Third Way is not about a range of policies, it is about the single policy of extending party power over the system.

When Tony Blair talks about New Labour, everything in it is in terms of the future. The institutions of the past—whether they be Old Labour, the House of Lords, the Constitution, the trade unions, the unity of the United Kingdom or even the Monarchy—have all become dispensable. Cool Britannia wants nothing to do with memory or the past. Its slogan has become: 'The past is bad, the present is good, the future will be even better and, in the meantime, just concentrate on East Enders and Sky Sports.'

In essence, New Labour, while constantly talking about 'the people', has recognised that big business and the lords of the media are the only 'people' it really has to concern itself with. Blair has gone to school in Clinton's America, where Huxley's prophecies are well underway to fulfilment and where money, media and government are all partners in power. In America television is writing an end to Caxton and his age of print and the advent of an era when Huxley's form of death for democratic culture will steal upon us with a smile. As Professor Postman declares, public consciousness has not yet assimilated the point that technology is ideology. Technology enables us to know about things without really understanding them, but, ultimately, we are only allowed to know what the news editor determines is news. If Rupert Murdoch decides what is good or bad, it becomes very important that he thinks your party is the good one. When a people have their interest in their past removed; when they have been entertained with superficial soundbites; when they have lost all real terms of reference with everything but the present; when their capacity for rational analysis has been removed; and when their government, either alone or in partnership, has effective control over the information they receive— then they may safely be consulted by referendum in which a choice, ostensibly said to be theirs, has already effectively been made by others on their behalf.

REFERENDUMS AND REALITY
Some five months before the 22 May 1998 referendum which endorsed the Belfast Agreement, I wrote:

> In the coming months the British and Irish governments, with the aid of the Irish American lobby, will seek, by a massive propaganda campaign, to persuade the pro-Union people that the benefits of a terrorist controlled ceasefire are a fair price to pay for the sacrifice of the Union and their British identity.

The government and the Northern Ireland Office were already putting everything into place. Officials of the semi-independent British Information Service were sacked, for what was now required were not civil servants, but government agents. By early 1998 the Northern Ireland Office had its own propaganda department hand-picked to implement its policies at government expense. By 4 March it had issued an 'Information Strategy Document', a composite publicity plan that was submitted to Mo Mowlam, the Secretary of State. A copy of it was briefed to all her junior ministers and high-level civil servants. This document said:

> We are embarking on what, in effect, will be the most crucial election campaign in Northern Ireland's history. During the next ten weeks we need to convince the Northern Ireland public both of the importance of what is at stake and also to convince them that not only is agreement possible, but they have a vital role to play in endorsing it.

What follows in that document is a master plan for deception and propaganda that uses every technique known to the totalitarian powers and adds to it the technology of the present. Here are some extracts:

> Key messages repeated at every opportunity . . .

The message that is not afraid to recognise and build on the public's desire for peace to build a momentum for both the referendum and the Assembly elections . . .

The message is to be reinforced and the public need to be in no doubt about how a deal will improve every aspect of their quality of life. It requires a concerted effort by every minister and department in every speech, interview and meeting . . .

Given that a central part of the government's approach is that we are not imposing a deal, but giving the people a choice, ministers should talk directly to people . . .

We will develop key lines which will underpin the whole campaign . . .

We will only be able to effectively refine the message and respond to apparent concerns if we have an effective monitoring system . . .

Under the title 'Champions', representative figures in wider groups, whose opinions were respected, were to be harnessed to the government's cause, such as archbishops and other church leaders, heads of community organisations, trade union figures and the leaders of industry. Paragraph fourteen counselled that while

> any overt manipulations could only be counter-productive, a carefully coordinated timetable of statements from the [Champions] will be helpful in giving our message credibility among those they represent. It has the benefit of providing a fresh face for the message and ensuring that it is not only the government which is seen to be selling the process.

Paragraph sixteen stated:

> Advertising on its own will not convince the public to vote in favour of the referendum, but it is the only means whereby we would be in total control of the message and be guaranteed near universal coverage if we use TV. But serious consideration needs to be given to the timing and content of any messages, because it could be seen as "big government" imposing its view . . . For that and reasons of government propriety, the focus should be on selling the concept of an agreed future. The central message will be "It's Your Choice". Initially that choice will be posed as being between the failure of the past and the future towards which we

are making progress. Once an agreement is in place, the message will
change to encouraging people to vote for this future.

Other paragraphs advised the suppression of unfavourable opinion polls.
These are but selections from a document containing concepts of
propaganda and public deception that have no place in a civilised
society.[2]

FOR WHOM THE BELL TOLLS

Millions of pounds were thrown into the government campaign. The full
resources of the civil service and the government were placed at the
disposal of the 'yes' campaign, in which not only the Prime Minister, the
Chancellor and other senior members of the government participated,
but also Mr John Major, Mr William Hague and shadow government
spokesmen. May I point out that the government's behaviour would have
been unlawful in the Republic of Ireland, where legislation exists to
ensure that both sides of a referendum issue are placed before the voters
so that they are fairly and equally informed of the arguments for and
against.

It was this element which Lord Neill addressed in his recent
report. His committee was highly critical of the way in which the Welsh
referendum was conducted. It was disturbed by evidence that the Welsh
campaign was very one-sided, with the last minute 'no' campaign
seriously underfunded, while the government spent large sums of money
distributing literature to every household in Wales. What is even more
disturbing is the committee's total silence on the Northern Ireland
referendum, where the abuse was even greater. The outcome of 71%
voting 'yes' and 29% voting 'no' reflected to within one point the total
percentage of time on Northern Ireland television and column inches in
the three main Northern Ireland newspapers afforded to the 'yes'
campaign versus the 'no' campaign.

Perhaps of even greater significance for any future referendums,
either on entry into monetary union or constitutional reform, is the likely
attitude of the Minister for Home Affairs, Mr Jack Straw, to the Neill
Committee's criticisms, as predicted in the *Guardian* on 21 October
1998:

> The government will ignore the advice of Lord Neill's Committee. It
> will put an official booklet of the government's case into every house

---

[2] See Appendix.

before the [next] referendum. Mr Straw will not accept Lord Neill's recommendations for a ban on the publication of government literature about the issues on which people are to vote. Mr Straw does not appear to understand the difference between obtaining an electoral mandate to hold a referendum and one entitling the government to use the public purse to advance its view of what the electorate should do. If the government has a mandate to enter monetary union, it should do so, but if its mandate is simply to let the people decide in a referendum, it should not interfere directly in that decision.

The reason for Mr Straw's attitude is clear. Referendums, which have never been a feature of the British political system, are only of value when the government can ensure the result it desires. This is why they have been so popular with absolutist regimes. In conclusion, no man is an island, and neither is any region of the United Kingdom. When the bell tolled for Northern Ireland, it tolled for everyone in this state who values democratic government, pluralism and individual freedom.

Thirty-four

Information Control in Ulster[1]

INTRODUCTION

The most basic right of a free people in a democratic society is that of expressing their dissent against prevailing opinion. The hallmark of a repressive regime is the attempted suppression of views contrary to its own. Communications technology in its present state has made suppression in its crude form of the concentration camp and the gulag no longer viable in the western world, but, paradoxically, it has enabled governments to achieve the same ends in a more subtle and effective form. The use and abuse of the media in forming and controlling public opinion has enabled nominally democratic governments to undermine and, perhaps, ultimately silence those who oppose their aims. No longer do the agents of control knock on the door at night. Instead, they are invited in by switching on the television and radio.

While the techniques and technology of persuasion and control have become infinitely more sophisticated, the principles of their use remain relatively constant. Just as George Orwell's Napoleon Pig endlessly repeated 'Four legs good, two legs bad', the primary object of propaganda remains that of embedding an image in the public consciousness. Those who dissent can only be motivated by false ideas, inimical to the social peace and good government that the ruler seeks to dispense. Stalin destroyed the opinions of his liberal opponents not by answering their questions, but by attacking their alleged motivations. This technique of fixing in the public mind a malign image of the state's opponents is far from new. Terms such as 'enemies of the people', 'social saboteurs', 'opponents of peace' and 'war-mongers' have all been used to denigrate those who question the validity of a popular opinion manufactured by the agencies of government. Nor are the techniques of social and political control confined to undemocratic forms of government. As Isaiah Berlin remarked, it matters little to the individual if his freedom is curtailed by a dictator or an elected government. Whether in Stalin's Russia, where one was sent to the gulag, or in a part of the United Kingdom, where one is effectively silenced by exclusion from the mass media, the voice of dissent is equally stifled.

The present British government, more than any other, is committed to maximum control over the information made available to the public. It has purged the British Information Service as an independent source and has rendered it an instrument of government

---

[1] *Belfast Telegraph*, 2 March 2000.

propaganda. It has established a News Unit for the specific purpose of countering the alleged distortion of those reputable newspapers which are independent enough to criticise the government's policies. The Prime Minister continues to be fed the reports of private opinion polls and focus groups, which enable him to assess the pulse of the people and, ultimately, to manipulate them. The pre-election promises of effective Freedom of Information laws remain largely unfulfilled. Even former members of the government express a growing fear about the rise of the executive's power, its growing lack of accountability to Parliament and its control of dissenting opinion within its own party.

INFORMATION CONTROL IN NORTHERN IRELAND
Nowhere in the United Kingdom have these developments been more evident than in Northern Ireland. Official government documents outlining the methods for persuading the people to vote 'yes' in the referendum reveal the total extent to which organised propaganda was used. The endlessly repeated message was as simple as 'Napoleon Pig's "yes" is good, "no" is bad'. The objective was to convince a majority that by voting 'yes' they were not only good people, but that those who voted 'no' were bad people against peace. By the repeated assertion that there was no alternative to the Belfast Agreement as a mechanism for peace, the message was reinforced that those who opposed it were simply wreckers. Since every decent person wants peace, the effect of such propaganda was to place them in a Catch 22 situation. If they wanted peace, they had to be in favour of the Belfast Agreement, for there was allegedly no other way. If they were against the Agreement, they must be against peace; as such, they were at best people unwilling to share power and at worst sectarian extremists.

Like Stalin, the government's tactic was neither to consider nor to answer the reasonable grounds for opposition to those who said 'no'. It was sufficient to denigrate their motivation, while endorsing the good faith of terrorists and murderers. Truth cannot be suppressed indefinitely, for it is ultimately exposed by time and circumstance. Those who advocated a 'no' vote have had the validity of their arguments proved by subsequent events. The Agreement has enabled hundreds of convicted terrorists, guilty of the most horrendous crimes, to have early release. The murderer of Lance Bombardier Restorick, among others, will be released inside of eighteen months, if not sooner. The Agreement has demoralised the RUC and provided for its reform to meet the demands of those who terrorised the entire community. It has created all-

Ireland bodies with executive powers and placed in government, for a time, the political representatives of a fully armed terrorist group.

Upon all of these rational grounds of objection, the 'no' parties made their case and displayed political judgement by placing no faith in the pledges of a Prime Minister who has since dishonoured them. Despite the validity of their arguments for voting 'no', those who did so continue to be the subject of epithets like 'rejectionist Unionists' from former terrorists whom government propaganda has afforded celebrity status. Many disillusioned 'yes' voters continue to be subjected to psychological pressure and are reluctant to admit publicly their change of heart. Many still fear that in an atmosphere of government-fostered political correctness, open opposition might prejudice their business or professional prospects, because government policy is to withhold approval and patronage from those who oppose it.

Such pressures are only different in degree, rather than in principle, from those exerted in totalitarian states where strict adherence to the party line was a requirement for any sort of preferment, and opposition led to exclusion or worse. Where a state imposes penalties, either directly or indirectly, upon those who oppose its policy; where a compliant media lends itself, knowingly or unwittingly, to the uncritical approval of government policy; where those in positions of influence, lay and clerical, allow themselves to be used as opponents of democratic dissent—then in such a state liberty and freedom may ultimately perish.

Thirty-five

Epilogue

INTRODUCTION

History reveals two opposing principles in British politics. The first, encapsulated in the aphorism attributed to the Whig/Liberal Prime Minister, Lord Palmerston, is that 'England has no long term friends or enemies, only interests'. The second, declared by the three-times Conservative Prime Minister, Lord Salisbury, states that 'buying off the barbarians was a fatal vice', while the failure by a state to assert its sovereignty and act according to its right 'takes the heart out of defence, dissolves cohesion and splits up an organised society into a mob of struggling interests'. In 1938 Neville Chamberlain followed Palmerston's dictum by sacrificing the Czechs to keep bombs out of London and failed. In 1940 Winston Churchill acted according to the country's right, resisted the barbarians and saved not only Britain, but also Europe, from fascist domination.

In Northern Ireland, as this book hopefully has revealed, successive British governments have yielded to Salisbury's 'fatal vice'. In following what appeared to them to be England's interest of confining bombs and violence to another part of the United Kingdom, they have adopted policies designed to buy off terrorist barbarism and have failed to assert their sovereignty. Northern Ireland has become semi-detached, the quality of the British citizenship of its people has been devalued and a foreign state whose policies are inimical to its perceived interest has been permitted to share in its governance. Such is not surprising, since consecutive British governments have had no heart for defence and no cohesion of purpose, with the result that society in Northern Ireland has become a mob of struggling interests.

The policy of appeasing terrorism in aid of a political imperative to keep bombs off the mainland has been the driving force of the mis-named peace process. In pursuit of this objective, the principles of democratic government have been distorted and the rule of law subverted. Each government declaration about the primacy of democratic engagement has been broken, and every position adopted requiring terrorist organisations to eschew violence and abandon their arsenals has been resiled from. At every point when weak and vacillating governments have attempted to impose the norms of democratic governance, their resolution has been literally blown away by terrorist bombs on the British mainland. Violence, and the continuing threat of violence, have dictated every aspect of the peace process—and will continue to do so. History provides few, if any, instances of political terrorists ceasing their activity until either their objectives have been achieved or they are defeated by the forces of democracy. The record of attempts to civilise terrorists by including their representatives in government—from the inclusion of Hitler's National Socialists to that of Mr Foday Sankoh in Sierra Leone—presents a dismal picture of failure.

THE DILEMMA OF DEVOLUTION
The claim that devolved government in Northern Ireland accords with democratic principles and is in keeping with regional devolution policies in Scotland and Wales is without truth. Whatever the reasons for devolution in those parts of the United Kingdom, they, at least, conform to the fundamental precepts of representative democracy. The party, or parties, forming the devolved government must either by themselves, or in coalition, represent the majority of those elected—subject to the protection which all democracies must afford to the fundamental rights of minorities, a condition which is now ensured by the United Kingdom's adoption of Europe's Charter of Human Rights. In a true democracy the electorate must have the right to dismiss the government in freely held elections, a principle that democracies insisted Slobodan Milosevic had to observe. Such is the position in Scotland and Wales. Devolution in these regions has the declared objective of providing more accessible, more sensitive and more accountable government. Should any government fail to meet these standards, the electorate may remove it from power.

*   *   *

The purpose of devolution in Northern Ireland is very different. Its real objective is to neutralise the power of the democratic majority and to create transitional institutions that will, over time, move Northern Ireland out of the United Kingdom and into the Irish Republic. This is the price which the British government is prepared to pay to avoid mainland terror. The devolved arrangements for Northern Ireland have produced a political Caliban incapable of change and designed to stagnate, while the all-Ireland bodies to which it is linked expand and develop.   Apologists for this process refer to it as 'compromised democracy' in the interests of peace. The undemocratic and enforced consensus upon which it is built dictate that future elections will,. in broad terms, return the same parties in largely similar numbers of nationalists and Unionists. The same parties will exercise their power to nominate the same or other ministers from within their own ranks. No matter how incompetent the last executive, the electorate, by their votes, will be unable to replace them in any real sense. The entire fundamental principle of government and opposition has been made redundant. Inevitably, the stock of both the Northern Ireland Assembly and its Executive will sink as political apathy and disenchantment rises. The impotence of the Assembly to effectively improve the lot of its citizens is manifest. Its public expenditure on essential services is limited by the amount of money allotted to it by the central government.

Since the British Treasury controls both the purse strings and overall policy, the devolved government's function is reduced, in real terms, to an administrative role. It is saddled with responsibility for carving up a predetermined cake among competing interests and subjected to national policies unsuited to Northern Ireland's economic and social difficulties. Agriculture, Northern Ireland's largest industry, has been unfairly devastated by the central government's incompetence over the BSE crisis. Its indigenous haulage industry is on the verge of extinction due to punitive fuel taxes and a massive smuggling operation controlled by terrorists, which is largely ignored by Westminster. The textile sector, faced with competition from cheaper labour in the Far East, is rapidly disappearing; heavy industry, meanwhile, hovers on the brink of oblivion. By interposing a local assembly with limited powers between it and the people, the central government distances itself from culpability, while spending vast amounts of money on objectives designed to further its own interests of appeasing terrorism and aiding disengagement from Northern Ireland. The influence of the devolved government is limited to adding its own largely impotent voice to those of the people who suffer.

THE RULE OF LAW

But it is not only in their distortion of democratic principles that successive British governments stand indicted. In their pursuit of political self-interest, they have violated all accepted standards by which the rule of law is enforced. As Justice Robert Jackson of the American Supreme Court puts it, 'the legal professions in all countries know that there are only two real choices of government open to a people. It may be governed by law or it may be governed by the will of one, or of a group, of men'. In yielding to terrorists, the British government has consigned large tracts of its sovereign territory, and huge numbers of its citizens, to their will. Violations of the rule of law in aid of government policy are, in effect, destroying the infrastructure of society in Northern Ireland, a society from which Britain wishes later to disengage.

The government's policy imperative to keep political violence off of the British mainland is presently served by an IRA ceasefire limited to the cessation of attacks on security personnel and economic targets. Repeated rulings by the government as to what constitutes a breach of that ceasefire have not precluded the IRA from murdering, maiming, exiling and intimidating those people nominally belonging to its own community and living within the areas over which it exercises *de facto* jurisdiction. The same indulgence is extended to the loyalist terror groups in the areas they control. In deciding whether any atrocity amounts to a ceasefire, the Secretary of State for Northern Ireland assesses the facts 'in the round'. The decision is not legal, but political. To make a positive decision would entail excluding the political party fronting the terrorist group responsible from participation in government. Since this might entail the exclusion of Sinn Fein, whose inclusion is considered politically vital, attributions of an act of terrorism to the IRA are either suppressed or the act dismissed as not amounting 'in the round' to a breach of the ceasefire.

This political licence, granted in violation of the rule of law, has led to an explosion in paramilitary crime which is not only destroying the fabric of society in the terrorist-controlled ghettos, but which is now expanding into every strata of Northern Ireland life. The opposing terrorist factions are becoming both more ambitious and financially sophisticated. Like the Mafia, they have moved into areas of legitimate business and, like that organisation and its 'families', they feud over territory and, from time to time, even cooperate. Profit from drugs, smuggling, extortion and protection rackets finance their arsenals. Like the Mafia, they have their front politicians allegedly espousing political ideals, but taking their real orders from the terrorist groups with which even the British government is forced to admit they are inextricably linked. The equation is simple: the price of England's peace is the destruction of the social framework of both the nationalist and unionist working class people living in large public housing estates. The effects have not yet fully impinged on the professional and commercial classes who are, for the time being, insulated by money and place, but, sooner rather than later, the blight will fall upon them, too.

PRISONERS, POLICE REFORM AND POLITICAL EXPEDIENCY
In the past successive British governments rightly claimed that there were no political prisoners in Northern Ireland. Those convicted and sentenced after due process had been found guilty of offences deemed to be crimes in any civilised democracy. In enforcing the rule of law, over 300 men and women of the RUC gave their lives and over nine thousand suffered serious injury. The judges who administered the law had to be

guarded night and day, and a number of them paid with their lives or suffered grave injuries. Yet in pursuance of a policy of yielding to terrorism, and in breach of the pledges publicly given by the Prime Minister, those guilty of the most horrific crimes have been granted early release from prison. Serial murderers of up to twelve human beings who were sentenced to life imprisonment have been released after eighteen months. Brutal psychopaths with the most tenuous of political connections have been set free. The morale of the RUC, the confidence of the bereaved and the belief of decent people in the rule of law have been shattered.

Not only do members of the RUC observe those whom they risked their lives to bring to justice set free amongst those whom they terrorised, the police themselves have now become the subject of reforms that place the political representatives of republican terror in positions of authority over them. While terrorists refuse not only to disarm, but are actively increasing their arsenals, those responsible for the enforcement of the rule of law are being demoralised and their service denigrated. Against a rising tide of paramilitary criminality backed by increasing stocks of weaponry, the means of combating crime and terror are being fatally weakened and the rule of law subverted. Experienced senior officers, demoralised by the political surrender to terrorism, are leaving the force. For them, and the officers who continue to serve, the award of the George's Cross was, effectively, a posthumous one for the RUC. Northern Ireland has, indeed, become a place where the government has no heart for defence, where social cohesion has dissolved and where a society, once organised, has become a mob of struggling interests.

Those who oppose the catalogue of concessions to terrorism, who object to the breach of democratic principles and who complain about the failure to enforce the rule of law are dismissed as 'dissidents', 'rejectionist Unionists' and 'sectarian bigots'. 'What is the alternative?' echoes the government mantra. The larger question as to 'what is the alternative to the appeasement of terrorism, the sacrifice of democracy and the subversion of the rule of law?' is never even addressed. When such issues are raised, government policies are justified as 'risks for peace'. Truth and clarity have been sacrificed for spin and ambiguity. The latter has been turned into a virtue by describing it as 'constructive', while presentational spin has replaced substance. Whatever is required to be done or said to solve a present political difficulty makes the saying or doing of it right. Truth, principles, justice and morality may all be sacrificed in aid of political expediency. The Stalinist approach of attempting to destroy the valid arguments of opponents by attributing to them a malign motivation has become the standard ploy of government ministers.

A DEMOCRATIC ALTERNATIVE

There is, of course, an alternative to the present policies of the British and Irish governments as well as those of the SDLP and Sinn Fein. This alternative is to apply the democratic principles to which the peace process was originally pledged when it was launched with the Joint Government Declaration at Downing Street in December 1993. Paragraph ten confirmed that 'Democratically mandated parties which establish a commitment to exclusively peaceful methods and which have shown that they abide by the democratic process are free to participate fully in democratic politics and to join in dialogue'. The democratic requirement was a permanent end to violence and a commitment to exclusively peaceful methods. There was no question but that all parties and governments understood that the price to be paid for democratic participation, first in negotiations and then in any agreed institutions of government, was a permanent end to violence of all kinds and the decommissioning of weapons. Dick Spring, the then Foreign Minister of the Irish government, put the matter clearly in Dail Eireann: 'Questions were raised on how to determine a permanent cessation of violence. We are talking about the handing up of arms and are insisting that it would not be simply a temporary cessation of violence to see what the political process offers.'

This statement underlines the most basic principle of democratic government as understood in every country where it is practised. Democratic government cannot coexist with political parties wedded to the use of violence to bring about political change in circumstances where the democratic process for advocating such change is available to them. The subsequent history of the peace process entails the successive abandonment of every established principle of democracy in order to support the policy requirement of keeping bombs off of the mainland. The present British government has dismally failed to recognise that the problem it must deal with is that of terrorism *per se*, rather than any particular exponent of terror with whom it from time to time negotiates. What does it matter if the Provisional IRA, temporarily satisfied with a string of political concessions, is replaced by a Real IRA posing a similar threat to the mainland and making even more exorbitant demands than the IRA would presently settle for?

*   *   *

The truth is that there are no political demands presently made by Sinn Fein/IRA that are not shared by the SDLP, the Irish Republic and the Real IRA. All are agreed that there should be an end to partition. All demand self-determination based upon the votes of all the people on the island of Ireland. All claim that Ireland should be united as a single sovereign state. All these parties know that the threat of a terrorist campaign on the mainland has been the biggest single factor in convincing Britain that she should first become a facilitator, and then a persuader, of the pro-Union people towards a united Ireland solution. It matters little, therefore, to these groups as to who or what organisations should constitute the cutting edge of violence that is the precursor for political concessions and appeasement. All of the components within the pan-nationalist front have a vested interest in ensuring that any settlement within the ambit of the United Kingdom is not permissible. By using violence, or the threat of violence, Northern Ireland is to be kept in a semi-permanent state of political instability. By allowing of no other alternative but that of Irish unity, pan-nationalism ensures that other solutions receive no consideration. Political violence precludes the examination of other options, and, on that basis, the political objectives of terrorism must be conceded, objectives that happily coincide with those of constitutional nationalism.

CATEGORIES OF BRITISH CITIZENSHIP

British citizens fall into two categories. Category one constitutes the first class variety. They live on the British mainland and can vote for the three major national parties: Labour, Conservative and Liberal Democrat. These parties organise in every mainland constituency and aspire to state power. The mainland citizens are first class because, by their votes, they can make or break governments. They constitute over ninety-seven percent of the total population. Category two comprises the second class citizens of Northern Ireland who are, effectively, excluded from the national party system and whose votes have little or no effect on which national party will form the government. While they have votes, they are, essentially, disenfranchised. By executing or threatening to execute a policy of mainland violence directed against the first class citizens to whom governments are answerable, the IRA exerts political pressure for the meeting of their demands by requiring the sacrifice of the interests of the second class citizens in Northern Ireland, a place in which Britain no longer has any selfish economic or strategic interest for remaining.

At the beginning of the peace process some nominal observance was paid to the principles of democracy and the rule of law. Increasingly, however, Northern Ireland and her second class citizens have become expendable—like the Czechs in 1938. Few Unionists doubt that currently British realism would admit that Irish unity could probably not be avoided in the long run and that England is only interested in seeing unity brought about by peaceful development. As in 1938, all of this has to be shrouded in what is now termed 'constructive ambiguity'. The British government dare not declare openly to its people that in their alleged interest its policy is directed to meeting the demands of terrorism. Instead, capitulation is disguised as a peace process, and conflict resolution with armed terrorists is passed off as a political settlement. Unfortunately, the intransigence of Sinn Fein/IRA in determining to remain armed, coupled with the political foolishness of constitutional nationalism in humiliating those Unionists naive enough to cooperate in their own destruction, has alerted the vast body of Unionists to the reality of the peace process. Increasingly incensed at the duplicity used to gain their support for the Belfast Agreement, they are withdrawing that support for an arrangement that has offered them no benefit. The Agreement, and the institutions it spawned, are now collapsing as a result of their own inherent defects. Ambiguities must, over time, be ultimately resolved, and their ongoing resolution in favour of nationalism is rapidly destroying Unionist belief in the Agreement and those Unionist leaders who endorsed it.

*   *   *

The time has come for both the British and Irish governments to realise that for the foreseeable future there is only one course of action to pursue, and that is to govern truly in the best interests of the vast majority of the people of Northern Ireland. Such a course demands the application of the normal rules by which democracy operates and the protection of citizens by the enforcement of the rule of law.

Today in Northern Ireland few, if any, citizens would oppose the principle that everyone, regardless of race, religion or political aspiration pursued within the law, is fully entitled to equality of treatment in every aspect of human activity. Scarcely anyone would object to the most comprehensive cooperation with the Irish Republic in any area of mutual benefit. Little or no dissent would be expressed regarding the fullest expression of a joint cultural heritage in sports, culture and the arts. Most would agree that cultural and ethnic differences are capable of resolution in a spirit of compromise. But all of this is more capable of achievement within the pluralism that already exists in an increasingly multi-cultural United Kingdom than it is ever likely to be achieved in the smaller and infinitely more socially and religiously homogenous Republic of Ireland. Perhaps the best evidence of this conclusion is the fact that currently almost one million people born in the Republic of Ireland work and live in the United Kingdom as the country of their choice. A settlement within the United Kingdom is not only possible, but desirable. Such a solution requires the British government to offer citizenship of equal value to all of its citizens, to actively suppress violent political terrorism rather than rewarding it and to restore true democracy and the enforcement of the rule of law within its own sovereign territory.

POSTSCRIPT
In moments of introspection, one wonders to what extent anything said, done or written makes a real difference in people's lives. Then something happens which renews one's hope and restores belief that the truth cannot be suppressed indefinitely and that ideas do matter. In January 2001, shortly before this book went to print, I read an article in the *Observer* by the respected journalist, Henry McDonald. The subject matter was the brutal beating of a sixteen-year-old boy with an IQ of 45 and a mental age of eight. The beating was carried out *by a Provisional IRA punishment squad* in the presence of the boy's sick mother and his younger siblings. The mother of this socially disadvantaged family living in a West Belfast republican enclave made this final comment about the peace process to Henry McDonald: 'There is no peace process for people like me. Nobody seems to care what is happening. It seems that as long as there are no bombs in England or policemen or soldiers being shot, than anything goes. People like us don't count in the peace process.' Her statement struck a chord and renewed my faith that ideas and their dissemination do matter to everyone.

Appendix

The Peace Process in Northern Ireland: Documentary Extracts

Downing Street Declaration

Paragraph Four

The Prime Minister, on behalf of the British Government, reaffirms that they will uphold the democratic wish of a greater number of the people of Northern Ireland on the issue of whether they prefer to support the Union or a sovereign united Ireland. On this basis, he reiterates, on behalf of the British Government, that they have no selfish strategic or economic interest in Northern Ireland. Their primary interest is to see peace, stability and reconciliation established by agreement among all the people who inhabit the island, and they will work together with the Irish Government to achieve such an agreement, which will embrace the totality of relationships. The role of the British Government will be to encourage, facilitate and enable the achievement of such agreement over a period through a process of dialogue and co-operation based on full respect for the rights and identities of both traditions in Ireland. They accept that such agreement may, as of right, take the form of agreed structures for the island as a whole, including a united Ireland achieved by peaceful means on the following basis. The British Government agree that it is for the people of the island of Ireland alone, by agreement between the two parts respectively, to exercise their right of self-determination on the basis of consent, freely and concurrently given, North and South, to bring about a united Ireland, if that is their wish. They reaffirm as a binding obligation that they will, for their part, introduce the necessary legislation to give effect to this, or equally to any measure of agreement on future relationships in Ireland which the people living in Ireland may themselves freely so determine without external impediment. They believe that the people of Britain would wish, in friendship to all sides, to enable the people of Ireland to reach agreement on how they may live together in harmony and in partnership, with respect for their diverse traditions, and with full recognition of the special links and the unique relationship which exist between the peoples of Britain and Ireland.

Paragraph Five

The Taoiseach, on behalf of the Irish Government, considers that the lessons of Irish history, and especially of Northern Ireland, show that stability and well-being will not be found under any political system which is refused allegiance or rejected on grounds of identity by a significant minority of those governed by it. For this reason, it would be wrong to attempt to impose a united Ireland, in the absence of the freely given consent of a majority of the people of Northern Ireland. He accepts, on behalf of the Irish Government, that the democratic right of self-determination by the people of Ireland as a whole must be achieved and exercised with and subject to the agreement and consent of a majority of the people of Northern Ireland and must, consistent with justice and equity, respect the democratic dignity and the civil rights and religious liberties of both communities, including:

* the right of free political thought;
* the right of freedom and expression of religion;
* the right to pursue democratically national and political aspirations;
* the right to seek constitutional change by peaceful and legitimate means;
* the right to live wherever one chooses without hindrance;
* the right to equal opportunity in all social and economic activity, regardless of class, creed, sex or colour.

These would be reflected in any future political and constitutional arrangements emerging from a new and more broadly based agreement.

Paragraph Seven

Both Governments accept that Irish unity would he achieved only by those who favour this outcome persuading those who do not, peacefully and without coercion or violence, and that, if in the future a majority of the people of Northern Ireland are so persuaded, both Governments will support and give legislative effect to their wish. But, notwithstanding the solemn affirmation by both Governments in the Anglo-Irish Agreement that any change in the status of Northern Ireland would only come about with the consent of a majority of the people of Northern Ireland, the Taoiseach also recognises the continuing uncertainties and misgivings which dominate so much of Northern Unionist attitudes towards the rest of Ireland. He believes that we stand at a stage of our history when the genuine feelings of all traditions in the North must be recognised and acknowledged. He appeals to both traditions at this time to grasp the opportunity for a fresh start and a new beginning, which could hold such promise for all our lives and the generations to come. He asks the people of Northern Ireland to look on the people of the Republic as friends, who share their grief and shame over all the suffering of the last quarter of a century, and who want to develop the best possible relationship with them, a relationship in which trust and new understanding can flourish and grow. The Taoiseach also acknowledges the presence in the Constitution of the Republic of elements which are deeply resented by Northern Unionists, but which at the same time reflect hopes and ideals which lie deep in the hearts of many Irish men and women North and South. But as we move towards a new era of understanding in which new relationships of trust may grow and bring peace to the island of Ireland, the Taoiseach believes that the time has come to consider together how best the hopes and identities of all can be expressed in more balanced ways, which no longer engender division and the lack of trust to which he has referred. He confirms that, in the event of an overall settlement, the Irish Government will, as part of a balanced constitutional accommodation, put forward and support proposals for change in the Irish Constitution which would fully reflect the principle of consent in Northern Ireland.

Paragraph Nine
The British and Irish Governments will seek, along with the Northern Ireland constitutional parties through a process of political dialogue, to create institutions and structures which, while respecting the diversity of the people of Ireland, would enable them to work together in all areas of common interest. This will help over a period to build the trust necessary to end past divisions, leading to an agreed and peaceful future. Such structures would, of course, include institutional recognition of the special links that exist between the peoples of Britain and Ireland as part of the totality of relationships, while taking account of newly forged links with the rest of Europe.

Paragraph Ten
The British and Irish Governments reiterate that the achievement of peace must involve a permanent end to the use of, or support for, paramilitary violence. They confirm that, in these circumstances, democratically mandated parties which establish a commitment to exclusively peaceful methods and which have shown that they abide by the democratic process, are free to participate fully in democratic politics and to join in dialogue in due course between the Governments and the political parties on the way ahead.

The Mitchell Report

Paragraph Twenty (The Mitchell Principles)
Accordingly, we recommend that the parties to such negotiations affirm their total and absolute commitment:

> a. To democratic and exclusively peaceful means of resolving political issues;
> b. To the total disarmament of all paramilitary organisations;
> c. To agree that such disarmament must be verifiable to the satisfaction of an independent commission;
> d. To renounce for themselves, and to oppose any effort by others, to use force, or threaten to use force, to influence the course or the outcome of all-party negotiations;
> e. To agree to abide by the terms of any agreement reached in all-party negotiations and to resort to democratic and exclusively peaceful methods in trying to alter any aspect of that outcome with which they may disagree; and,
> f. To urge that "punishment" killings and beatings stop and to take effective steps to prevent such actions.

Paragraph Thirty-four
The British and Irish Governments will seek, along with the Northern Ireland constitutional parties through a process of political dialogue, to create institutions and structures which, while respecting the diversity of the people of Ireland, would enable them to work together in all areas of common interest. This will help over a period to build the trust necessary to end past divisions, leading to an agreed and peaceful future. Such structures would, of course, include institutional recognition of the special links that exist between the peoples of Britain and Ireland as part of the totality of relationships, while taking account of newly forged links with the rest of Europe.

Paragraph Thirty-five
In addition, it offers the parties an opportunity to use the process of decommissioning to build confidence one step at a time during negotiations. As progress is made on political issues, even modest mutual steps on decommissioning could help create the atmosphere needed for further steps in a progressive pattern of mounting trust and confidence.

Framework Document

Paragraph Twenty

The British Government reaffirm that they will uphold the democratic wish of a greater number of the people of Northern Ireland on the issue of whether they prefer to support the Union or a sovereign united Ireland. On this basis, they reiterate that they have no selfish strategic or economic interest in Northern Ireland. For as long as the democratic wish of the people of Northern Ireland is for no change in its present status, the British Government pledge that their jurisdiction there will be exercised with rigorous impartiality on behalf of all the people of Northern Ireland in their diversity. It will be founded on the principles outlined in the previous paragraph with emphasis on full respect for, and equality of, civil, political, social and cultural rights and freedom from discrimination for all citizens, on parity of esteem, and on just and equal treatment for the identity, ethos and aspirations of both communities. The British Government will discharge their responsibilities in a way which does not prejudice the freedom of the people of Northern Ireland to determine, by peaceful and democratic means, its future constitutional status, whether in remaining a part of the United Kingdom or in forming part of a united Ireland. They will be equally cognisant of either option and open to its democratic realisation, and will not impede the latter option, their primary interest being to see peace, stability and reconciliation established by agreement among the people who inhabit the island. This new approach for Northern Ireland, based on the continuing willingness to accept the will of a majority of the people there, will be enshrined in British constitutional legislation embodying the principles and commitments in the Joint Declaration and this Framework Document, either by amendment of the Government of Ireland Act 1920 or by its replacement by appropriate new legislation, and appropriate new provisions entrenched by agreement.

Paragraph Twenty-one

As part of an agreement confirming the foregoing understanding between the two Governments on constitutional issues, the Irish Government will introduce and support proposals for change in the Irish Constitution to implement the commitments in the Joint Declaration. These changes in the Irish Constitution will fully reflect the principle of consent in Northern Ireland and demonstrably be such that no territorial claim of right to jurisdiction over Northern Ireland contrary to the will of a majority of its people is asserted, while maintaining the existing birthright of everyone born in either jurisdiction in Ireland to be part, as of right, of the Irish nation. They will enable a new Agreement to be ratified which will include, as part of a new and equitable dispensation for Northern Ireland embodying the principles and commitments in the Joint Declaration and this Framework Document, recognition by both Governments of the legitimacy of whatever choice is freely exercised by a majority of the people of Northern Ireland with regard to its constitutional status, whether they prefer to continue to support the Union or a sovereign united Ireland.

Paragraph Twenty-four
Both Governments consider that new institutions should be created to cater adequately for present and future political, social and economic inter-connections on the island of Ireland, enabling representatives of the main traditions, North and South, to enter agreed dynamic, new, co-operative and constructive relationships.

Paragraph Thirty-five
Both Governments envisage that all decisions within the body would be by agreement between the two sides. The Heads of Department on each side would operate within the overall terms of reference mandated by legislation in the two sovereign Parliaments. They would exercise their powers in accordance with the rules for democratic authority and accountability for this function in force in the Oireachtas and in new institutions in Northern Ireland. The operation of the North/South body's functions would be subject to regular scrutiny in agreed political institutions in Northern Ireland and the Oireachtas respectively.

Paragraph Forty
Both Governments intend that under such a new Agreement a standing Intergovernmental Conference will be maintained, chaired by the designated Irish Minister and by the Secretary of State for Northern Ireland. It would be supported by a Permanent Secretariat of civil servants from both Governments.

Paragraph Forty-two
The Conference will provide a continuing institutional expression for the Irish Government's recognised concern and role in relation to Northern Ireland. The Irish Government will put forward views and proposals on issues falling within the ambit of the new Conference or involving both Governments, and determined efforts will be made to resolve any

differences between the two Governments. The Conference will be the principal instrument for an intensification of the co-operation and partnership between both Governments, with particular reference to the principles contained in the Joint Declaration, in this Framework Document and in the new Agreement, on a wide range of issues concerned with Northern Ireland and with the relations between the two parts of the island of Ireland. It will facilitate the promotion of lasting peace, stability, justice and reconciliation among the people of the island of Ireland and maintenance of effective security co-operation between the two Governments.

Paragraph Forty-seven
In the event that devolved institutions in Northern Ireland ceased to operate, and direct rule from Westminster was reintroduced, the British Government agree that other arrangements would be made to implement the commitment to promote co-operation at all levels between the people, North and South, representing both traditions in Ireland, as agreed by the two Governments in the Joint Declaration, and to ensure that the co-operation that had been developed through the North/South body be maintained.

Belfast Agreement

Section on Decommissioning
1. Participants recall their agreement in the Procedural Motion adopted on 24 September 1997 "that the resolution of the decommissioning issue is an indispensable part of the process of negotiation", and also recall the provisions of paragraph 25 of Strand 1 above.
2. They note the progress made by the Independent International Commission on Decommissioning and the Governments in developing schemes which can represent a workable basis for achieving the decommissioning of illegally-held arms in the possession of paramilitary groups.
3. All participants accordingly reaffirm their commitment to the total disarmament of all paramilitary organisations. They also confirm their intention to continue to work constructively and in good faith with the Independent Commission, and to use any influence they may have, to achieve the decommissioning of all paramilitary arms within two years following endorsement in referendums North and South of the

agreement and in the context of the implementation of the overall settlement.

4. The Independent Commission will monitor, review and verify progress on decommissioning of illegal arms, and will report to both Governments at regular intervals.

6. Both Governments will take all necessary steps to facilitate the decommissioning process to include bringing the relevant schemes into force by the end of June.

Patten Commission: Terms of Reference

Taking account of the principles on policing as set out in the agreement, the Commission will inquire into policing in Northern Ireland and, on the basis of its findings, bring forward proposals for future policing structures and arrangements, including means of encouraging widespread community support for those arrangements.

Its proposals on policing should be designed to ensure that policing arrangements, including composition, recruitment, training, culture, ethos and symbols, are such that in a new approach Northern Ireland has a police service that can enjoy widespread support from, and is seen as an integral part of, the community as a whole.

Its proposals should include recommendations covering any issues such as re-training, job placement and educational and professional development required in the transition to policing in a peaceful society.

Its proposals should also be designed to ensure that:
> * the police service is structured, managed and resourced so that it can be effective in discharging its full range of functions (including proposals on any necessary arrangements for the transition to policing in a normal   peaceful society);
> * the police service is delivered in constructive and inclusive partnerships with the community at all levels with the maximum delegation of authority and responsibility;
> * the legislative and constitutional framework requires the impartial discharge of policing functions and conforms with internationally accepted norms in relation to policing standards;
> * the police operate within a clear framework of accountability to the law and the community they serve, so:
>> - they are constrained by, accountable to and act only within the law;

- their powers and procedures, like the law they enforce, are clearly established and publicly available;
- there are open, accessible and independent means of investigating and adjudicating upon complaints against the police;
- there are clearly established arrangements enabling local people, and their political representatives, to articulate their views and concerns about policing and to establish publicly policing priorities and influence policing policies, subject to safeguards to ensure police impartiality and freedom from partisan political control;
- there are arrangements for accountability and for the effective, efficient and economic use of resources in achieving policing objectives;
- there are means to ensure independent professional scrutiny and inspection of the police service to ensure that proper professional standards are maintained;

* the scope for structured co-operation with the Garda Siochana and other police forces is addressed; and
* the management of public order events which can impose exceptional demands on policing resources is also addressed.

The Commission should focus on policing issues, but if it identifies other aspects of the criminal justice system relevant to its work on policing, including the role of the police in prosecution, then it should draw the attention of the Government to those matters.

The Commission should consult widely, including with non-governmental expert organisations, and through such focus groups as they consider it appropriate to establish.

The Government proposes to establish the Commission as soon as possible, with the aim of it starting work as soon as possible and publishing its final report by Summer 1999.

Information Strategy

The following is a copy of a widely distributed Northern Ireland Office memorandum outlining the government's proposed publicity campaign leading up to the referendum on the Belfast Agreement, held on 22 May 1998.

2. We are embarking on what in effect will be the most crucial election campaign in Northern Ireland's history. During the next ten weeks we need to convince the Northern Ireland public both of the importance of what is at stake, and also convince them that not only is agreement possible, but they have a vital role to play in endorsing it.

3. If we are to do that then the government's message needs to be clear, simple and direct. It needs to prioritise its key messages, and keep repeating them at every opportunity, to reinforce the big picture, even while it deals with the detail. It should be a message that is not afraid to recognize and build on the public's desire for peace, and uses that, in parallel with the progress in the talks, to build a momentum as we approach the referendum and subsequently the election to a new administration.

4. But that will require a sustained, committed and coherent effort right across government. The message needs to be reinforced on every conceivable opportunity and the benefits of an agreement underlined in every possible way. The Northern Ireland public needs to be in no doubt about how a deal will improve every aspect of their quality of life. We need to convey that message. That means a concerted effort by all ministers and departments in every speech, interview and meeting. The momentum towards an agreement and the people's decision in a referendum must become a central part of every message government sends whether the context is the economy, health, or even agriculture. It can no longer be an add-on at the end of the speech. It must be the central part of every piece of communication we do. That will not only help flesh out what an agreement would mean for the everyday life of people here, but also keep the message fresh by introducing different faces delivering the message.

5. If we can also find different formats in which to deliver the message the impact would be all the greater. Given that a central part of the government's approach is that we are not imposing a deal, but giving the people a choice, it is particularly apt to look for occasions in which ministers will be able to talk directly to people rather than at them. The ideal are situations in which question and answer sessions can develop. These would not be designed to focus on the minutiae of the talks, but rather to underline the historic opportunity facing the Province. We need to look for the right occasion and location, and devote sufficient resources to ensure that it delivers the right result. While vigorous

questioning is, if anything, to be welcomed, equally a succession of shouting marches will be counter-productive. Help from divisions and departments will therefore be needed in selecting and preparing such occasions.

Key Themes and Lines

6. Considerable work has already been done on identifying the key themes and messages which will underpin our efforts between now and the referendum, and many of those were reflected in the round of interviews by ministers last weekend. But this effort needs to be sustained. We will develop key lines which will underpin the whole campaign. These, in turn, should be updated on a weekly basis, or more often if necessary, to inform and structure our response to the changing course of events. In practical terms, we propose listing these key lines at the start of the Weekly Information Bulletin to serve as a ready reminder. This then would provide a starting point for [a] daily handling meeting. Any necessary amendment or update to the lines would be circulated following the meeting as happens at present. We intend to start this practice next week. We will also be reviewing the effectiveness of lines on a weekly basis . . .

Monitoring

7. But we will only be able to effectively refine the message and respond to apparent concerns, if we have an effective monitoring system. Essentially this will include a survey of media coverage, particularly changes in tone and attitude; the intelligence gleaned from informal contacts with key media people; and similar input from officials in NIO divisions and departments, as part of their normal community contacts. For our part we are conscious that there will be an immediacy to this campaign which will be reflected most notably by the broadcast media. We need, therefore, to enhance our early warning capacity to allow us to be in a situation to take the initiative, before others set their own agenda. We intend therefore to supplement our existing morning digest, cuttings, and broadcast transcripts by a more considered view of reaction carried on the airwaves. This in turn will feed into our updating of lines at the morning meeting. In addition we will be undertaking a similar service at lunchtime as well as teatime. Again we would propose re-visiting the daily lines as necessary.

Key Audiences

8. But the media is not the only audience we are playing to. There are the voters themselves, and we need to target and monitor our message towards key groups. Amongst those, at the broadest, are the main elements of unionism and nationalism. But also we need to know how

other groups, such as the young, first time voter, and the East of the Province 'middle class silent majority' type, are responding.

Focus and Research Groups

9. A key requirement in developing our communications strategy will be a continuing flow of information about public attitudes and response. On some occasions this will be helpful to our cause and on others not so. It will be important therefore to ensure that not all of the results of opinion polling, etc. will be in the public domain.

10. It would be open to us to encourage some degree of public opinion polling by, for example, newspapers and current affairs programmes, where we believe the results are likely to be supportive. Some of this can be encouraged during meetings and briefings of senior media people.

11. We have now commissioned . . . both quantitative and qualitative research [to be] carried out, without it being seen to be Government inspired. This applies whether we are doing any advertising or not . . . Particularly for quantitative research we could expect to have preliminary results within a week to 10 days of commissioning: qualitative research (involving small selective groups representative of social, religious and geographical sectors) might take 2-3 weeks.

12. Further and more in-depth work through focus groups has been instigated . . . and a detailed paper will follow later this week.

Champions

13. Each focus group should be representative of a section of the wider community. Those wider groups in turn each have someone they look up to as a representative figure. We should, where possible, be enlisting the help of those people to champion our cause, e.g. . . . church leaders, the heads of community organizations and trade unions . . .

14. While any overt manipulation could only be counter-productive, a carefully co-ordinated timetable of statements from these people will be helpful in giving our message credibility with those they represent. It has the added benefit of providing a fresh face for that message, and ensuring that it is not only the government which is seen to be selling the process.

15. While [this] office can do its part, it is essential that other divisions and departments use all their available contacts not only to identify suitable people, but also to advise on how best to cultivate their support. [Another office] is co-ordinating a database of key movers and shakers from all sections of the community.

Advertising

16. Advertising on its own will not convince the public to vote in favour of the referendum. But as part of an integrated campaign it could play a

crucial role in alerting the public to the precisely what is at stake. It is the only means where we would be in total control of the message and be guaranteed near universal coverage if we use TV. But serious consideration needs to be given to the timing and content of any messages because it could be seen as 'big government' imposing its view, which would be entirely counter-productive. For that, and reasons of government impropriety, the focus should be on selling the concept of an agreed future rather than its precise details. The central message will be 'It's your choice'. Initially that choice will be posed as being between the failure of the past and the future towards which we are making progress. Once an agreement is in place, the message will change to encouraging people to vote for their future.

Internet

17. This is clearly a medium which we cannot afford to ignore. It provides an opportunity to offer instantly updated information to a world-wide audience and at a very modest cost. The revamped NIO site is already attracting a very high level of interest and visits and many of our regular media and other clients are now taking their feed of press releases, etc., from our internet site; the value is clearly proven.

18. The probability is that we should have a dedicated site for the Referendum/Settlement and [this] office is now looking urgently at how this work should be carried forward.

Identifying Opportunities

19. An essential element in the planning process will be a rolling composite list of forthcoming events and announcements which will provide platforms for speeches and interviews together with early warning of issues which may present potential difficulties in presentational terms. This will be updated and circulated weekly . . . We will create targeted opportunities such as Woman and Youth conferences.

20. This list will allow us to see at a glance the range of opportunities and the variety of audiences already in the programme, and to consider and develop ideas for reaching audiences not covered.

21. There are about 10-12 current affairs broadcast programmes with which [this] office will liaise closely thus allowing us to have early warning of programmes into which we might wish to have input. We will also wish from time to time to offer suggestions for other programmes which would improve knowledge and understanding of the process and the prospects for a satisfactory outcome.

Briefing

22. We will wish to put more emphasis on briefing of media people generally, both to ensure that they are fully informed and to encourage them to develop their own ideas for programmes on the Talks process and later the Referendum. We will be particularly anxious to use this means of exerting some influence on the content and quality of media coverage. The many weekly newspapers around Northern Ireland offer considerable scope for us to present our message and the editors of these papers should feature in the efforts of Ministers to cultivate the media.

23. The work of meeting and briefing media representatives should be spread around all of the Ministerial team and there is no reason why on occasions officials shouldn't carry some of this burden . . .

24. None of this work will obviate the need for some form of "regular message from the Talks" briefing of those who regularly cover the process. This might be done at both the start and finish of the Talks week . . . These sessions might be undertaken on 'off the record' lobby terms.

25. To complement this for the national media [we] propose to explore with the Prime Minister's Press Secretary the possibility of a once-weekly briefing on Northern Ireland affairs as part of or immediately following the regular No. 10 lobby briefing.

26. [We] also intend to use the opportunity of Thursday's IGC to open dialogue with [Dublin] as to how we and Dublin can co-ordinate our messages to better effect and avoid unhelpful clashes.

Select Bibliography of Political Writings by Robert McCartney

Political Pamphlets

Liberty and Authority in Ireland
    Londonderry: Field Day Pamphlet, 1985

The McCartney Report on Consent
    Belfast: UK/Unionist Party, 1997

The McCartney Report on the Framework Documents
    Belfast: UK/Unionist Party, 1997

Chapters in Books

'Priests, Politicians and Pluralism', in John Wilson Foster (ed.), *The Idea of the Union: Statements and Critiques in Support of the Union of Great Britain and Northern Ireland* (Vancouver: Belcouver Press, 1995).

'A Tale of Two Governments', in John Wilson Foster (ed.), *The Idea of the Union: Statements and Critiques in Support of the Union of Great Britain and Northern Ireland* (Vancouver: Belcouver Press, 1995).

Sovereignty and Seduction', in John Wilson Foster (ed.), *The Idea of the Union: Statements and Critiques in Support of the Union of Great Britain and Northern Ireland* (Vancouver: Belcouver Press, 1995).

'The Union and the Economic Future of Northern Ireland', in Richard English and Joseph Morrison Skelly, *Ideas Matter: Essays in Honour of Conor Cruise O'Brien* (Dublin: Poolbeg Press, 1998).

Newspapers and Magazines

Bangor Spectator
'Déjà Vu?', 24 July 1997

Belfast News Letter
'Leaders' Strategy will Doom the Union', 14 April 1987
'Beware Cosmetic Formula . . . it Means a Sell-out', 27 April 1987
'Making Votes Matter to the Government', 27 May 1987
'Hume, Adams and Clausewitz', 9 September 1988
'Humpty's Great Fall', 6 February 1989
'Dance of Dinosaurs', 5 May 1989

'A Shabby Neighbour is Courted', 22 March 1990
'New Strategy Essential to Block Hume-Adams', 14 September 1994
'Unionists Must Talk to Each Other', 21 November 1995
'The Union Needs Unity', 20 March 1996
'The Defence of the Union', 24 April 1996
'Since December 1993 When the Two Governments', 13 June 1996
'Emperor Major's Peace Exposed', 9 July 1996
'What a Sham in Cause of Peace', 5 February 1997
'Edward Carson was Passionately Committed . . . ', 28 June 1997
'Decommissioning—A Demand of Democracy', 16 July 1997
'Murder of Billy Wright is Detonator', 2 January 1998
'Visit to the Maze Means Parties are Irrelevant', 13 January 1998
'The Joint-Government Proposition on Agreement', 14 January 1998
'No Secret Author Critical of Peace Process', 18 January 1998
'A Process of Corruption', 24 February 1998
'Mowlam Confident there will be an Agreement', 18 March 1998
'There is no Going Back', 19 May 1998
'Patten Report Just Part of a Process', 18 September 1999
'Nightmare Scenario Becoming Reality', 25 October 1999
'Credibility in Hands of UUC', 24 May 2000

Belfast Telegraph
'The Case for Equal Citizenship', 25 August 1986
'Peace at any Price', 30 November 1993
'The Threat to the Union', 16 December 1993
'Peace for Whom?', 26 January 1994
'Has IRA Hijacked Peace?', 3 February 1994
'The Peace that Never Was', 17 August 1994
'Deadly Myth of Democracy', 31 August 1994
'Mirage of Peace', 5 September 1994
'Major Joins in the Humpty Game', 10 September 1994
'Why Major's Guarantees Lack Credibility', 22 September 1994
'Echoes of Sunningdale', 3 October 1994
'Cost of Unification is Too Dear a Price for the Poor', 28 October 1994
'Question They Will Not Answer', 8 December 1994
'Parity of Esteem had got Little to do with Civil Rights', 19 January 1995
'Division and Deception are Major's Tools', 8 February 1995
'Conditional Surrender', 21 February 1995
'Solutions Plagued by a Lack of Vision', 4 April 1995
'Where the Unionists are Going Wrong in the '90s', 19 June 1995
'The President's Men', 2 November 1995

'Just How Far Can We Go to Pay the Price of Peace?' 12 March 1996.
'Governments Primed Drumcree Powder Keg', 18 July 1996
'The Last Illusion Shattered', 11 October 1996
'Mr John Bruton in a Recent Article . . . ', 17 February 1997
'Unionist Disharmony Spells Danger', 14 May 1997
'Many in Northern Ireland Favourable to My Views', 22 September 1997
'Kelly's Inverse Logic', 27 August 1997
'A Classic Piece of Fudge', 14 January 1998
'Placating Terror will Cost Dearly', 11 January 1999
'Major Proves that the Truth Will Out', 20 October 1999
'No Declaration that the War is Over', 25 November 1999
'Canary Wharf, IRA Arms and Mandelson', 15 February 2000
'Does Tony Blair Pull Too Many Strings?' 2 March 2000
'Guns or Butter?' 19 May 2000
'The Ends Never Justify the Means', 2 August 2000
'For Whom the Bell Tolls', 18 September 2000.
'Dr Jekyll and Mr Hyde', 22 November 2000.

Daily Telegraph
'And Now a Ceasefire?', 17 June 1996.
'No Long-Term Friends, Only Interests', 14 April 1998

Irish News
'The Lillis Connection in Hume-Adams Talks', 6 September 1993
'People of Northern Ireland Encouraged to vote "Yes"', 19 May 1998

Irish Times
'Only One Bull Bellows in Fianna Fail', 24 October 1984
'Finding a Fudge to Quell Unionist Discontent', 26 January 1998
'Isaiah Berlin in "Two Concepts of Liberty"', *Irish Times*, 25 May 1998
'Confusion of the Long-term Strategy of Process', 26 September 1998
'Democracy Will Die Without Decommissioning', 17 November 1998
'North's Bright Future Fast Becoming a Nightmare', 12 January 1999.
'Illusionists are Taking the Public for a Political Spin', 2 April 1999
'They Walk Alone', 26 June 1999
'Ahern and Blair Should Decide on IRA Violence', 9 August 1999
'Terms of Patten Report Politically Explosive', 8 September 1999

News of the World
'To the Average Mainland Briton, the Orangemen . . .', 23 June 1997

Observer
'Devolution is a Sham', 20 February 2000

Parliamentary Brief
'Selling Peace and Selling Out', October, 1994

Spectator
'Why the UK/Unionists are not at the Talks', 6 November 1997

The Times
'Patten Report Finishes What IRA Started', 28 October 1999.

Index